بِسْمِ اللهِ الرَّحْمٰنِ الرَّحِيْمِ

In the Name of Allah, Most Gracious, Ever Merciful

AHMADIYYA MUSLIM MOSQUES AROUND THE WORLD — A PICTORIAL PRESENTATION

Khilafat Centenary Edition, U.S.A.

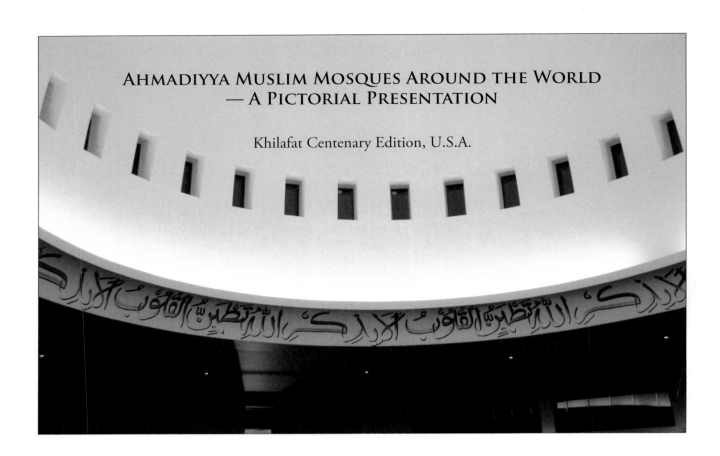

AHMADIYYA MUSLIM MOSQUES AROUND THE WORLD — A PICTORIAL PRESENTATION

Khilafat Centenary Edition, U.S.A.

Published by:
The Ahmadiyya Muslim Community, U.S.A.
15000 Good Hope Road
Silver Spring, MD 20905

Printed and bound in the U.S.A. by
Quebecor World Book Services, Versailles, Kentucky

ISBN: 1-882494-51-2

The First Ahmadiyya Muslim Mosque Built by Hadhrat Mirza Ghulam Ahmad[as] in 1883 in Qadian, India

Masjid Mubarak, in Qadian, India, is the first Ahmadiyya Muslim Mosque to be constructed. Hadhrat Mirza Ghulam Ahmad[as] built this mosque in 1883.

Contents

1 Introduction

49 Africa

306 South

Brazil **307**   French Antilles **310**   Guyana **311**   Suriname **314**   Trinidad and Tobago **318**

America

321 Oceania

Australia **322**   Fiji Islands **332**   New Zealand **340** Tuvalu **344**

346 Epilogue

Holding Fast by the Rope of Allah **346**   Glossary **349** Annotated Bibliography **350**   Acknowledgments **351**

Editor's Note

Chairman
Dr. Ahsanullah Zafar
(*Amir Jama'at USA*)

Editor
Anwer Mahmood Khan

Layout/Design/Fact Checks
Arshad Mahmood Khan
Ahsan Mahmood Khan
Ata ul Malik Khan

Translations
Imam Mubasher Ahmad
Anis Shaikh
Khalid Ahmad

Copy Editing
Amjad Mahmood Khan
Sabiha Ahmad Khan
Saddia Ahmad Khan
Amtul Hakeem Khan

Cover Design
Salman Sajid

Centerfold Design
Sajid Maqsood

Consultants
Hasan Hakeem
Syed Sajid Ahmad

Printer
Basharat M. Mirza

A study of human nature reveals two distinct aspects of one's life: the individual, which includes the fulfillment of personal needs; and the collective, which includes the fulfillment of societal needs. Often times, an individual foregoes his personal needs for the sake of a larger societal good. The religion of Islam, being a religion rooted in human nature, uses spirituality to address both these needs. The divine scripture of Islam—The Holy Qur'an—elucidates the purpose of one's life on earth in the following verse:

Anwer Mahmood Khan

"*We have not created man and Jinn but to worship God.*" (51:57)

The primary mode of worship in Islam, *Salat*, is prescribed five times daily, and every Muslim is required to offer *Salat* at the prescribed times. *Salat* in and of itself can be performed individually or collectively. Collective *Salat*, however, carries a reward twenty-seven times greater than individual *Salat*. Collective *Salat* therefore constitutes the preeminent form of worship in Islam.

The *Masjid*, or mosque, is a spiritual sanctuary for worshippers to offer both individual and collective *Salat*. Muslims stand shoulder to shoulder in rows and follow the *Imam*, or leader, in carrying out the rituals of *Salat*.

Owing to its vital importance, the *Masjid*, like all houses of worship, is paid special emphasis in the Holy Qur'an. Indeed, Allah promises to protect the sanctity of the *Masjid* thus:

"*Those who have been driven out from their homes unjustly only because they said, 'Our Lord is Allah.' And if Allah had not repelled some people by means of others, cloisters and churches and synagogues and mosques, wherein the name of Allah is oft remembered, would surely have been destroyed. And Allah will, surely, help him who helps Him. Allah is, indeed, Powerful, Mighty.*" (22:41).

The Prophet of Islam, Muhammad[sa], reportedly said: "A person who builds a mosque for Allah's sake, Allah builds a better house in heaven for that person." (*Sahi Muslim*).

The founder of the Ahmadiyya Muslim Community, *Hadhrat* Mirza Ghulam Ahmad[as], also stressed the importance of building mosques: "The foundation stone of the renaissance of Islam and a superior world order have been laid. Now mosques will be built and people will enter therein and join the Divine Movement in droves." (*Noorul Haq*, Vol. 2, p. 42).

Honoring the venerable tradition of the *Masjid* in Islam, the Ahmadiyya Muslim Community now has built over 15,000 mosques around the world. Such unprecedented growth has not come without struggle. Segments of the Islamic world bitterly oppose efforts by Ahmadi Muslims to build mosques. In Pakistan, for example, penal code provisions prohibit Ahmadi Muslims from calling their houses of worship "mosques." Militant clerics also have supported the destruction of some 120 Ahmadi mosques in Pakistan over the past two decades. Nevertheless, despite being persecuted, the Community continues to remain steadfast through its mosque-building efforts.

To commemorate 100 years of *Khilafat*, the spiritual institution of successorship in Islam and Ahmadiyyat, this publication attempts to chronicle the stunning advancement of the Community over the past century. In particular, we capture through pictures and narrative the history of the *Masjid* in Islam and Ahmadiyyat. We also pay homage to the tireless efforts of the *khulufa*, the spiritual leaders of the Community, to build mosques and provide guidance to millions.

We begin with the First House of Worship, the Holy *Ka'aba*, located in Makkah, Saudi Arabia. By examining the significance of this magnificent structure, we encapsulate the essential aspects of the tradition of *Masjid* in Islam from which the Community derives inspiration. Next, we provide various perspectives on the tradition of *Masjid* by the *Hadhrat* Mirza Ghulam Ahmad[as] and his *khulufa*. We then provide several accounts by esteemed scholars on the significance and impact of the *Masjid*. Finally, we travel the world highlighting the history and beauty of the Ahmadiyya Muslim mosques in over 60 countries, from the Mediterranean hillsides of Albania to the South Pacific waters of Tuvalu. We also pay special tribute to the historic visits of the Ahmadiyya *khulufa* to many of these countries.

This humble publication could not have been possible without the mercy and blessings of Allah. I wish to thank His Holiness, *Hadhrat Mirza Masroor Ahmad*[aba], *Khalifatul Masih V*, for his spiritual guidance for this project, from its inception to its completion. I also am grateful to the *Amir* of the USA *Jama'at*, Ahsanullah Zafr, for his valuable support. I also want to acknowledge the efforts of numerous contributors who dedicated countless hours towards this task. A list of these individuals can be found in the acknowledgments section at the end of this publication. May Allah bless them all. *Ameen.*

We pray that Allah continues to safeguard the mosques of the Community, and indeed all houses of worship around the world. May He continue to make them a source of peace and prosperity for all citizens of the world. *Ameen.*

Anwer Mahmood Khan
May 27, 2008
Chino Hills, California

Message from Hadhrat Khalifatul Masih V [aba]
Supreme Head of the Worldwide Ahmadiyya Muslim Community

Dear Respected *Amir Sahib, Jama'at Ahmadiyya* USA
Assalamo Alaikum wa Rahmatullahe wa Barakatahu

Alhumdolillah that *Jama'at* Ahmadiyya USA is enabled by God's grace to publish a historic souvenir on the occasion of *Khilafat* Ahmadiyya Centenary to illustrate one hundred years of *Jama'at* Ahmadiyya's services for the progress of Islam and the establishment of the Holy Prophet Muhammad's [sa] exalted status. In particular, it prominently features the Ahmadiyya *Jama'at's* good fortune to facilitate the building of mosques all over the world. In humankind's spiritual history, it is a magnificent and extraordinary feat that a community which emerged from the tiny village of Qadian, India has been able to construct mosques in all the countries and continents of the world!

Hadhrat Mirza Masroor Ahmad[aba], *Khalifatul Masih V*, is the supreme head of the worldwide Ahmadiyya Muslim Community.

In 1894, after the appearance of the universally witnessed sign of the eclipses of the moon and the sun, *Hadhrat* Promised Messiah [as] said that the foundation stone for the renaissance of Islam and the blessed institution to promote goodness had been laid down, and mosques would now be constructed, and people would start entering the religion of God in multitudes. He said:

> "Eclipses of the moon and the sun are manifestations of beauty and glory; and this event is a bright and glorious indication for renaissance and spiritual revolutions. It is the keystone to set forth an establishment to promote goodness, build mosques, and debilitate places of idol-worship. Thus the heavenly powers shall conquer the earthly powers…and God shall show a luminous lamp to His people, and they will enter God's religion in great multitudes." (*Ruhani Khaza'in*, Vol. 8, p. 238).

After that, the Promised Messiah [as] also launched a vigorous appeal for the construction of mosques, and explaining the necessity of mosques, he said:

> "At this time, our *Jama'at* is in a great need for mosques. A mosque is a house of God. In whatever village or city our *Jama'at* establishes a mosque, be assured then that the foundation for the *Jama'at's* progress has been laid there. In any

village or city where there are only a few Muslims, or no Muslims at all, and Islam has to progress there, then a mosque needs to be built there; then God Himself shall attract Muslims to that place." (*Malfoozat*, Vol. 7, p. 119)

The foundation laid down by the Promised Messiah[as] to construct mosques was followed by the Second Manifestation of Power – the *Khulufa-e-Ahmadiyyat* – who continued to build mosques all over the world. Responding positively to the call of the *khulufa*, Ahmadis graciously offered their wealth in the way of Allah, and Ahmadi women presented their bracelets and other valuable jewelry. Whether it is in Europe, America, Asia or Africa, Ahmadiyya mosques are being built in all the countries of the world where the name of God in being exalted. *Alhumdolillah ala zalik*! Always remember that mosques are built to glorify, praise and worship Allah the Exalted, the Most High. As Allah says:

$$مَسٰجِدُ يُذْكَرُ فِيْهَا اسْمُ اللّٰهِ كَثِيْرًا$$

"Mosques, wherein the name of Allah is oft commemorated." The Holy Prophet Muhammad[sa] says: "Mosques are for the remembrance of Allah the Exalted, and for the recitation of the Holy Qur'an." Also remember that the doors of mosques are open for all worshippers without any discrimination of color or race. Moreover, a mosque gives us the lesson that all humans are equal in the sight of God, whether they are rich or poor. Another message attached with mosques is to maintain peace and security: Love for all, hatred for none! Mosques teach us to remain united. As God is One in the Heavens, similarly the worshippers of One God should become united on the earth, and they should discard all hatred, grudges and hostility from their hearts.

Thus, you have to spread this message of peace all over America; indeed, the entire world. You have to bring the whole world under the banner of the Holy Prophet Muhammad[sa]. May Allah the Exalted grant us the ability to build the most mosques in the world, and may He bless us with the opportunity to render true worship of the Unique and One God! May He make us heirs of all the blessings and spiritual light attached with the establishment of the mosques. *Ameen*.

Wassalam,

Humbly,

Mirza Masroor Ahmad
Khalifatul Masih V

Message from Wakil e A'ala
On the Construction of Mosques Around the World

Mukaram wa Muhtaram Amir Sahib USA, Assalamo Alaikum wa Rahmatullahe wa Barakatahu.

I hope, by the Grace of Allah, you are doing well.

I am happy to know that *Jama'at* Ahmadiyya USA is publishing a pictorial souvenir about Ahmadiyya Mosques constructed around the world, on the occasion of the *Khilafat* Centenary in 2008. This souvenir would include the pictures of mosques that were constructed and managed by chapters of the Ahmadiyya Muslim Community throughout the world. This special souvenir will not only reflect the efforts made by *Jama'at* Ahmadiyya, in the construction of Mosques worldwide, but will also rejuvenate the faith of its readers.

The Holy Prophet Muhammad[sa] has said:

> For those who will construct Allah's house in this world, Allah will construct a similar house in paradise.

In accord with this statement, the Muslim *Ummah* has constructed countless mosques in various parts of the world during the last fourteen hundred years. However, with the coming of *Hadhrat* Mirza Ghulam Ahmad, the Promised Messiah[as], the following of this directive of the Holy Prophet[sa] has been taken up with a renewed sense of direction and objective.

Hadhrat Ahmad[as] stated:

> At this time there is a dire need of mosques for our *Jama'at*. This is a house of God. In the village or town where our mosque is established, the foundation for the progress of the *Jama'at* has already been laid. If there is a town or city where there are no Muslims, or very few of them, and in that town the progress of Islam is desired, then a mosque should be constructed there. (*Malfoozat*, vol 5, p. 93).

Chaudhry Hameedullah is *Wakil ul A'ala, Anjuman Tehrik e Jadid*, Rabwah, Pakistan.

Thus, the Ahmadiyya Muslim Community has constructed many mosques to introduce Islam and to continue its progress. *Hadhrat Khalifatul Masih V*[aba], in his Friday Sermon of October 22, 2004, said:

> *Hadhrat Musleh Maood*[ra] once expressed the desire that if we have two thousand and five hundred mosques in Europe then the pace of progress will increase many fold. May Allah bestow this ability to the members of our *Jama'at* that soon they may construct mosques here in that number.

After laying the foundation stone of the London Mosque in 1924, *Jama'at* Ahmadiyya constructed many mosques around the world or the propagation of Islam. It has constructed mosques in Sweden, Denmark, Germany and in several African countries. *Hadhrat Khalifatul Masih III*[ra], during the time of his *khilafat*, laid the foundation stone of Basharat Mosque in Spain. This mosque was inaugurated during the *khilafat* of *Hadhrat Khalifatul Masih IV*[rh].

Similarly, *Hadhrat Khalifatul Masih IV*[rh] laid the foundation stone of Baitul Huda Mosque in

The construction of Baitul Huda Mosque in Sydney, Australia. The Ahmadiyya Muslim Community has built thousands of mosques around the world, for the purpose of spreading the peaceful teachings of Islam and to promote interfaith harmony in all nations of the world.

Australia and initiated the propagation of Islam on the Australian continent. A project of constructing one hundred Mosques in Germany, which started at the time of *Khilafat e Rabbiya* has seen much progress in the time of *Khalifatul Masih V* [aba].

The construction work of Baitul Futuh Mosque in the United Kingdom was started at the time of *Hadhrat Khalifatul Masih IV* [rh], but its opening ceremony was done by our beloved *Imam, Hadhrat Khalifatul Masih V* [aba]. The journey of the Ahmadiyya Muslim Community to spread Islam's message of peace outside of India is still continuing. There are many mosques that have been constructed and completed outside India and Pakistan. *Hadhrat Khalifatul Masih V* [aba], while drawing our attention to the real purpose of constructing mosques, said:

Remember the victory of Islam and Ahmadiyyat is tied with keeping these mosques occupied with supplicants. Thus, O Ahmadis, get up and run towards the mosques and keep them occupied with prayers, so we may see the day of triumph of Islam according to the promises of Allah.

God willing, may we all, in compliance with the directives of our dear *Imam* [aba], be the ones who will keep these mosques occupied. May we pay close attention to the real beauty of the mosques, in the form of our regular offering of prayers in them. May Allah with His extreme Mercy, not only give us the ability to construct more mosques in the world, but also give us the ability to keep them occupied with prayers. *Ameen.*

Wassalam,

Chaudhry Hameedullah
Rabwah, Pakistan.

Message from the Amir of the U.S.A. Jama'at

وَّاَنَّ الْمَسٰجِدَ لِلّٰهِ فَلَا تَدْعُوْا مَعَ اللّٰهِ اَحَدًا ۞

And all the places of worship belong to Allah; so call not on anyone beside Allah." (72:19)

Dr. Ahsanullah Zafar is the *Amir* of the Ahmadiyya Muslim Community, U.S.A.

It is befitting that we celebrate this *Khilafat* Jubilee commemorative on Ahmadiyya *Masajid* (Ahmadiyya Mosques) worldwide with the above-mentioned Quranic verse. Our Mosques truly fall under the verse's dictates since we are guided by *Hadhrat Khalifatul Masih V* [aba] and the traditions of the *Jama'at* Ahmadiyya.

Some of our mosques are grand to our eyes, while most are simple. The richness of mosques is not from their artistry, but from the humility of the worshippers inside. Allah's Blessings are glowing on the faces of Ahmadi Muslims as they spend time in the mosques. The talk is of divine promises of peace and prosperity. The attitude is of supporting and not disturbing the world where we live and flourish. There is the peaceful belief that this world and Allah's blessings in the hereafter are a continuum.

Our purpose as a *Jama'at* is to carry the message given to the Promised Messiah [as]. We do that by living in harmony in the message when we come together in Ahmadiyya mosques. We welcome people of other faiths, to see us, to meet us, to share with us the message and teachings of Islam.

I join everyone in a prayer that Allah helps us place this commemorative for the best use in celebration of the Centenary of *Khilafat e Ahmadiyya*.

Wassalam,
Khaksar,

Ahsanullah Zafar
May 27, 2008

Quranic Verses About the First House of Allah
The Importance of the Sacred Mosque

وَإِذْ جَعَلْنَا الْبَيْتَ مَثَابَةً لِّلنَّاسِ وَأَمْنًا وَاتَّخِذُوا مِن مَّقَامِ إِبْرَاهِيمَ مُصَلَّى وَعَهِدْنَا إِلَى إِبْرَاهِيمَ وَإِسْمَاعِيلَ أَن طَهِّرَا بَيْتِيَ لِلطَّائِفِينَ وَالْعَاكِفِينَ وَالرُّكَّعِ السُّجُودِ ۩

And remember the time when We made the House a resort for mankind and a place of security; and take ye the station of Abraham as a place of Prayer. And We commanded Abraham and Ishmael, saying, 'Purfiy My House for those who perform the circuit, and those remain therein for devotion and those who fall prostrate in prayer. (2:126)

وَمِنْ حَيْثُ خَرَجْتَ فَوَلِّ وَجْهَكَ شَطْرَ الْمَسْجِدِ الْحَرَامِ وَإِنَّهُ لَلْحَقُّ مِن رَّبِّكَ وَمَا اللهُ بِغَافِلٍ عَمَّا تَعْمَلُونَ ۩

From wheresoever thou comest forth, turn thy face twoards the Sacred Mosque; for that is indeed the truth from thy Lord. And Allah is not unmindful of what you do. (2:150)

إِنَّ أَوَّلَ بَيْتٍ وُضِعَ لِلنَّاسِ لَلَّذِي بِبَكَّةَ مُبَارَكًا وَهُدًى لِّلْعَالَمِينَ ۩

The first House founded for mankind is that at (Mecca), abounding in blessings and guidance for all peoples. (3:97)

فِيهِ آيَاتٌ بَيِّنَاتٌ مَّقَامُ إِبْرَاهِيمَ وَمَن دَخَلَهُ كَانَ آمِنًا وَلِلَّهِ عَلَى النَّاسِ حِجُّ الْبَيْتِ مَنِ اسْتَطَاعَ إِلَيْهِ سَبِيلًا وَمَن كَفَرَ فَإِنَّ اللهَ غَنِيٌّ عَنِ الْعَالَمِينَ ۩

In it are manifest Signs; it is the place of Abraham; and whoso enters it, enters peace. And pilgrimage to the House is a duty which men -- those who can find a way thither -- owe to Allah. And whoever disbelieves, let him remember that Allah is surely independent of all creatures. (3:98)

وَلَا يَجْرِمَنَّكُمْ شَنَآنُ قَوْمٍ أَن صَدُّوكُمْ عَنِ الْمَسْجِدِ الْحَرَامِ أَن تَعْتَدُوا وَتَعَاوَنُوا عَلَى الْبِرِّ وَالتَّقْوَى وَلَا تَعَاوَنُوا عَلَى الْإِثْمِ وَالْعُدْوَانِ وَاتَّقُوا اللهَ إِنَّ اللهَ شَدِيدُ الْعِقَابِ ۩

And let not the enmity of a people, that they hindered you from the Sacred Mosque, incite you to transgress. And help one another in righteousness and piety; but help not one another in sin and transgression. And fear Allah; surely, Allah is severe in punishment. (5:3)

جَعَلَ اللهُ الْكَعْبَةَ الْبَيْتَ الْحَرَامَ قِيَامًا لِّلنَّاسِ وَالشَّهْرَ الْحَرَامَ وَالْهَدْيَ وَالْقَلَائِدَ ذَلِكَ لِتَعْلَمُوا أَنَّ اللهَ يَعْلَمُ مَا فِي السَّمَاوَاتِ وَمَا فِي الْأَرْضِ وَأَنَّ اللهَ بِكُلِّ شَيْءٍ عَلِيمٌ ۩

Allah has made the Ka'aba, the inviolable House, as a means of support and uplift for mankind, as also the Sacred Month and the offerings and animals with collars. That is so that you may know that Allah knows what is in the heavens and what is in the earth, and that Allah knows all things well. (5:98)

وَمَا لَهُمْ أَلَّا يُعَذِّبَهُمُ اللهُ وَهُمْ يَصُدُّونَ عَنِ الْمَسْجِدِ الْحَرَامِ وَمَا كَانُوا أَوْلِيَاءَهُ إِنْ أَوْلِيَاؤُهُ

And what excuse have they now that Allah should not punish them, when they hinder men from the Sacred Mosque, and they are not its true guardians ? Its true guardians are only those who are righteous, but most of them know not. (8:35)

وَالْبَيْتِ الْمَعْمُورِ ۩ وَالسَّقْفِ الْمَرْفُوعِ ۩

By the frequented House, and by the elevated roof. (52:5-6)

The Holy Ka'aba
The Sacred Heart of Islam

Masjid Al-Haram (The Sacred Mosque) is the holiest site of the Islamic faith. Here, millions of Muslims arrive here each year to perform the sacred pilgrimage ceremonies associated with the Hajj, one of the "five pillars" of belief in Islam.

HISTORICAL FACTS

Foundation

- It is believed that *Hadhrat* Adam[as] built the Holy *Ka'aba*, which was the first house of worship. Later, the Holy *Ka'aba* was renovated by *Hadhrat* Ibrahim[as] and his son, *Hadhrat* Ismail[as].

Dimensions of Original Structure

- Originally, the *Ka'aba* was about 50×30 ft. in area, and was roofless and rectangular in shape.
- It is believed that *Hadhrat* Ibrahim[as] raised the foundation of the original structure and offered a prayer, which is recorded in the Qur'an, to God.
- There was one space left for the door in the east wall that was leveled to the ground.
- The current area of *Hateem* outside the *Ka'aba* was included in the original structure.
- The walls were 13.5 feet high. The *Ka'aba* was on an elevated hillside in Mecca.

Renovation by the Quresh tribe

Five years before Muhammad[sa] announced that he was a prophet of God, the *Ka'aba* was renovated by the tribe of Quresh. They assembled and collected funds to rebuild the *Ka'aba*, which had been ravaged by fire. They appointed Baqoom, an Abyssinian mason, to lead the effort. The renovation began with great enthusiasm and was proceeding appropriately until the placement of the Black Stone came into question. This created a great dispute as to who would have the honor of placing it. The most senior among the Quresh, Abdullah bin Umar bin Makhzoom, historically is noted as stating, "O

G.M. Farooq

A view of the Ka'aba from inside a portion of Masjid Al-Haram (The Sacred Mosque).

Quresh, come to an agreement concerning that over which you are disputing. Let the first man who enters through the gate of this mosque decide the matter for you."

The first man to enter through the gate of the mosque was Muhammad[sa]. When the Quresh saw him, they said, "Here is *Al-Amin* [the trustworthy one]! We agree to accept Muhammad's decision." They then explained to Muhammad[sa] their dilemma. Upon hearing this, Muhammad[sa] asked for a cloak to be brought to him. He then placed the Black Stone on the cloak and then instructed the leader of each tribe to take an edge of the cloak and lift up the Black Stone together. When they had done as he had instructed, and the Black Stone was now on the lifted cloak and in a position to be placed within its resting place, Muhammad[sa] himself then set the Black Stone in its place. (*Seerat Ibne Hasham*, 1, 233-234; p. 35).

The Holy Prophet[sa] expressed his displeasure about the renovation of the *Ka'aba* to his wife *Hadhrat* Ayesha[ra]. He said: "Were it not that your people are still so close to the time of *Kufr*, I would have knocked the *Ka'aba* down and rebuilt it with two doors, a door through which people can enter and a door through which they could exit and I would have brought the doors to the ground level" (*Bukhari* and *Muslim*).

He further stated: "Your people placed the door at an elevated level so anyone seeking entrance to the *Ka'aba* would need their consent. They would permit or deprive entry to whomsoever they would like. The area of *Hateem* was part of the Abrahamic Plan, but your people ran out of funds when they were installing the roof, and, hence, they left that area." (*Bukhari* and *Muslim*)

A nighttime view of Masjid Al-Haram (The Sacred Mosque) as seen from one of its entrances.

Renovation by Abdullah bin Zubair[ra] in 64 Hijri
- Fulfilling the wishes of the Holy Prophet[sa], Abdullah bin Zubair[ra] built two doors at the ground level.
- Abdullah bin Zubair[ra] raised the walls to 40.5 feet by incorporating the *Hateem* area in the structure.
- A small window at the upper side of the wall was installed for circulation of air and light.
- Abdullah bin Zubair[ra] purchased the surrounding homes for 10,000 Dinars to include in the open space around the *Ka'aba*.

Renovation by Hajjaj bin Yousuf
- Unfortunately Hajjaj reconstructed the *Ka'aba* after the pattern of the Quresh and later regretted this when he learned that the Holy Prophet's specifications were realized by Abdullah bin Zubair[ra].

Renovation by Sultan Murad Khan in 1040 Hijri
- In the year 1038, a devastating flood destroyed the structure of the *Ka'aba* and its renovation once again became necessary. Sultan Murad Khan undertook this project and renovated the *Ka'aba* along Hajaj bin Yousuf's structural guidelines.

Modern Renovations in the Saudi Era
- The beginning of the Saudi Era was marked by many new renovations and additions to the structure of the *Ka'aba*. A few are highlighted in **Table 1**.

Ka'aba is the Center of Dry Land
- Dr. M. A. Shaltout, President of the Research Center for the Sun and Geophysical Studies in Cairo, Egypt, performed extensive research and came to the conclusion that Mecca is the geographical center of both the Old and New World. The Old World consists of three continents, Africa, Europe and Asia. When a circle is drawn with Mecca in the center, the 8000 km^2 area covers the borders of

Table 1. Modern Renovations of the Ka'aba in the Saudi Era			
Parameters	Before Saudi Era	Additions	Current total
Total area	193,000 m^2	163,000 m^2	356,000 m^2
Capacity of worshippers	410,000	773,000	1.2 million
Minarets	7	2	9
Main entrances	3	1	4
Ordinary entrances	27	18	45
Basement entrances	4	2	6
Escalators	7	4	11
Doors	27	14	41
Restrooms	5000	4000	9000

these continents. When this circle is drawn to a diameter of 13,000 km^2, it would cover the borders of the three new continents formed in the New World (North America, South America and Australia).

Extensions of *Ka'aba*

■   In 638, *Hadhrat* Umar Farooq [ra] expanded the *Ka'aba* prayer area by demolishing the homes around it.

■   In 646, *Hadhrat* Uthman [ra] continued this extension by purchasing adjacent homes and expanding the facilities.

■   In 684, *Hadhrat* Abdullah bin Zubair [ra] extended the area by buying a large estate for 10,000 Dinars; he also built corridors within the *Ka'aba*.

■   In 709, Waleed added beautiful corridors with elaborate designs.

■   In 745, Abu Jafar Al Mansoor made a large extension on the north side of the *Ka'aba* and created several *Mehrabs* and modified the corridors with elaborate designs.

■   In 771, Mehdi Abbasi made huge extensions of the *Ka'aba* at least twice during his reign.

■   In 875, Abu Jafar Ahmad renovated the roof, reinforced the walls, and made extensions for the worshippers.

■   Abul Fazal Al Muqtadar had a large door built and named it *Bab e Ibrahim* and also built two large palaces nearby. These extensions added an area of 81.5 × 98 feet to the existing facilities.

■   Organizing worshippers in circular rows around the *Ka'aba* began in the reign of Governor Khalid bin Abdullah in 100 Hijri. *Hadhrat* Ata deduced this from the Qur'an (39:75).

■   Black Stone: Dimensions: Height = 1.1 m; Length = 25 cm; Width = 17 cm.

■   The Holy Prophet [sa] has been reported to say that the Black Stone came from the heavens and it was whiter than milk but the human sins turned it black. (*Tirmidhi Kitabul Haj, Hadith* 877).

■   The circuit around *Ka'aba* begins and ends with this landmark. The Holy Prophet [sa] used to touch and kiss this stone.

■   It is reported that *Hadhrat* Umar [ra] kissed the Black Stone and said: "I know that you are only a stone and can neither do harm nor bring benefit. Had I not seen Allah's Messenger kissing you, I would not have kissed you" (*Al Bukhari*, 1597).

Objectives of the Ka'aba
(From Friday Sermons, April 7 and 14, 1967 of *Hadhrat Khalifatul Masih* III[rh])

Hadhrat *Khalifatul Masih* III[rh], in a series of Friday sermons, enumerated twenty-three objectives of the *Ka'aba* as follows:

■ The *Ka'aba* was formed for all humanity, and thus negates all forms of discrimination.

■ The *Ka'aba* is a blessed place presenting a complete *Shariah* (Islamic law).

■ It serves as a guidance for all people.

■ No nation has an unfair advantage over others for its use in worship.

■ Implicit in this objective is a prediction that in latter days select nations would pose themselves to be leaders while others are subjects. The Holy Qur'an refutes this ideology.

■ From this venue, the perfect guidance for humankind will be established through the advent of Islam as past messengers were limited in both scope and time.

■ Manifest signs are embedded in the *Ka'aba*.

■ A nation will be formed whose members will demonstrate the signs of Allah as living proof of ultimate and everlasting successes.

■ It is the station of *Hadhrat* Ibrahim[as] – a state of complete submission to Allah's will.

■ People of this nation would demonstrate total submission to God's will out of pure love that would produce immense sacrifices.

■ Whoso enters the *Ka'aba* is safe, and whoso performs the modes of worship dictated by the *Shariah* sincerely will be in God's protection with his or her previous sins being forgiven.

■ Pilgrimage to this House is a duty for all who posses the ability to reach it. It is not restricted to the residents of Arabia, but is open to all who can reach it. As such, it becomes a meeting point for the entire world.

■ This house is a place of unification; while people were divided into factions, this House will assemble them as one nation, thereby removing all man-made boundaries.

■ This house is a place of security. No other formula to establish world peace will succeed save the formula created through this House of one mankind without differentiation.

■ Take the station of *Hadhrat* Ibrahim[as] as a place of prayer to create a nation that reflects the submission of Ibrahim[as] to Allah with full sincerity.

■ Purify my House, this house will teach the ways of purification as in a university.

■ This house will serve as a meeting place for the citizens of all nations who come for visitation and comfort.

■ A nation of devotees to this House of Allah will be established.

■ A nation shall be created from among those who bow down and fall prostrate in prayers and will consist of true worshippers of God.

■ This town will be protected from the onslaught of all invaders. The Prophet of Islam[sa] who was raised from here also will be in Allah's protection, and the *Shariah* revealed to him will be divinely protected.

■ Provisions of fruits for its dwellers. This indicates that those who sacrifice everything for the sake of Allah are immensely rewarded with delicious fruits in this world and the next.

■ Oh our Lord, accept our prayers – the nation created with *Baitullah* will continuously and deeply indulge in prayers that will serve as a message for humankind.

■ Oh Allah, make our offspring a people submissive to Thee so that they should recognize the Prophet that will be sent to them and become a nation of those who submit to Thee.

REFERENCES

El-Nagah, Hadeer Abo. *The Ka'ba is the Center of the World*. Dar Al-Manarah, Egypt: 2000.

Maubood, Muhammad Abdul. *Tarikh Makkah Muqarammah (History of Mecca)*. Maktabah Rahmaniyya, Lahore: 1988.

Masjid e Nabawi
The Prophet's Mosque

Masjid e Nabawi (The Prophet's Mosque) is located in the city of Madinah in Saudi Arabia. It is one of the most famous mosques in the world.

The traditional story regarding this mosque relates that the Holy Prophet Muhammad [sa] departed the town of Quba on Friday, October 4, 622 C.E. As he arrived in Madinah, and his camel rested at a spot, he decided to build a mosque at that very spot. This parcel of land belonged to two orphan children, Sahal and Sohail, who offered to give it as a gift to the Prophet of God [sa]. He, however, decided to buy it for ten Dinars and laid the foundation stone of what came to be known as the Prophet's Mosque on October 16, 622 C.E.

According to *Hadhrat* Ayesha[ra], the Prophet of God [sa] laid down the first stone, and *Hadhrat* Abu Bakar[ra], *Hadhrat* Umar Farooq[ra] and *Hadhrat* Uthman[ra] laid down the next three stones, respectively. After the foundation was laid down with stones, the walls were raised with unbaked bricks. The Holy Prophet Muhammad [sa] carried out the construction work himself by fetching the bricks. On one occasion, he was carrying a large pile that reached his chest. Seeing this, one of his companions, *Hadhrat* Asyad bin Hafeer[ra], offered to lend him a hand. To this, the Prophet Muhammad [sa] responded: "Carry on and fetch another pile. To earn virtues in the way of Allah, you are not in greater need than I." (*Jammaul Qawaid*, 67:1).

■ This mosque measured 30 x 35 m². It had three doors on its south, east and west sides. With the change of the *qibla*, a south side door was closed, and a north door was installed.

■ A platform for *Ashabus Suffa* (the poor companions of the Prophet [sa]) was made outside the mosque near the northeast end.

■ At first, the mosque had no roof, but a roof that was made with the trunks and branches of palm trees, and which provided only a little shelter, was added later.

■ In the year 628 C.E., the Prophet [sa] constructed the second extension, increasing the area of the mosque to 2,475 m².

■ *Hadhrat* Umar Farooq[ra] extended the structure by five meters to the south, ten meters to the west and fifteen meters to the north, thereby increasing the total area to 3,575 m².

■ In 649 C.E., *Hadhrat* Usman[ra] extended the mosque by an additional 496 m², thereby increasing the total area to 4,071 m².

■ In 706 C.E., Waleed bin Abdul Malik expanded the total area of the mosque to 6,440 m². There still was no prayer niche, or *mehrab*, for the Imam in the Prophet's Mosque until 706 CE, when *Hadhrat* Umar bin Abdul Aziz[ra] added the architectural feature from where the Friday sermon could be delivered.

■ Khalifa Mahdi Abbasi extended the Mosque's

Hasan Gopalani

A closer look at the entrance to Masjid e Nabawi (The Prophet's Mosque). The mosque is visited frequently throughout the year, but especially during the annual Hajj (piligrimage ceremony) performed by Muslims arriving from all over the world.

north end by 2,450 m^2, bringing the total area of the mosque to 8,890 m^2.

■ In 1257 C.E., a fire broke out in the mosque. Khalifa Al-Mustasim renovated it over the next few years.

■ Renovation and maintenance of the mosque continued until 1474 C.E. Malik Qayatbai added another 120 m^2, which resulted in a total area of 9,010 m^2.

■ From 1848 to 1860, Sultan Abdul Majeed added a new gate on the north side and carried out further extensions, resulting in a total area of 10,303 m^2.

Doors of the Mosque

The Saud Family, under the leadership of Shah Abdul Aziz, undertook a massive expansion that increased the area of the mosque to 16,327 m^2. Currently, over 750,000 worshippers can offer *Salat* in the mosque. The Saudi expansion

included ten beautiful, sturdy, and easily operable doors. Although each one weighs 2.5 tons, the doors can be opened or closed with a slight push or pull of a finger. Some of these doors have historical significance:

Bab un Nabi. This door stood adjacent to the Prophet's [sa] quarters and is thus named after him. It was later replaced with a window with web wire.

Bab e Ali. This door was in front of *Hadhrat Ali's* [ra] quarters, but was later closed during expansion.

Bab e Usman, also known as *Bab e Jibreel.* The Prophet[sa] would enter the Mosque via this door. "*Bab e Jibreel*" refers to an incident when the Angel Gabriel appeared to and spoke with the Prophet[sa] during the Battle of the Ditch.

Bab e Rabota or *Bab un Nisa.* This door was situated in front of the quarters of a woman named Rabta, who was the daughter of Al Abbas-al-Saqah. The door was installed at the time of *Hadhrat* Umar [ra] per instructions given by the Prophet[sa]. These instructions called for the construction of a door solely for the purpose of affording female worshippers privacy during entry and exit at the mosque.

Bab ur Rahmat. It is related that the name "*Bab ur Rahmat*" (Door of God's Grace) is derived from an incident in which the prayers of the Prophet [sa] were accepted. The tradition relates that a man entered the mosque through this door while the Prophet [sa] was delivering the Friday sermon. The man told the Prophet [sa] of a severe drought that was falling on the land and begged the Prophet [sa] to pray for rain. The Prophet [sa] prayed, and it began to rain for an entire week. On the following Friday, the man came again and requested the Prophet [sa] to pray for the rains to stop. The Prophet [sa] again prayed and the rain stopped. This door was named *Bab ur Rahmat* in honor of this incident.

In addition to these five doors, the Saudi family added five more doors.

Beginning of Adhan

The call for prayers, or *adhan*, is observed five times a day for the 1.5 billion Muslims all over the world. Most do not realize that this ritual is the result of much prayer and consultation among the Prophet [sa] and his companions.

The Prophet [sa] and his companions consulted about how best to call the followers to prayer. Three suggestions were presented, including lighting a flame, beating a gong, and blowing a trumpet. The Prophet[sa] rejected all these suggestions and adjourned the meeting.

Hadhrat Abdullah bin Zaid [ra] came back and was quite concerned and kept on thinking. During the night, he had a waking vision in which he saw a man wrapped in two green sheets come to him with a gong in his hand. *Hadhrat* Abdullah [ra] asked him to sell this gong to him. The man replied: what would you do with it? *Hadhrat* Abdullah [ra] replied: I would assemble worshippers for *Salat*. To this the man remarked: Shouldn't I tell you a better way? *Hadhrat* Abdullah [ra] responded in

the affirmative. The man shared the words of the present call for prayers and asked *Hadhrat* Abdullah [ra] to recite with him.

After he woke up, he related this entire vision to Prophet [sa]. The Prophet [sa] remarked: God willing, this vision is true. He further instructed *Hadhrat* Zaid [ra] to find *Hadhrat* Bilal [ra] and teach him these words and ask *Hadhrat* Bilal [ra] to call these phrases. As this was going on, *Hadhrat* Umar [ra] appeared to the Prophet[sa] and said: I saw the same vision that was shown to *Hadhrat* Zaid[ra]. The Prophet[sa] thanked Allah and said all praise belongs to Allah. (*Sunan Abu Daud*)

■ The Prophet[sa] frequently commented on the rewards for offering *Salat/Itekaf* in this Mosque. He said: With the exception of *Masjid e Haram*, offering *Salat* in my mosque carries a thousand-fold rewards.

■ *Hadhrat* Anas bin Malik[ra] reports: Anyone who offers *Salat* at home will receive the reward of one *Salat*; if this *Salat* is offered in the neighborhood mosque, the reward will be twenty-five fold; if this *Salat* is offered in *Jamay Masjid* (a large mosque that can hold a large congregation), the reward will increase 500 fold. In *Masjid* e Aqsa, this reward becomes 5,000 fold, and in the Prophet's Mosque, this reward increases 50,000 fold, while the reward in Masjid e Haram is 100,000 fold. (*Ibn e Maja*, 102)

■ The Prophet[sa] said: "I am the last prophet, just like my mosque is the last mosque."

■ *Hadhrat* Anas[ra] reports that the Holy Prophet[ra] said: Anyone who offers forty *Salat* in congregation will be protected from hellfire and relieved from the evil of hypocrisy.

REFERENCES

■ Maubood, Muhammad Abdul. *Tarikh Madina Muqarammah (History of Medina)*. Maktabah Rahmaniyya, Lahore: 1988.

■ Mubarakpuri, Shaikh Safiur Rahman. *History of Medina*. Darus Salam Books, Riyadh: 2002.

Qibla e Awwal
The Dome of the Rock

A view of Masjid Qubbat as Sakhrah (The Dome of the Rock), which is located on the Temple Mount in Jerusalem.

The sanctuary known as *Qubbat as Sakhrah* (The Dome of the Rock) was completed by 'Abd al Malik ibn Marwan in 691 C.E. This sacred building is believed to rest on Mt. Moriah in the Old City of Jerusalem. This mountain, also known as the Temple Mount, was the site where *Hadhrat Suleiman*[as] (The Prophet Solomon[as]) built the first temple (known as *Baitul Muqaddas*), which was completed in 957 B.C.E.

It was towards the direction of this site that the Holy Prophet Muhammad [sa] and his companions [ra] would pray (i.e., it was the first *Qibla*). Muslims believe that upon receiving a revelation from God the direction of the *Qibla* was changed towards the Sacred Mosque in Makkah, Arabia. This revelation is recorded in the Holy Qur'an:

"Verily, We see thee turning thy face often to heaven; surely, then, will We make thee turn to the Qiblah which thou likest. So, turn thy face towards the Sacred Mosque; and wherever you be, turn your faces towards it." (2: 145).

The switch in *Qiblah* occurred as the Holy Prophetsa was offering Salat in the mosque now known as *Masjid Qiblatain* (the Mosque with Two Qiblas - described on page 12).

The First Temple was destroyed by Nebuchanezzar II of Babylonia, when he sacked Jerusalem in 586 B.C.E. The temple was rebuilt beginning 20 B.C.E, but was again destroyed in 70 C.E.

The Cave of Hira
The Prophet's Sanctuary

Prophet Muhammad[sa] was endowed with the deep love of the Creator right from his early youth. When he reached his thirties, his love of God and love of His worship began to possess him more and more. To get away from the mischiefs and vices of the people of Mecca, the Prophet[sa] often would retire to a secluded cave atop the lofty Mount Hira. At Hira, he would worship God day and night, praying ardently for the uplift of humanity. When he was forty years of age, he saw an angel commanding him to recite. The Prophet[sa] said in reply that he did not know what or how to recite. The heavenly figure insisted and at last made the Prophet[sa] recite the following verses:

Recite thou in the name of thy Lord Who created, created man from a clot of blood. Recite! And thy Lord is the Most Beneficent, Who taught man by the pen, taught man what he knew not.
— Holy Qur'an (96:2-6).

Hence, this cave became the initiation place of the greatest spiritual revolution mankind ever has witnessed, the advent of Islam. The Promised Messiah, *Hadhrat* Ahmad[as] described this spiritual revolution:

Have you any notion what was the strange event which took place in the desert country of Arabia when hundreds of thousands of people were revived within a brief period? Those who were blind obtained sight and those who were dumb began to speak of the understanding of the Divine. And the world underwent a revolution which has never been heard or seen before. It was the supplications during dark nights of one who had lost himself in God, which raised a clamor in the world and manifested such wonders as appeared impossible in the case of that unlearned helpless one.
— *Blessings of Prayer by Hadhrat Mirza Ghulam Ahmad*[as], p. 10.

Masjid Quba
Islam's First Mosque

This is the very first mosque outside Mecca whose foundation was laid by the Prophet Muhammad[sa] himself. It was built during the Prophet[as]'s migration to Medina, when he took a short stay at the city of Quba, three miles north of Medina. He worked as a laborer to construct this house of Allah.

Within a few days, the mosque was completed. The Prophet[sa] continued to have a special attachment with the Quba Mosque; he visited it every week even after his migration to Medina.

Some righteous scholars have attributed the following verse to be related to this mosque:
"*A mosque that was founded upon piety from the very first day, is surely more worthy than thou*

should stand therein to lead the prayer service."
— Holy Qur'an (9:108)

The Quba Mosque

Masjid Qiblatain
The Mosque with Two Directions

The *Masjid* Qiblatain (Mosque with two *Qiblas*) is the historic location where the Prophet Muhammad [sa], according to Muslim belief, was instructed during prayer to switch from facing the Dome of the Rock in Jerusalem to the Sacred Mosque in Makkah (The Holy Qur'an, 2:145). From that point onwards, Muslims always have performed their daily prayers facing Makkah, a symbol of their collective worship within a single mosque.

The Charter of Freedom
The religion of Islam and freedom of worship

"This is the document which Muhammad, son of Abdullah, God's Prophet, Warner and Bearer of glad tidings, has caused to be written so that there should remain no excuse for those coming after. I have caused this document to be written for Christians of the East and the West, for those who live near, and for those of distant lands, for the Christians living at present and for those who will come after, for those Christians who are known to us and for those as well whom we do not know...I promise that any monk of wayfarer who will seek my help on the mountains, in forests, deserts or habitations, or in places of worship, I will repel his enemies with all my friends and helpers, with all my relatives and with all those who profess to follow me and will defend him, because they are my covenant. And I will defend the covenanted against the persecution, injury, and embarrassment by their enemies in lieu of the poll tax they have promised to pay. If they prefer to defend their properties and persons by themselves, they will be allowed to do so and will not be put to any inconvenience on that account. No bishop will be expelled from his bishoprice,

no monk from his monastery, no priest from his place of worship, and no pilgrim will be detained in his pilgrimage. None of their churches and other places of worship will be desolated or detroyed or demolished. No material of their churches will be used for building mosques or houses for the Muslims; any Muslim so doing will be regarded as recalcitrant to God and His prophet. Monks and bishops will be subject to no tax or indemnity whether they live in forests or on the rivers, or in the East or West, North or South. I give them my word of honor. They are on my promise and covenant and will enjoy perfect immunity from all sorts of inconveniences. Every help shall be given them in the repair of their churches. They shall be absolved from wearing arms. They shall be protected by the Muslims. Let this document be not disobeyed until Judgment Day."

(Transcribed and adapted from the *Commentary on the Holy Qur'an* by *Hadhrat* Mirza Bashiruddin Mahmood Ahmad, Vol. 4, pp. 1755-1756).

The Holy Prophet[sa] on Praying in the Mosque
by Maulana Shamshad Ahmad Nasir

The purpose of creation of humans is the love and worship of Allah. It is for this sole purpose that Allah raised the Holy Prophet Muhammad[sa] in this world. The Holy Prophet[sa] through his actions and acts of worship has left an exemplary model for all Muslims in perpetuity. From the early days of Islam, five *salat* are mandated for Muslims. The purpose of *salat* is to be in Allah's presence and win His pleasure. *Salat* is the only means how one can acquire these goals. In the context of *Ahadith*, I will attempt to shed light on the central role of mosques and the importance of congregational prayers.

In Chapter *Alhijra* of *Sahih Bukhari*, *Hadhrat* Imam Bukhari quoted the incident of migration as cited by *Hadhrat* Aisha[ra], in which she states that the very first thing the Holy Prophet Muhammad[sa] did after reaching Madinah was to build a mosque. This action of the Prophet[sa] demonstrates that the mosque is the foundation of Islamic society. The mosque is a place for spiritual, moral, intellectual and material guidance.

The following *Ahadith* illustrate the importance that the Prophet[sa] gave to mosques:

■ A person who builds a mosque for Allah's sake, Allah builds a better house in heaven for that person. (*Sahi Muslim*, Chapter *Fazlul Banaul Masajid*).

■ A believer in a mosque is like a fish in water.

■ The most liked buildings in cities to Allah are the mosques (Muslim book of mosques, Chapter *Fazlul Jaloos fee Mosulaho baadas Subh*).

■ *Hadhrat* Abu Huraira[ra] narrates that Holy Prophet Muhammad[sa] said that whenever people gather together in one of the houses of Allah for recitation of the Holy Qur'an and teaching it to one another, comfort descends upon them, mercy covers them, angels spread their wings over them, and Allah makes mention of them to those around Him (*Sahi Muslim*).

Imam Shamshad A. Nasir is Missionary for the Southwestern region of the U.S. Ahmadiyya Muslim Community.

■ In another *hadith* narrated by *Hadhrat* Abu Huraira[ra], the Holy Prophet Muhammad[sa] said: "Shall I tell you something whereby Allah would wipe out your sins and raise your status? Those present said: Certainly, Messenger of Allah. He said: Performing the ablution carefully even in difficulty, frequent walking to the mosque, and waiting eagerly for the next salat after one is finished. This is your striving in the cause of Allah." (*Sahi Muslim*).

■ *Hadhrat* Buraidah[ra] relates that the Holy Prophet Muhammad[sa] said, "Give glad tidings of full light on the Day of Judgment to those who walk to the mosque in the dark of night." (*Abu Daud* and *Tirmidhi*).

The Holy Prophet Muhammad[sa] emphasized the importance of mosques because they are the place where people join to worship God. Great emphasis is therefore given to congregational prayers in the sayings of the Holy Prophet of Islam[sa]. The one who is regular in prayer establishes the religion, and the one who stops praying, drops the faith and destroys the building of religion.

■ The Holy Prophet Muhammad[sa] worshipped Allah in the true sense and spirit of the word, and every moment of his life and every breath he took was spent in the remembrance of Allah to the extent that, even at the time of his death, the last will he made was with the words of *Salat*. He said: "O Muslims, take special care of your prayers, offer congregational prayers in a timely manner, and exhort others to this important obligation. Remember, prayer, which is a bond between the

Creator and Creation, never breaks".

■ *Hadhrat* Abu Huraira [ra] narrates that the Holy Prophet Muhammad [sa] said that the person who goes to the mosque in the morning and evening, Allah prepares for him or her a spiritual sanctuary in paradise (*Bukhari* and *Muslim*).

■ *Hadhrat* Abu Huraira [ra] further narrates that a person who performs ablution carefully at home and then proceeds to the mosque to fulfill his obligation to Allah, Allah wipes out his sin with his first step and elevates his stature with the next step (*Muslim*).

■ Jarir bin Abdullah [ra] narrates that one night we were with the Holy Prophet Muhammad [sa] and there was a full moon. The Holy Prophet [sa] looked towards the moon and said that you would see your Lord the same way you see the moon, i.e., without any obstruction. If you can do anything to have this, then do not be negligent in offering the morning prayers or afternoon prayers, *Salat e Fajr* and *Salat e Asr*.

■ *Hadhrat* Barida [ra] narrates that the Holy Prophet [sa] said that the person who is neglects *Asr* prayers wastes away all his deeds.

■ *Hadhrat* Abu Saeed Khudri [ra] narrates that the Holy Prophet [sa] said that when you see someone coming for worship in the mosque then you should vouch for that person as a believer because Allah says that, "Only those people populate Allah's mosques who believe in God and the Day of Judgment" (*Tirmidhi Kitabutafsir*, Chapter *Al Tauba*).

■ *Hadhrat* Ibn Umar [ra] narrates that the Holy Prophet [sa] said that the reward for offering congregational prayers is twenty seven times more than when one offers prayers by himself.

■ *Hadhrat* Abu Huraira [ra] narrates that the Holy Prophet [sa] said that offering congregational prayers is twenty five times better than offering prayers privately in home or away from home. Whoever among you performs ablution properly and comes to mosque only for prayers then Allah forgives one mistake for each step he takes and raises his stature until he enters the mosque. And when he enters the mosque and waits for prayers he is considered to have joined in prayers, and angels pray for him that 'Oh Allah forgive him' and 'Oh Allah have mercy on him'. This condition remains until he gets busy with some other work or conversation (*Sahi Bukhari, Kitabus Salat Fil Masjid*).

The subject matter of these *Ahadith* is very clear. The Holy Prophet [sa] in different ways impressed upon his followers the importance of congregational prayers, especially those offered in the mosque with other members of the community.

Masjid e Nabawi (The Prophet's Mosque) in Madinah.

Introduction to Ahmadiyyat
A brief overview of the Ahmadiyya Muslim Community

The Ahmadiyya Muslim Community (AMC) is a dynamic, fast growing international revival movement within Islam. Founded in 1889, AMC spans over 180 countries with membership exceeding tens of millions.

AMC is the only Islamic organization to believe that the long-awaited messiah has come in the person of Mirza Ghulam Ahmad (1835-1908) of Qadian. Ahmad[as] claimed to be the metaphorical second coming of Jesus[as] of Nazareth and the divine guide, whose advent was foretold by the Prophet of Islam, Muhammad[sa]. AMC believes that God sent Ahmad[as], like Jesus[as], to end religious wars, condemn bloodshed and reinstitute morality, justice and peace. Ahmad's[as] advent has brought about an unprecedented era of Islamic revival. He divested Islam of fanatical beliefs and practices by vigorously championing Islam's true and essential teachings. True to Muhammad's[sa] prophecy, he also has united the family of religions under the single banner of the true Islam by safeguarding the teachings of Abraham[as], Jesus[as], Moses[as], Krishna[as], Buddha[as], Confucius[as], Guru Nanak[as], Lao Tzu[as] and Zoroaster[as].

AMC is the leading Islamic organization to categorically reject terrorism in any form. Over a century ago, *Hadhrat* Ahmad[as] emphatically declared that an aggressive "*jihad by the sword*" has no place in Islam. In its place, he taught his followers to wage a bloodless, intellectual "*jihad of the pen*" to defend Islam. To this end, Ahmad[as] penned over 80 books and tens of thousands of letters, delivered hundreds of lectures, and engaged in scores of public debates. His rigorous and rational defenses of Islam unsettled conventional Muslim thinking. As part of its effort to revive Islam, AMC continues to spread Ahmad's[as] teachings of moderation and restraint in the face of bitter opposition from the Muslim world.

Similarly, AMC is the only Islamic organization to endorse a separation of mosque and state. Over a century ago, *Hadhrat* Ahmad[as] taught his followers to protect the sanctity of both religion and government by becoming righteous souls as well as loyal citizens. He cautioned against irrational interpretations of Quranic pronouncements and misapplications of Islamic law. He continually voiced his concerns over protecting the rights of God's creatures. Today, AMC continues to be an advocate for universal human rights and protections for religious and other minorities. It champions the empowerment and education of women. Its members are among the most law-abiding, educated, and engaged Muslims in the world.

AMC is the foremost Islamic organization with a central spiritual leader. Over a century ago, Ahmad[as] reminded his followers of God's promise to safeguard the message of Islam through *khilafat* (the spiritual institution of successorship to prophethood). AMC believes that only spiritual successorship can uphold the true values of Islam and unite humanity. Five spiritual leaders have succeeded *Hadhrat* Ahmad[as] since his demise in 1908. AMC's fifth and current spiritual head, Mirza Masroor Ahmad, resides in the United Kingdom. Under the leadership of its spiritual successors, AMC has now built over 15,000 mosques, over 500 schools, and over 30 hospitals. It has translated the Holy Qur'an into over 60 languages. It propagates the true teachings of Islam and the message of peace and tolerance through a twenty-four hour satellite television channel (MTA), the Internet (alislam.org) and print (Islam International Publications). It has been at the forefront of worldwide disaster relief through an independent charitable organization, Humanity First.

LOVE FOR ALL HATRED FOR NONE

The Conditions of Ba'ait
Initiation into Ahmadiyyat

www.alislam.org

1 The initiate shall solemnly promise that he shall abstain from *Shirk* (association of any partner with God) right up to the day of his death.

3 That he shall regularly offer five daily prayers in accordance with the commandments of God and the Holy Prophet; and shall try his best to be regular in offering the *Tahajjud* (pre-dawn superogatory prayers) and invoking *Darood* (blessings) on the Holy Prophet; that he shall make it his daily routine to ask forgiveness for his sins, to remember the boutnies of God and to praise and glorify Him.

5 That he shall remain faithful to God in all circumstances of life, in sorrow and happiness, adversity and prosperity, in felicity and trials; and shall in all conditions remain resigned to the decree of Allah and keep himself ready to face all kinds of indignities and sufferings in His way and shall never turn away from it at the onslaught of any misfortune; on the contrary, he shall march forward.

7 That he shall entirely give up pride and vanity and shall pass all his life in lowliness, humbleness, cheerfulness, forbearance and meekness.

9 That he shall keep himself occupied in the service of God's creatures, for His sake only; and shall endeavor to benefit mankind to the best of his God-given abilities and powers.

2 That he shall keep away from falsehood, fornication, adultery, trespasses of the eye, debauchery, disssipation, cruelty, dishonesty, mischief and rebellion; and will not permit himself to be carried away by passions, however strong they may be.

4 That under the impulse of any passions, he shall cause no harm whatsoever to the creatures of Allah in general, and Muslims in particular, neither by his tongue nor by his hands nor by any other means.

6 That he shall refrain from following un-Islamic customs and lustful inclinations, and shall completely submit himself to the authority of the Holy Quran; and shall make the word of God and the sayings of the Holy Prophet the guiding principles in every walk of his life.

8 That he shall hold faith, the honor of faith, and the cause of Islam dearer to him than his life, wealth, honor, children and all other dear ones.

10 That he shall enter into a bond of brotherhood with this humble servant of God, pledging obedience to me in everything good, for the sake of Allah, and remain faithful to it till the day of his death; that he shall exert such a high devotion in the observance of this bond as is not be found in any other wordly relationship and connections demanding devoted dutifulness.

Perspectives on Mosques
by Hadhrat Mirza Ghulam Ahmad [as], the Founder of Ahmadiyyat

"The only condition is that the building of the mosque be based on sincere motives and that it be undertaken solely for God with no ulterior motives or evil intentions. Then Allah will bestow His blessings. It is not important that the mosque have a finished and beautiful structure. Merely allocate a parcel of land and establish a boundary demarcation, and any simple construction of bamboo or leaves could be used to secure the structure from rains. Allah does not like any superficial décor. The Prophet's Mosque was built with a few palm leaves and branches and continued like that until *Hadhrat* Usman[ra] gave that structure a finished look, as he had a passion for construction […] Therefore, our community should have a mosque with our own prayer leader who would lead and speak in that mosque. Members of our community should offer congregational prayers together in such mosques. There is blessing in assembly and unity. Disunity creates discord. This is the time when we need unity and togetherness and should forego trivial things that would create discord."

— *Malfoozat*, Vol. 7, p. 219.

The foundation for Masjid Mubarak, in Qadian, India, was laid by Hadhrat Mirza Ghulam Ahmad [as], the founder of the Ahmadiyya Muslim Community and the Promised Messiah.

Hadhrat Mirza Ghulam Ahmad [as]
The Promised Messiah and *Mahdi*
1835-1908

Hadhrat Mirza Ghulam Ahmad [as] was born on February 13, 1835, in Qadian, India. In his youth, he was deeply immersed in the study of the Holy Qur'an and often was seen in the mosque in ardent supplications. Those who knew hin would call him a *Maseetar*, a person who has fallen in love with the mosque and frequently stays there. In 1882, he was commissioned by God to be the Divine Reformer. He understood very well that a long arduous task of reformation lay ahead. In 1889, under the Divine command, he founded the Ahmadiyya Muslim Community. He was bestowed with Divine revelations. One of his revelations was: "I shall give you a large party of Islam." At that time, only a handful of people accepted him as the Messiah, but today his followers exceed tens of millions in over 189 countries.

Perspectives on Mosques
by Hadhrat Hakim Maulvi Nooruddin [ra], Khalifatul Masih I

After the establishment of Talimul Islam High School and major growth in Qadian, *Hadhrat Khalifatul Masih I* [ra] developed the northern area of Qadian and named it Darul Uloom. The first construction in this area was that of Noor Mosque. *Hadhrat Khalifatul Masih I* [ra] laid the foundation of Noor Mosque after Fajr prayers on March 5, 1910, and on April 22, offered Asar prayers to inaugurate the mosque. He presented *Darsul Qur'an* of *Sura* Al-Anbiyya and declared:

"Today Allah has taught me such beautiful words for prayers that I am amazed." He said further: *"I can swear that the foundation of this mosque is based on achieving the pleasure of Allah and is solely based on Taqwa . . ."* (*History of Ahmadiyyat*, Vol. 4, p. 330).

The Noor Mosque was completed in 1910. A custodian was appointed in November 1, 1910. In 1912-1913, a large area was added to convene annual gatherings of the community.

In his sermon of February 12, 1909, *Hadhrat Khalifatul Masih I* [ra] presented a commentary on verse 155 of *Sura* Al-Baqarah and explained why people, out of bigotry and jealousy, forbid worshippers to enter the mosques. He said:

The elements of insult have increased in these people to the extent that if one of them would have the power regarding the mosque, they will forbid those people to enter the mosque who disagree with them. Such a person does not realize that the other person also glorifies the name of the same God. By so doing, this person will cause the mosques to be deserted rather than populated. Muslim Mosques were not separate until the Twelfth Century; after that the Sunni and Shia Mosques got separated, then Wahabis and non-Wahabis separated themselves, and now there is no limit. These people were not ashamed that the Mosque in Mecca is one, the Mosque in Madinah is the same, the Qur'an is the same, the Prophet[sa] is the same and the Creator Allah is also the same, so why are we creating this discord? They should all enter the Mosque with the awe, majesty and fear of Allah in their hearts. (Khutbat e Noor, p. 390).

Jama'at Ahmadiyya, Qadian, India

The foundation stone for Noor Mosque, Qadian, was laid on March 5, 1910, by Hadhrat Khalifatul Masih I [ra]. On April 23, 1910, *Hadhrat Khalifatul Masih I* [ra] inaugurated the mosque.

Hadhrat Al-Haj Hakim Maulvi Nuruddin[ra]
Khalifatul Masih I
1841-1914

Hadhrat Hakim Maulvi Nuruddin[ra], *Khalifatul Masih I*, was born in 1841 in Bhera, India. He was a descendant of *Hadhrat* Umar Farooq[ra], the Second *Khalifa* of Islam. He was a very learned man and studied from practically all of the famous religious institutions of India. He also had the privilege of staying in the holy cities of Mecca and Medina. He was a great scholar, a talented physician and an expert theologian. When the Promised Messiah[as] initiated the *Ba'ait* on March 23, 1889, *Hadhrat* Nuruddin[ra] was the first to pledge allegiance to him.

His obedience to the Promised Messiah[as] was exemplary. The Promised Messiah[as] once said, "(Nuruddin) obeys me in every respect and as the pulse is governed by the heart beat, similarly he follows me. I find him lost in securing my pleasure and appreciation. How nice it would be if everybody from among my followers were Nuruddin." (*Aina Kamalat-i-Islam*).

Hadhrat Nurrudin[ra] served Ahmadiyyat for six years as *khalifa* and did his utmost for the Community's uplift and progress. He studied and taught the Qur'an and wrote many books. He passed away in Qadian, India on March 13, 1914.

Perspectives on Mosques
by Hadhrat Mirza Bashiruddin Mahmood Ahmad [ra], Khalifatul Masih II

"Muslims make use of mosques for purposes of congregational prayers, but this is not due to any feeling that the buildings of these mosques possess any peculiar sanctity for the purposes of divine worship. A mosque is built to enable the Muslims of the neighborhood to assemble for the purpose of congregational prayers. Mosques facilitate the performance of collective worship and are used for other religious and social purposes also. No particular ceremony is required for consecrating mosques and dedicating them to the worship of God, as is the case with temples and churches. Any building that is used for the purpose of congregational prayers by the Muslims is a mosque.

No structural design has been prescribed for a mosque, nor is a mosque divided into naves and transepts, nor does it possess anything resembling an altar. There are no pictures or images in a mosque nor relics of saints. The Muslims gather for Divine worship in the simplest possible manner and Islamic religious services are free from all artistic and emotional distractions. There is no music or singing, no temple dances, no priestly vestments, no burning of candles and no attempt to create an emotional atmosphere by the aid or organs or incense. The light inside a mosque is not dimmed artificially to create an atmosphere of awe and no images of saints divert the attention of worshippers from God. At the appointed hour the worshippers collect in the mosque and arrange themselves in rows to indicate that, having concluded their individual worship in their homes or in the mosque, they are now ready to offer collective worship to God.

Mosques are used not solely for the purposes of congregational and individual worship but for all kinds of religious and intellectual pursuits. They serve as schools and for the celebration of marriages, as courts of law and places of meeting where plans are settled for the social and economic progress of the community."

(Extracted from *Commentary of the Holy Qur'an*, Vol. 1, pp. ccxiv-ccxivi)

Jama'at Ahmadiyya, United Kingdom

The foundation stone for the Fazal Mosque in London was laid by Hadhrat Khalifatul Masih II [ra] on October, 19, 1924.

Hadhrat Mirza Bashiruddin Mahmood Ahmad[ra]
Khalifatul Masih II
1889-1965

Hadhrat Mirza Bashiruddin Mahmood Ahmad[ra], *Khalifatul Masih II*, was born on January 12, 1889. His birth was the fulfillment of a great prophecy, which was vouchsafed to the Promised Messiah[as] in advance in the form of a divine revelation. In this revelation, 51 immaculate characteristics were described regarding a "promised son" to the *Hadhrat* Mirza Ghulam Ahmad[as].

The larger commentary of the Holy Qur'an (*Tafseer-e-Kabeer*) and the concise commentary of the Holy Qur'an (*Tafseer-e-Saghir*) are among his greatest works. He also initiated a scheme known as *Tehrik-e-Jadid* in 1934, which faciliated the construction of Ahmadiyya mosques and missions throughout the world. He organized the *Jama'at* into several auxiliary organizations in order to strengthen the general body of the *Jama'at*. Under his leadership, Ahmadiyyat progressed rapidly and reached 75 countries of the world.

Hadhrat Khalifatul Masih II [ra] breathed his last on November 8, 1965, marking the end of an incredibly blessed and productive 51 years as second *khalifa*.

Perspectives on Mosques
by Hadhrat Mirza Nasir Ahmad [rh], Khalifatul Masih III

"The Holy Qur'an lays down clearly that a mosque, which is the house of God, belongs to no human being and that all places of worship belong to Allah. Man simply performs the function of a custodian. Therefore, the doors of a mosque are open to all those who desire to worship the One and only True God. It is, however, quite clear that no god except God is permitted to be worshipped in a mosque. This restriction is reasonable and no legitimate objection can be raised against it. Hence the idols and images that some people worship are not allowed to be brought into the mosque, but anyone who wants to worship the One and only True God with a sincere heart and without any ulterior motive may worship Him freely in a mosque. Allah grants this permission and commands us not to stand in his or her way. This would be clear from the practice and traditions of the Holy Prophet Muhammad[sa], on whom be peace. When the Jews of Khaiber and the Christians of Najran came under Muslim government, the Prophet Muhammad[sa] gave them complete freedom of belief and worship. It has been reliably reported that when the Christians of Najran came to Madinah the Prophet Muhammad[sa] permitted them to perform the rites of their worship in their own way in the Prophet's Mosque. When some companions of the Prophet Muhammad[sa] objected to this, he reprimanded them by reminding them that a mosque belongs to Allah. Therefore, the Christians turned their faces to the East and prayed in their own way. The Holy Qur'an states: *"All places of worship belong to Allah: So call not on anyone beside Allah. When the servant of Allah stands up praying to Him, they crowd upon him, well nigh suffocating him."*

(Excerpt from the inaugural address of Hadhrat Khalifatul Masih III [rh] in Sweden)

Jama'at Ahmadiyya, Denmark

On July 21, 1967, Hadhrat Khalifatul Masih II [rh] inaugurated the Nusrat Jahan Mosque in Copenhagen, Denmark.

Hadhrat Mirza Nasir Ahmad[rh]
Khalifatul Masih III
1909-1982

Hadhrat Mirza Nasir Ahmad[rh], *Khalifatul Masih III*, was born on November 15, 1909, the eldest son of the second *khalifa, Hadhrat* Mirza Bashiruddin Mahmood Ahmad[ra].

Hadhrat Khalifatul Masih III[rh] committed the entire Holy Qur'an to memory in his early childhood. He was educated at Baliol College in Oxford, England, and later was appointed the President of several key auxiliary organizations including *Majlis Khuddamul Ahmadiyya* and the Central *Ansarullah* Organization. He was elected as the third successor of the Promised Messiah[as] on November 8, 1965.

Among his notable achievements was the initiation of the *Nusrat Jehan* Scheme for the uplift of education and healthcare in six West African nations. He also introduced the slogan, "Love for All, Hatred for None" to the worldwide Ahmadiyya community, and initiated the Centennial Jubilee Scheme in 1973. During his *khilafat*, the famous revelation of the Promised Messiah[as]: "Kings shall seek blessings from thy garments," was fulfilled when Al Haj F.M. Singhate, the Governor-General of The Gambia, accepted Ahmadiyyat. *Hadhrat* Mirza Nasir Ahmad[rh]'s leadership as the third *khalifa* extended for over 17 years. He breathed his last on June 9, 1982.

Perspectives on Mosques
by Hadhrat Mirza Tahir Ahmad [rh], Khalifatul Masih IV

"The building of places of worship, such as mosques, dedicated to the one and only one God, is indeed among the noblest of tasks, but alas, the places of worship are sometimes built with mixed intentions. They are not always entirely and purely dedicated to the worship of Allah alone.

Islam stands out among religions in its total commitment to the unity of God. Yet it does not permit its adherents to interfere with the beliefs and practices of idolatrous religions. The principle teaching in this regard, without compromise, is given in Chapter 2, Verse 257 of the Holy Qur'an: "There is no compulsion in religion."

This contains, indeed, the fundamental principle of religious practices and beliefs. This principle also implies that those who believe in the unity of God cannot be denied the right to worship in mosques. The doors of the Muslim mosques must therefore always remain open to the followers of all religions, who believe in the unity of God. As far as physical access is concerned, even idolaters are not denied. That which is forbidden is only to pay homage to anyone besides God. The Muslim places of worship must entirely remain dedicated to God alone in all sincerity.

It must be remembered that, according to Islam, the status of a place of worship, in the sight of Allah, is not related to physical grandeur or outstanding architectural design. The greatness of a mosque depends entirely on the fear of God and the sincerity with which the worshippers bow and prostrate therein."

(Excerpt from the message of *Hadhrat Khalifatul Masih IV* [rh] at the inauguration of Baitur Rahman Mosque, Silver Spring, Maryland).

Jama'at Ahmadiyya, Spain

On September 10, 1982, Hadhrat Khalifatul Masih IV [rh] *inaugurated Basharat Mosque in Pedro Abad, Spain.*

Hadhrat Mirza Tahir Ahmad [rh]
Khalifatul Masih IV
1928-2003

Hadhrat Mirza Tahir Ahmad [rh], *Khalifatul Maih IV*, was born on December 18, 1928 in Qadian. He was the son of *Hadhrat* Mirza Bashiruddin Mahmood Ahmad [ra], *Khalifatul Masih II*.

After graduating from *Jamia Ahmadiyya* (Training Academy) in Rabwah, he pursued further education at the School of Oriental and African Studies in England for 2 1/2 years. He then dedicated his life for the service of Ahmadiyyat, serving as, among other things, in-charge of *Waqf-e-Jadid* and President of *Majlis Khuddamul Ahmadiyya*. After the passing of *Hadhrat Khalifatul Masih III* [rh] in 1982, Mirza Tahir Ahmad [rh] was elected the fourth *khalifa*. Due to escalating persecution in Pakistan, he moved to England in 1984. During his *khilafat*, Ahmadiyyat grew exponentially and an unprecedented expansion of mosques took place worldwide. Muslim Television Ahmadiyya was also initated under his *khilafat* in 1992.

Hadhrat Khalifatul Masih IV [rh] was known for his excellent oratory skills and writing. He authored several landmark books including *Murder in the Name of Allah, Islam's Response to Contemporary Issues, Christianity - A Journey from Facts to Fiction* and *Revelation, Rationality, Knowledge, and Truth*. He passed away in England on April 19, 2003.

Perspectives on Mosques

Hadhrat Mirza Masroor Ahmad [aba], Khalifatul Masih V

"It is a great blessing of Allah on the Ahmadiyya Community that He is enabling us to build mosques in every region and every city of the world. Always remember that the dues of building mosques can only be honored when one goes to the mosque with the intention that people should gather there for worship of God and purely for worship of God. Only then will one be truly rewarded and only then will each believer be deemed as paying the dues of the purpose of his creation; will be deemed as fulfilling the objective for which Allah the Exalted has created man. Allah declares in the Holy Qur'an: "And I have not created the *Jinn* and the men but that they may worship me." (51:57). Therefore, whether one is a person of great position, is a person of great rank and grandeur, is a very wealthy person, or is a very poor person, Allah the Exalted has stated the objective of the creation of both kinds of people as this alone that they worship Him.

These mosques signify that everyone, rich and poor, gathers in one place and discarding all worldly positions and ranks stands together most humbly in the presence of Allah to worship Him. So that they may turn to God, bow before Him as one entity and seek His blessings. When worship of God is observed as one entity, so that the grace of His blessings is increased more than before, then Allah the Exalted also rewards such worship twenty-seven times more. If one harbors discriminatory feelings of wanting to stand next to such and such and not wishing to stand next to such and such or that such and such has newly taken their *Ba'ait* and one presumes their status to be less than one, then, despite the fact that one is in a mosque for the worship of God, one is not worthy of this reward."

(From Friday Sermon delivered by *Hadhrat Khalifatul Masih V* [aba] at the newly built mosque in Porto Novo, Bénin in April, 2008).

Jama'at Ahmadiyya, United Kingdom

Hadhrat Khalifatul Masih V [aba] *inaugurated Baitul Futuh Mosque in Morden, U.K.*

Hadhrat Mirza Masroor Ahmad[aba]
Khalifatul Masih V
1950-Present

Sahibzada Mirza Masroor Ahmad[aba] was born on September 15, 1950 in Rabwah, Pakistan. He is the son of *Hadhrat Sahibzada* Mirza Mansoor Ahmad[ra], a grandson of the Promised Messiah[as].

In 1977, he devoted his life for Islam, and as directed by *Khalifatul Masih III*[rh], *Hadhrat* Mirza Masroor Ahmad[aba] proceeded to Ghana under the Nusrat Jahan Scheme. This social, educational and economic development scheme supports a large number of hospitals and schools in West Africa. He was the founding principal of the Ahmadiyya Secondary School Salaga, a school in the northern region of Ghana, where he served for two years. In 1985, Mirza Masroor Ahmad[aba] returned to Pakistan and in 1997, *Hadhrat Khalifatul Masih IV*[rh] appointed him as *Nazir e A'ala* (chief executive director) of Sadr Anjuman Ahmadiyya Pakistan as well as the local Amir.

In 1999, *Sahibzada* Mirza Masroor Ahmad[aba] had the additional distinction of becoming a prisoner in the name of Allah, in Rabwah, Pakistan. He was released later that year. He was elected fifth *khalifa* on April 22, 2003, and has overseen the rapid progress of Ahmadiyyat over the last 5 years.

The Significance and Etiquettes of a Mosque

by Maulana Daud Hanif

A "Mosque" (in Arabic, "*Masjid*") refers to a place built solely for the worship of Allah. Therefore, no polytheistic practice or worship can be performed in it. The Holy Prophet Muhammad[sa] has made things easy for us and has given a broad significance regarding the use of the term "mosque" by stating that "The whole Earth has been made a Mosque for me." So, worship can be performed in all clean and quiet places of the world whether roofed or unroofed, inside or outdoors. However, the construction of a mosque is considered to be a very meritorious deed in Islam. The Prophet Muhammad [sa] has also said: "He who builds a Mosque for Allah, Allah builds a house for him in paradise." The purpose of worship is to develop closer ties with the Creator, so mosques are built in every Muslim village and town to facilitate the believers to achieve this objective individually as well as collectively.

In the early days of Islam, mosques, besides being used for the worship of God, were also centers used for educational, training, social, cultural and administrative purposes. This is still true today, but often separate buildings are now erected for social, cultural and political activities and gatherings, while mosques are reserved mostly for worship, religious ceremonies, and education.

Mosques are simple structures. Their domes and minarets distinguish them outwardly from other places of worship, including churches, synagogues and temples. At times, mosques have intricate Islamic art work and tiles that have distinguished them from other buildings. However, inside mosques there are no divisions, pews, naves, transepts or anything that resembles an altar. There are no pictures, images or artistic beauty displayed, nor is music or singing carried out in the mosque. In short, there are no artificial ways adopted to create an atmosphere of awe in the worshipper.

There are no special places reserved in the

mosque for any individuals except for the Imam (the leader for the congregation), which is in the center of the mosque in the front row. The rest of the believers make straight rows behind the Imam and stand shoulder to shoulder without

Imam Daud Hanif is a Naib Ameer and Missionary in Charge of the Ahmadiyya Muslim Community in the U.S.

any distinction of any kind. However, men and women offer their prayers in separate prayer halls and there is no mixing of genders in the congregation.

Believers gather in their neighborhood mosque five times every day for divine worship and offer prayers individually as well as in the congregation in the simplest manner. A mosque allows one to be near truthful friends and company, and offers an excellent and equal opportunity to rise to the highest pinnacles of spiritual progress. However, believers — men and women alike — will derive benefit from the mosque according to their own personal endeavors, sincerity, devotion and sacrifices.

Etiquettes of the Mosque

■ A mosque symbolically represents the Sacred Mosque in Makkah, Arabia, about which God says in the Holy Qur'an: "Purify My House for those who perform the circuit and for those who remain therein for devotion and those who bow down and fall prostrate in Prayer." So a mosque should always be kept clean and pure for worshippers. Thus, the cleaning of a mosque and its surroundings is a directive of God and a very meritorious task. Conversely, littering or spitting in the mosque, on its walls, stairs, elevators or

28 Essay | Mosque Etiquettes

Müde Yavuz

A mosque in Izmir Alsancak, Turkey.

parlors, is loathsome and prohibited.

■ One should go to the mosque with a clean body, clean clothes and a pure mind. Brushing one's teeth and performing *Wudhu* (ablution) at home or in the mosque before offering prayers is obligatory, and the conservative use of perfume or cologne is recommended. The Holy Prophet[sa] has prohibited the eating of such foods that could produce offensive bad breath and odors, such as raw onions and garlic, before going to the mosque.

■ One should proceed to the mosque with dignity, keeping a normal pace. It is unseemly to run or rush towards prayer.

■ Upon entering the mosque, worshippers are encouraged to recite the following prayer quietly. In Arabic: *Bismillahissalato Wassalamo Ala Rasoolillahi. Allahummaghfir li Zonubi Waftah li Abwaaba Rahmatika.* Translation: "In the name of Allah I enter; peace and blessings be upon the Prophet of Allah. O Allah! Forgive me my sins and open the doors of Your Mercy upon me."

■ Entering the prayer hall with shoes/footwear can add dirt to the carpets/mats where worshippers bow down and offer their prostrations during prayer. It is therefore not permitted.

■ After entering the mosque, one should offer two voluntary prostrations in prayer (known as *Nawafil*) as a *Tahayyatul-Masjid* (means of purifying the mosque) before seating oneself on the floor or carpet provided time is available before the congregational prayers.

■ After one offers her *Nawafil/Sunnah* (voluntary forms of prostration) and is waiting for the congregational *Salat* to begin, the remaining time should be spent in the remembrance of Allah. This is achieved by invoking *Durood*, or silent prayers, upon the Holy Prophet[sa].

■ Seating in the mosque should begin from the first row sitting as close to the Imam as possible. On the women's side, where the Imam is not present, this translates to sitting as far forward (i.e., towards the first row) as possible. In case the first row is full, one should sit quietly in the second, or third, and so on. Worshippers are encouraged to sit shoulder to shoulder, leaving no gaps between any two people.

■ Every row begins exactly from behind the Imam (or, on the women's side, the front row) and spreads equally on both sides, keeping the Imam always in front of the the center of the row. The rows must be kept straight and stand shoulder to shoulder without a gap between two people.

■ Gaps in the rows must be filled by person(s) nearest the gaps. Do not jump over anothers' shoulders to fill the gap.

■ Passing in front of a worshipper without respecting the line of demarcation is prohibited. In the absence of a line of demarcation, however, leave enough room for the worshiper to have space to perform prostrations and pass beyond that space.

■ Religious talks and speeches, meetings and discussions concerning the community, or those that concern matters of a national interest are permissible in the mosque, provided that they do not disturb the worshippers.

■ One should not stand with arms on one's

back. Sitting in unorganized groups, leaning against walls or stretching/extending out one's legs while sitting in the mosque is not allowed. Of Course the sick and disabled are allowed to sit as is possible for them.

■ Announcements regarding articles lost outside the mosque are not permissible in the mosque. Discussions concerning trade, business and the conversations of a similar nature are also prohibited inside the mosque during salat times

■ The placing of carved images or the hanging of curtains portraying images or photos is not permissible in the mosque.

■ Talking, while others are still engaged in *Sunnah* or *Nawafil*, is not permissible. Similarly, making noise or behaving in a manner that could distract or disturb worshippers is not permitted in the mosque.

■ Mothers with infants or small children should remain in the rooms usually allocated in the mosque for that purpose. Men with children accompanying them should also move to another room or go temporarily outside the men's prayer area if their child is becoming loud or boisterous. Young children should not be left unattended at any time by respective guardians for reasons of safety and security as well as to ensure peace and silence during worship.

■ After the completion of the obligatory prayers, *Tasbihaat* (invocations) should be offered. Specifically, one should quietly utter 'Subhanallah' (Holy is Allah), 'Alhamdolillah' (All Praise belongs to Allah) and 'Allaho-Akbar' (Allah is Great) 33 times each, and this ritual should be concluded with 'La Ilaha illallah' (There is no God but Allah). The remaining *Sunnah/Nafl* (voluntary prayers) should then be offered.

■ Conversation, after completion of obligatory Prayers and *Sunnah*, is permitted. Worshippers should introduce themselves to others to increase their circle of acquaintances. They should be cheerful and extend a cordial welcome to guests and visitors in order to strengthen mutual relationships. This is true for both women and men in their respective prayer areas.

■ Upon leaving the mosque, the following prayer should be offered quietly. (In Arabic): *Bismillahissalato Wassalamo Ala Rasoolillahi. Allahummaghfir li Zonubi Waftah li Abwaaba Fadhleka.* Translation: 'In the name of Allah, I enter here. Peace and Blessings be upon the Prophet of Allah. O Allah! Forgive me my sins and open the doors of Your bounties upon me.'

Jumu'a, or Friday Prayer, Etiquettes

■ Taking a bath before *Jumu'a* prayers is a tradition of the Holy Prophet[sa], and he has also emphasized it greatly.

■ Arriving at the mosque early is much more blessed than arriving late. The Holy Prophet[sa] said, "He who arrives at the mosque for *Jumu'a* in the earliest hour earns a reward equivalent to the sacrifice of a camel; the one coming next earns the reward of slaughtering a cow; after that of a goat; after that of a hen, and after that of an egg." (*Al Bukhari* and *Muslim*)

■ Scholars and learned people should sit closest to the Imam.

■ The sermon of the Imam on *Jumu'a* is a formal part of the prayer service. Therefore, worshippers must observe complete silence during the sermon, and listen to it attentively.

■ Talking & text messaging during the sermons is strictly prohibited. Even asking someone to observe silence is not allowed. It should be done only with a quiet gesture. Cellular phones should be turned off

■ Do not occupy a place vacated by someone temporarily, as they may intend to return.

The Holy Ka'aba is visited by thousands of worshippers daily.

Two Living Memoirs of the Holy Prophet[sa]
The holy book of Allah and the khulufa of the prophet
by Maulana Dost Muhammad Shahid

Abu Kharja, *Hadhrat* Zaid bin Saqib[ra], who was the Ansari Companion of the Prophet of Islam[sa], as well as one of the script writers of revelations, narrated the following *Hadith*:

> "The Prophet of Islam said that I am leaving behind two of my successors for you as my 'memoirs.' The first is the Book of Allah and the second is my 'Itarat.'"
> — *Durre Mansoor Siooti*, Vol. 4, p. 60.

The word *"Itarat"* connotes not only spiritual and physical descendants, but also contemplates the *khulufa*. This is clearly proven by a statement made by the first *khalifa, Hadhrat* Abu Bakr[ra]:

> "*Nahno Itarat Rasul Allah wa Baizatuhu.* [We are the descendants of the Prophet of Islam and the center of prophethood.]"
> — *Nahaya Ibn e Aseer.*

These words of *Hadhrat* Abu Bakr[ra] clearly are revealing of the system of *khilafat* and those who will lead it.

The Prophet of Islam[sa] delivered the following prayer for his *khulufa*:

> "*Allah Humma Ar hum, Khulfai Ala Zina Yatuna min Baadi, Alazi Yarauna Ahadeesi was sunnati, was ya Alamo nahan Naas.* [Oh my God, have mercy on my *khulufa* who will come after me and who will tell people my *Hadith* and my *Sunnah* and ask them to act accordingly.]"
> — *Jamia as Sageer us Siooti*, Vol. 1, p. 92.

The background of this grand prayer of the Prophet of Islam[sa] is this that Allah has mentioned in Holy Qur'an that Muslims should hold tight to the rope of Allah and not engage in divisions of their unity. It is proven from the *Hadith* of the Prophet of Islam[sa] that *"hub lallah"* or "the rope of Allah" refers to the Holy Qur'an and *"wala tafarraku"* means *"al Jamat,"* that is, a group that should stay connected with the *khalifa* of the time.
—*Durre Mansoor Siooti*, Vol. 2, p. 63.

Maulana Dost Muhammad Shahid is the Official Historian of the worldwide Ahmadiyya Muslim Community.

This further indicates that there is strong relation between the Holy Qur'an and the *khulufa*. Islam's progress depends upon *khilafat*. The *khulufa* are the living examples of the spirit of the Holy Qur'an. It is for this reason that the Prophet of Islam[sa], while mentioning the disorders of the latter days, said that in that age only the Book of Allah would guarantee protection to Muslims, because it has all the information about the new age as well as the ages that have passed. It will act as a judge and will give its verdicts when differences arise. It is the rope of Allah. It will always stay fresh and its extraordinary features will never go away.
—*Tirmizi*, Bab e Maa Jaa fil Qur'an.

The Prophet of Islam[sa] also left the following will for the Muslims:

> "*Fa alikum bisunti was suntan hul Khulfa e Rashedeen al Muhtadeen fa tamas kun bi has was ozoo elai ha bin nawajiz.* When you have too many differences among you, you should fully obey me and my *Khulufa e Rashideen*, the guided ones. You should embrace them and hold them tight the same way as you hold something with your teeth."

Moreover, the Prophet[sa] said:

"Faa in Raito Yauma is Khalifa tullah fil Arz e fal zim wa in nohi ka, Jiamoka wa okhe za Malik. [In the age that will be full of disorders, your duty is to see the *khalifa* of Allah on earth and hold on to him closely, even if your whole body is injured or starts bleeding and all your wealth is lost in doing so.]"

(*Masnad Ahmed Bin Hambul*, Vol. 5, p. 403)

The Prophet[sa] further remarked:

"Inna Rasul Allah Qala Ya tii Imam ul Ulama Bi Rabwah ta. [The Imam of the godly and scholarly people of Allah will come from an elevated land.]"

Hadhrat Imam Bukhari in his book *Kitab ul Ambiyya* has mentioned the views of *Hadhrat* Qaiza about "*Aseehabis*" — those who rebelled at the time of *Hadhrat* Abu Bakr[ra]. These rebellious individuals refused to obey *khilafat* and maintained:

"An Naqzt un Nabuwata Bi moti hi Fala natih ahada Badi. [After the Prophet[sa], the Prophethood has ended in any shape or form and after that we will not obey anybody.]"

There is a famous saying that history repeats itself. The *Aseehabis* in early Islamic history closely resemble members of the Lahori group of Ahmadis, who also refused to obey the *khulufa* of Ahmadiyyat.

The reader will be amazed to find out that the National Assembly of Pakistan passed a resolution on September 7, 1974, that showed a close resemblance to the point of view of the rebellious group at the time of *Hadhrat* Abu Bakr[ra]. That is to say, the resolution embodied defiance to *khilafat*. The drink that was prepared by those who denied *Hadhrat Khalifatul Masih I*[ra], the same drink was presented by the Parliamentary House of Pakistan in a different pitcher.

A final word of the Promised Messiah[as] showing the high office of *khilafat* and its grandeur and peace of heart for others is given in the following excerpt. While explaining the sixth level of *roohaniat* (spirituality) he writes:

"This is the same status at which the personal love of a *momin* [believer] reaches its peak and it attracts the personal love of Allah towards him, then the personal love of Allah enters the *momin* and engulfs him completely. This gives a new and extraordinary power to the *momin*. It gives such strength to his faith as if a new life as been infused into his dead heart. It actually enters into a *momin* and performs the work of the soul. This light illuminates all his faculties. He gets the support of the Angel Gabriel (*Roh ul Qudus*) [Holy Spirit] and those doors of knowledge and understanding are opened on him that are beyond the reach of human faculties. After he has traversed all the stations of spiritual progress, due to those virtual perfections that are bestowed upon him by the real perfections of God, a *momin* is given the title of '*Khalifa tullah*'(*khalifa* of Allah) in the Heavens. When a person stands before a mirror, all the features of his face are reflected perfectly in the mirror. In the same way the *momin* of that status not only gets rid of his inner self but also takes this work of the annihilation of his inner self and his humility to such a level, that nothing is left behind of his own self and he becomes just like a mirror. Then all the signs of goodness of Allah are gathered into him. Just as we say that a mirror that takes all the features of the person who stands before it, becomes the *khalifa* of the face, the same way a *momin* virtually takes the morals and attributes of God into him and takes on the status of a *khalifa* of God. He virtually becomes the reflection of the attributes of Allah. Like the way Allah is hidden behind so many curtains and his entity is infinite, so in the same way this perfect *momin* in his self is hidden behind so many curtains and is far off. The world cannot really understand the reality behind his person."

—*Zameema Braheen e Ahmadiyya*, Vol. 5, p. 81, first published in *Rohani Kahzain*, Vol. 21, pp. 241-242.

Mosques Around the World
An overview of Ahmadiyya mosques and missions

FROM MASJID MUBARAK, QADIAN (1883)

TO MASJID MUBARAK ABUJA, NIGERIA (2008)

Year	Mosques
1914	12
1965	365
1984	790
1985	822
1986	1,028
1987	1,402
1988	1,630
1989	2,290
1990	2,614
1991	3,205
1992	3,512
1993	3,830
1994	4,512
1995	5,274
1996	5,391
1997	6,306
1998	6,729
1999	8,253
2000	10,168
2001	12,738
2002	13,682
2003	13,908
2004	14,082
2005	14,401
2006	14,760
2007	15,055

During the period of *Hadhrat Khalifatul Masih I* [ra], mosques were built in Qadian, Lahore, Wazirabad, Dera Ghazi Khan, Jammun, and Patyala District. (*History of Ahmadiyyat*, Vol. 4, p. 640).

During the era of the second *Khalifat*, 343 mosques were built in 14 foreign countries. (Monthly *Khalid*, Dec. 1964, p. 76).

During the era of the third *Khalifa*, 425 mosques were built in foreign countries outside the Indo-Pak subcontinent. (*Khalid*, Syedna Nasir Issue, p. 214).

After 1984, during the period of fourth *Khalifa*, the mosques were added to the total in two ways: either the mosques that were newly built in various parts of the world; or thousands of mosques were added along with their *Imams* who accepted the Promised Messiah [as]. Our beloved *Khulufa*, in describing these figures at the annual *Jalsa Salana* United Kingdom, have been elaborating the total of newly built and pre-built mosques for the year.

All the figures presented in the chart are extracted from the addresses of *Hadhrat Khalifatul Masih IV* [th] delivered at the *Jalsa Salana* United Kingdom from 1985-2002 and that of *Hadhrat Khalifatul Masih V* [aba] from 2003 to 2007.

Hadhrat Khalifatul Masih V [aba], in his address on the second day at the United Kingdom *Jalsa* 2003, said:

"Several Prayer Leaders (Imams) at various mosques, when joining the Ahmadiyya fold, join with their mosque structures and all the followers whom they lead in these mosques. This year 227 mosques were added that include 121 newly built ones and 105 that were already built. During the nineteen years after migration 13,291 mosques have been added to the total, out of which 11,472 were prebuilt."
(*Al-Fazl International*, September 5, 2003; page 2)

Construction of Ahmadiyya Muslim Mosques

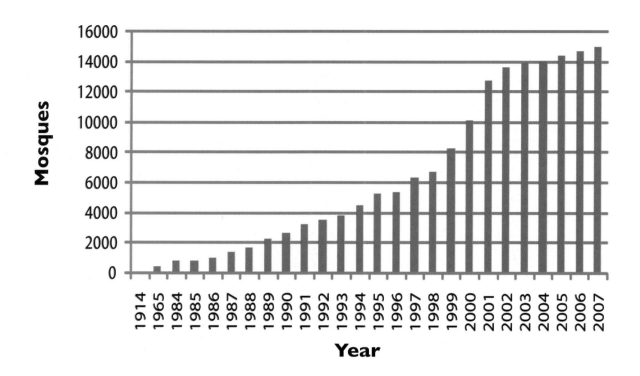

Masjid **Mubarak, Qadian (1883)**

This mosque was built by the Promised Messiah[as] in 1883. He received many revelations about this mosque, including: *"Both the blessor and the blessed is this mosque, and everything blessed takes place in it."*

Masjid **Mubarak Abuja, Nigeria (2008)**

This is the last mosque inaugurated by *Hadhrat Khalifatul Masih V*[aba] in the first century of *Khilafat*, on April 29, 2008, in Abuja, Nigeria

The Legacy of Hadhrat Khadija's [ra] Sacrifices
Mosques funded by Ahmadi Muslim women
by Dr. Shahnaz Butt, President, Lajna Imaillah USA

In the Holy Qur'an, we are guided by Almighty Allah: "You cannot attain to righteousness unless you spend out of that which you love; and whatever you spend, Allah surely knows it well" (Chapter 3, Verse 93).

The Holy Prophet Muhammad[sa] has said that whoever builds a mosque for Allah, Allah, The Exalted shall build a house for such a one in paradise.

As members of *Lajna Imaillah* (The Organization of Allah's Maid Servants), we recite the following as part of our Pledge to *Khilafat*: "I affirm that I shall always be ready to sacrifice my life, property, time and children for the cause of the faith and the community. I shall always adhere to the truth and shall always be prepared to make every sacrifice for the perpetuation of the Ahmadiyya *Khilafat*" (*Insha'Allah*).

Historically, the concept and philosophy of giving of ourselves, our abilities, our wealth and possessions in the way of Allah is not new to women. Every religion recounts many examples of pious and dedicated women who have rendered great services for the cause and propagation of their Faith. In fact, one of the most significant building blocks of Islam resulted from the sacrifices made by *Hadhrat* Hajra[as]. When *Hadhrat* Ibrahim[as] took *Hadhrat* Hajra[as] and *Hadhrat* Ismael[as] towards Makkah and left them there with a bag of dates and a container of water, *Hadhrat* Hajra[as] never once looked back and said 'If God, the Almighty, has commanded that we be left here, then He Himself will protect us. Why should we worry?' So she stayed there and Allah enabled the spring of *Zamzam* to gush out. Caravans began to stop and use the water from that spring by her permission and when a tribe was established there,

Hadhrat Ismael[as] was made their chief. It is from the womb of such heroic sacrifices that a prophet as magnificent as the Holy Prophet Muhammad[sa] emerged through the lineage of *Hadhrat* Ismael[as].

In the days of the Prophet[sa], women accomplished phenomenal deeds of sacrifice by giving their property, life and children for the propagation of Islam. In fact, whenever the Prophet[sa] had a need of special sacrifice, hesaw always used to appeal to women because he knew that once a woman decided to sacrifice, she would sacrifice to an extraordinary level. Once after Eid prayers, when the Prophet[sa] was in need of funds, he made an appeal to the women who immediately removed their jewelry and donated it to the fund. The Prophet[sa] told one of his Companions to collect the jewelry, so he walked around collecting the jewelry in a sack while the women were sitting with their faces covered by their veils. Presently a girl from a rich family took a gold bracelet off her arm and put it in the collection sack. When the Prophet[sa] saw that she had made a large donation for the sake of Allah, he said 'your other arm also begs to be saved from the fire of hell.' At this she donated her second bracelet as well.

During the age of the Promised Messiah[as], we also find that Ahmadi women have made extraordinary sacrifices; often times beyond their means and capability. The Promised Messiah[as] once said, "The Mosque has to be extended and for this purpose a request was made to members to contribute. Some members started giving their pledges. The Promised Messiah[as] said: "Let me go and ask my wife inside the house." So he went inside and then after a little while came back and said that my wife, (*Hadhrat* Amma Jaan) has pledged to sell her jewelry and give one thousand rupees in the fund to construct the Mosque."

Hadhrat Khalifatul Masih II [ra] writes: "In this age too, if we observe, we can see that women's sacrifices for the cause of religion, are not any less. In the 1920s, when I launched the movement to collect funds for the Berlin Mosque, women, who were a lot less in number than all of you sitting here, took off their jewelry and asked to sell it and add the money to the mosque fund. The women sacrificed so much at that time that within a month, they collected 100,000 rupees for the mosque."

Here are some examples of Mosques built by the sacrifices of Ahmadi Women:

The London Mosque. The Berlin Mosque could not be built because the German government had imposed some conditions causing the construction of the mosque to be more expensive. When the land purchased for the Berlin Mosque was sold, it generated 50,000 rupees in excess of the original price. That money was then used to build the London Mosque. In this way, the first Ahmadi Mosque in London, Fazal Mosque was built by the enormous sacrifices of women from Qadian who gave up jewelry, chickens and goats for this cause. The construction of this mosque was started on September 28, 1925 and inaugurated on October 3, 1926. To this day, thousands of Ahmadis visit the Fazal Mosque and send praises for the sacrifices of our earlier Ahmadi sisters.

The Holland Mosque. In 1950, *Hadhrat Khalifatul Masih II* [ra] made an appeal to Ahmadi women in Rabwah for donations for the Holland Mosque. In a sermon, dated May 12, 1950, *Hadhrat Khalifatul Masih II* [ra] said: "Furthermore, they (women) have given this contribution in a manner, that the less the money they have, the greater their spirit of giving. Although men possess more money, they have shown less courage in giving. Women possess less money, but they think about earning Allah's pleasure by sacrificing whatever they have, even though they do not have much." During *Jalsa Salana* in 1956, *Hadhrat Khalifatul Masih II* [ra] said: "This year,

Fazal Mosque in London was funded by the sacrifices of women from Qadian

by the Grace of Allah, a magnificent mosque has been built in Holland only with the help of Lajna's contribution. Ladies took the sole responsibility for the contribution for the Holland mosque. I had estimated one hundred thousand rupees for the project, but 174,000 rupees have been spent. They had provided a donation of 74,000 rupees. It means that there is a need for an additional amount of 96,000 rupees. Thus I encourage the ladies to collect 96,000 rupees quickly so that the Holland mosque can be theirs."

The Nusrat Jahan Mosque, Denmark. In 1964, *Hadhrat* Maryam Siddique[ra] proposed to *Hadhrat Khalifatul Masih II* [ra] that *Lajna Imaillah* build a mosque in Denmark. At that time, the Ahmadi women collected rupees 600,000.00. This first historic mosque was located in Copenhagen, Denmark and named Nusrat Jahan Mosque. During it's inauguration by *Hadhrat Khalifatul Masih III* [rh], on July 21, 1967, *Huzoor* [aba] said, "Our Master and Sole Sustainer! Make this house a house of peace and security. May Your glowing light illuminate every heart, and may all of our hearts be filled with the love of your most beloved, the chief benefactor of mankind, the Holy Prophet Muhammad[sa], Ameen."

The Khadijah Masjid, East Berlin, Germany. In 1989, *Hadhrat Khalifatul Masih IV* [rh] announced a scheme to construct one hundred mosques in Germany. Under this scheme the *Lajna* of

Germany also made a pledge to construct one mosque with contributions from Ahmadi women. On May 28, 2001, the *Lajna* Germany under the auspices of Amir *Jama'at* Germany, made a formal request to *Huzoor*[rh] to grant them permission. *Hadhrat Khalifatul Masih IV*[rh] granted them the permission and named the structure "Khadijah *Masjid*." Honoring the original request of *Hadhrat Khalifatul Masih II*[ra], the *Lajna* of Germany once again approached *Hadhrat Khalifatul Masih V*[aba] to grant them permission to construct "Khadijah *Masjid*". The permission was granted to them and they were instructed to work on the project with full speed.

In his sermon dated December 29, 2006, *Huzoor*[aba] said: In historical terms as well as in the current situation, the building of this mosque has been a challenge for the Community. It was a great wish of *Hadhrat Khalifatul Masih II*[ra] to have a mosque built in Berlin and donations were collected for this purpose. However due to the political situation of that time this donation was used for the construction of the Fazl Mosque in London. *Huzoor*[aba] said as it has been explained before these donations were collected by ladies of India, in particular Qadian. At that time one hundred thousand rupees was a huge amount and the bulk of this came from the disadvantaged women of Qadian who had donated their chickens and goats and other household items.

Huzoor[aba] said the Berlin mosque held great significance for him for it is after decades that the state of affairs have allowed for us to begin its construction. With the fall of the Berlin Wall, Allah has created the circumstances to fulfill our wish and we should be prompt in taking advantage of the agreeable situation. Directly addressing the congregation as well as the Ahmadis worldwide via MTA, *Huzoor*[aba] asked for prayers that all goes well on January 2, 2007, when the inauguration is

Thus we find that many Mosques were built worldwide by the financial sacrifices of Ahmadi women. In addition, we have several examples of women who either funded the construction of the mosques or donated land on an individual basis, and these are worthy of mention.

planned. *Hadhrat Khalifatul Masih V*[aba] said in his sermon: "My main objective and desire that has brought me here was to lay the foundation stone of the mosque of Berlin. From the minarets of our mosques the rays of the spiritual light, of the last and the perfect religion of Allah, will spread in all directions. These mosques will become the symbol of peace in this country."

Finally, the foundation stone for the Khadijah *Masjid* was laid on Jan 02, 2007 almost eighty four years after the first appeal of *Hadhrat Khalifatul Masih II*[ra] on Feb 02, 1923, to establish a mosque in Berlin, Germany. At the ceremony, *Hadhrat Khalifatul Masih V*[aba] laid the first foundation stone. The next stone was laid by *Sahibzadi* Amatus Subooh, wife of *Hadhrat Khalifatul Masih V*[aba]. The remaining foundation stones were all laid down by the executive members of *Lajna* Germany including the *Lajna* President of Germany.

Thus, we find that many mosques were built worldwide by the financial sacrifices of Ahmadi women. In addition, we have several examples of ladies who either funded the construction of the mosques or donated land on an individual basis, and these are worthy of mention.

Individual Contributions of Ahmadi Ladies towards Mosques or Land

Sisters Bilquis Ajibode in Nigeria, Shafya Okaray, in Bakare, Nigeria, Al Haja Fatima Ali for the Jamay Masjid Ajibade, Nigeria, and Sario in Abadan, Nigeria were instrumental in building these various Mosques all over Nigeria. Sister Khizar Sultana was responsible for the *Masjid* Khizar Sultana in Rabwah. Sister Maryam Bi donated the land for the Mosque in the Fiji Islands. The late Mrs. Maryam Bi donated a parcel of land in 1966 with the hope of building a mosque. Her children constructed *Masjid* Bilal on the land, which is located in Nasarwaqa, Vanua Levu. Sister Tooba Tabki donated a plot where Baitul Mahdi was built in the Fiji Islands. Its inauguration was performed on August 20, 2004. In Mauritius, the land was donated by Mrs. Zulekha Soodhun in 1944. Later on, it was reconstructed by *Maulana* Ismail Munir and completed by *Maulana* Aslam Qureshi and was called *Masjid* Mubarak in Mauritius. In 1958, Noor Mosque of Port - Louis was built in Pailles of wood and iron sheets during Missionary Fazal Ilahi Basir's stay. Mrs. Ghoolam Hussain funded the concrete reconstruction and *Sahibzada* Mirza Wasim Ahmad [rh] laid its foundation stone in 2002. *Maulana* Ataul Mujeeb Rashid inaugurated the first floor in 2003. Mrs. Salima Sookia donated a land in Stanley area of the city of Rose-Hill in 2000. It was inaugurated by *Hadhrat* Mirza Waseem Ahmad [rh] in 2001. It was financed on behalf of Khatoon Taujoo, Amina Taujoo and Mohammad Taujoo by M. Shams Taujoo. Similarly, many ladies in Ghana also donated mosques and land.

Close Relationship with Allah through the Service of Mosques

In 1950, Mrs. Aziza Walter accepted Ahmadiyyat in Holland. She loved The Hague Mosque that was built by Ahmadi women's contributions. The decoration of the *Mehrab* (Niche for the Imam) and writing the Quranic verses on the walls of the Hague Mosque were Sister Aziza's contributions. She was so involved in her prayers and supplications, that she developed a communicative link with Allah. Her prayers were accepted and she used to receive glad tidings from Allah. *Hadhrat* Ch. Zafrullah Khan [ra] used to request her for prayers; she would then pray

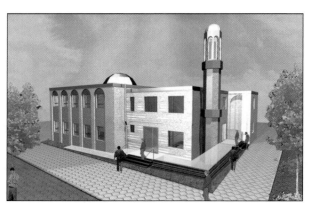

Artist's Rendition of the new Khadija Mosque in Berlin, Germany

and inform him of the outcome of her prayers.

Architectural Contributions

Sister Mubashira Mahmood is a young architect of Germany. She has designed three mosques including, the mosque in Offenbach funded by Majlis Ansarullah, the Mosque in Bremen, and will also be involved with the design of the Khadija Mosque, which will built in Berlin by *Lajna Imaillah. Hadhrat Khalifatul Masih V* [aba] has discussed these drawings in detail with her during her visits to these places.

In conclusion, women during all times in history, and especially Ahmadi women in the past 100 years, have proven repeatedly that they are willing and capable of making all kinds of sacrifices in the cause of their faith. *Hadhrat Khalifatul Masih II* [ra] prayed: "If Ahmadi women decide to take on the challenge and remain willing to make every kind of sacrifice for the sake of religion, then I assure you that many of you will still be alive when Islam becomes dominant and you will become the recipients of Allah's approval in this world and you will also become heirs to His rewards in the hereafter. I pray that you are able to serve Islam truthfully and may you always be the recipients of Allah Almighty's approval and blessings."

In keeping with the promise of Allah Almighty to the Promised Messiah [as], in a revelation that "I shall cause thy message to reach the corners of the earth," may Allah Almighty enable Ahmadi women to always be ready to sacrifice their life, property, time and children for the cause of the faith and always be prepared to make every sacrifice for the perpetuation of the Ahmadiyya Khilafat. *Ameen.*

Building Ahmadiyya Muslim Mosques
The contributions of the blessed women Hadhrat Ahmad's[as] family

Once *Hadhrat* Ahmad[as] appealed for funds to extend *Masjid* Mubarak in Qadian, India. Members immediately began to make pledges, including *Huzoor's*[as] wife, *Hadhrat* Syeda Nusrat Jehan Begum[ra] who pledged to sell her jewelry and give one thousand rupees to the mosque contruction fund.

Jama'at Ahmadiyya, Indonesia

Hadhrat Maryam Siddiqua, wife of Hadhrat Khalifatul Masih II[ra], is seen in Indonesia fundraising for a mosque.

Africa Speaks

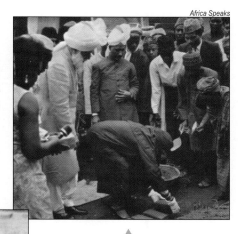

Jama'at Ahmadiyya, Switzerland

Hadhrat Nawab Amtul Hafeez Begum[ra], daughter of Hadhrat Ahmad[as], is seen laying the foundation of Mahmood Mosque in Zurich, Switzerland.

Hadhrat Mansoora Begum, wife of Hadhrat Khalifatul Masih III[rh] is seen laying the foundation of a mosque in Bo, Sierra Leone, 1970.

Jama'at Ahmadiyya, Australia

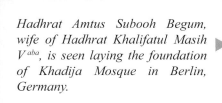

Jama'at Ahmadiyya, Germany

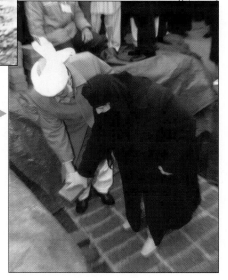

Hadhrat Amtus Subooh Begum, wife of Hadhrat Khalifatul Masih V[aba], is seen laying the foundation of Khadija Mosque in Berlin, Germany.

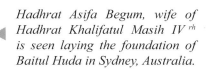

Hadhrat Asifa Begum, wife of Hadhrat Khalifatul Masih IV[rh] is seen laying the foundation of Baitul Huda in Sydney, Australia.

Qadian, Darul Aman
The birthplace of the Ahmadiyya Muslim Community

Masjid Mubarak and Minaratul Masih are festooned with colorful lights to mark the celebration of Jalsa Salana, Qadian in 2007.

Masjid Mubarak

In 1882, *Hadhrat* Mirza Ghulam Ahmad [as] was commissioned by God to be the Reformer of the Age. The very first task he addressed was the building of a mosque. Around 1883, he laid the foundation of the Mubarak mosque under the Divine command. He received several revelations about the task he just completed. Two of these revelations was as follows:

مبارک و مبارک و کل امر مبارک یجعل فیه

1. *Both blessor and the blessed is this mosque, and everything blessed takes place in it.*

الم نجعل لک سهولةً فی کل امر
بیت الفکر و بیت الزکر و من دخله کان آمنا

2. *Have We not made every thing easy for you. We bestowed upon you Baitul Zikr and Baitul Fikr and whosoever will enter the mosque with sincerity will attain peace.*

Minaratul Masih

The Holy Prophet Muhammad [sa] prophesied that the Promised Messiah would be raised near a white minaret, east of Damascus. This prophecy was fulfilled with the advent of *Hadhrat* Mirza Ghulam Ahmad [as] in Qadian, India, a city situated east of Damascus. *Hadhrat* Ahmad [as] decide to give the fulfillment of this prophecy a concrete shape. On March 13, 1903, he laid the foundation stone of ***Minaratul Masih***, with three objectives in mind:

- The *muezzin* should call out the *Adhan* from it five times daily.
- Bright lamps shall be fixed on the top of the minaret to serve as a symbolic source of illumination for the world.
- A clock shall be fitted on the top to strike the hours of the day for the benefit of the people. It shall indicate that present is the time when the doors of heaven are open and that there is no need of any holy war with the sword.

(Abdur Rahim Dard, *Life of Ahmad*, p. 50)

Masjid Aqsa

The Aqsa Mosque was built in 1876 by *Hadhrat* Mirza Ghulam Murtaza, the father of *Hadhrat* Ahmad [as].

On April 11, 1900, *Hadhrat* Ahmad [as] delivered the "Divinely inspired sermon" (*Khutba Ilahamiyya*) in this blessed mosque. Extensions of the mosque took place in 1900, 1910, and 1938. In 1903, a lofty minaret was built in the courtyard of the mosque, known as Minaratul Masih. On January 7, 1938, *Hadhrat Khalifatul Masih II* [ra] used a loudspeaker for the first time to deliver his Friday sermon in the Aqsa Mosque.

The Aqsa Mosque was built in Qadian in 1876.

Jama'at Officers Stationed in Qadian

Hafiz Dr. Saleh Muhammad Aladdin, Sadr, Sadr Anjuman Ahmadiyya, India

Maulana M. Inam Ghauri, Nazir-e-A'ala, Qadian

Dr. Mohammad Arif, Naib Amir of Qadian Jama'at

Maulana Muhammad Umar, Nazir Islaho Irshad, Qadian

Bait ud Dua

Attendees of Jalsa Salana, Qadian, wait their turn to offer prayers at Baitud Dua, the site where the founder of the Ahmadiyya Muslim Community, Hadhrat Mirza Ghulam Ahmad[as], used to offer his own prayers.

Other Mosques in Qadian

The Darul Futooh Mosque, in Qadian, India.

A view of Nasirabad Mosque, Qadian.

A scene from Jalsa Salana, Qadian in 2006.

Dr. Hameedur Rahman, Naib Amir USA, standing humbly in front of Huzoor^{aba} at Sarae Tahir in Qadian. Sarae Tahir has been built as a guest house by Dr. Rahman in the memory of Hadhrat Sahibzada Abdul Lateef Shaheed^{ra}.

Among the 313 who Decided to Stay
The steadfastness and devotion of Sahibzada Mirza Waseem Ahmad

Sahibzada Mirza Waseem Ahmad was the grandson of the Promised Messiah[as] and the son of *Hadhrat Khalifatul Masih II*[ra]. He served as the *Nazir-e-A'ala* and Sadr, Anjuman Ahmadiyya, India. He, along with 312 other *Dervishes*, was entrusted with the security of Qadian, India, during the violent partition between India and Pakistan in 1947-48. Until his demise in 2007, he remained true to his promise, and remained in Qadian serving the Ahmadiyya Muslim Community his entire life.

The Weekly Badr, Qadian, December 20/27, 2007

Sahibzada Mirza Waseem Ahmad

The Weekly Badr, Qadian, December 20/27, 2007

Huzoor [aba] *with Mirza Waseem Ahmad in 2005.*

"Huzoor [aba] said he was naturally concerned at [Mirza Waseem Ahmad's] passing away, in that a most assiduous elder has departed. He was not just my uncle, *Huzoor* [aba] observed. Rather, he was my right hand person and Allah had made him my great helper."

—Summary of Friday sermon delivered by *Hadhrat Khalifatul Masih V* [aba] on May 7, 2007 [from alislam.org].

Both lower photos: www.alislam.org

Thousands of mourners line Qadian's streets in anticipation of Mirza Sahib's funeral procession.

The Janaza (funeral) prayers for Sahibzada Mirza Waseem Ahmad.

Rabwah
A new home for the migrating Ahmadiyya Muslim Community

An aerial view of Rabwah, Pakistan as it appeared circa 1958.

An even earlier view, showing how the first Jalsa Salana in Rabwah was held in 1949. The large complex at the bottom of the photograph is the Langar Khana (where food is prepared for Jalsa guests).

The Aqsa Mosque in Rabwah, Pakistan.

The Yadgari Mosque marks the location where Hadhrat Khalifatul Masih II[ra] first offered prayers upon his arrival, and was the first mosque built in Rabwah.

A nighttime photo of the Aqsa Mosque main entrance.

Facts about Rabwah

Rabwah lies on the Lahore Sarghoda road, six miles from Chiniot across the Chenab River towards Sargodha. The town stretches 3 miles from west to east and two miles north to south. The foundation stone of Rabwah was laid by *Hadhrat Khalifatul Masih II*[ra] on September 20, 1948. *Huzoor*[rh] credited the establishment of Rabwah to *Hadhrat* Nawab Muhammad Din, a retired Deputy Commissioner, who acquired the original land lease. *Maulana* Jalaluddin Shams suggested the name '*Rabwah*' (In Arabic, 'elevated place') which is mentioned in the Holy Qur'an as the place of refuge granted by Allah to *Hadhrat Isa* (Jesus)[as] and *Hadhrat Maryam*[ra]. — From "Rabwah" by Raja Nasrullah Khan in *Jama'at U.K. Centenary Souvenir*, 1989.

The Hasan Iqbal Mosque in Rabwah, Pakistan.

The Tragic Outcome of Religious Intolerance
The destruction of Ahmadiyya mosques by radical extremists

"And who is more unjust than he who prohibits the name of Allah being glorified in Allah's Mosques and seeks to ruin them? It was not proper for such men to enter them except in fear. For them is disgrace in this world: and theirs shall be a great punishment in the next." (Holy Qur'an, 2:115).

This injunction of the Holy Qur'an is the magna carta of the freedom of worship for Muslim followers. In spite of the words of the Holy Qur'an, the persecution of the Ahmadiyya Muslim Community continues today.

Early on, the opposition did not involve any government or state regulations. This, however, changed in 1974, when Pakistan enacted a law to declare Ahmadis out of the pale of Islam; in direct contrast to the convictions of the Founder of Pakistan, Mohammad Ali Jinnah, who declared his policy with regards to religious practices three days prior to the nation's independence thus:

"If you change your past and work together in a spirit that every one of you . . . is first, second and last a citizen of this State with equal rights, privileges, and obligations, there will be no end to the progress you will make. We should begin to work in that spirit, and in the course all these angularities of the majority and minority communities, the Hindu community and the Muslim community -- because even as regard to Muslim you have Pathans, Punjabis, Shias, Sunnis, and so on -- will vanish. To my mind, this problem of religious differences has been the greatest hindrance in the progress of India. Therefore, we must learn a lesson from this. You are free; you are free to go to your temples, you are free to go to your mosques or to any other places of worship in this State of Pakistan. You may belong to any religion or caste or creed--that

has nothing to do with the business of the State. (Mohammad Ali Jinnah, Address at the Karachi Club, August 11, 1947).

Despite the peaceful proclamations of Jinnah, religious fanatics targeted minority religious groups only six years later, pushing a martial law declaring formal opposition to the message of Mirza Ghulam Ahmad [as], the founder of the Ahmadiyya Muslim Community.

In 1974, tensions heightened as Ahmadis were formally declared non-Muslim under a blasphemy law. This opened the floodgates for looting, vandalism, crime, and bigotry, all leveled against the Ahmadiyya Muslim Community. These hate crimes, which still exist today, are a flagrant violation of both international human rights and Quranic injunction.

To counter such opposition, *Hadhrat* Mirza Tahir Ahmad [rh], the fourth successor of the Ahmadiyya Muslim Community, enjoined followers to avoid responding in kind and to instead build mosques in every city of the world. Thus, while enemies of the community have pillaged and burned hundreds of mosques in Bangladesh, Indonesia, and Pakistan, the *Jama'at* has been blessed with 15,000 new mosques in the same period when 123 of Ahmadiyya Mosques were destroyed.

Eight killed, twenty injured in armed attack on the Ahmadiyya Mosque in Mandi Bahauddin.

The Plight of Ahmadiyya Mosques in Pakistan in Numbers
(1974 to December 31, 2006)

Number of mosques torched, destroyed or forcibly occupied in 1974	13
Number of Ahmadiyya Mosques demolished	20
Number of Ahmadiyya Mosques sealed by the authorities	25
Number of Ahmadiyya Mosques set on fire	11
Number of Ahmadiyya Mosques forcibly occupied	14
Number of Ahmadiyya Mosques barred from construction	35

Source: www.thepersecution.org

Some images of Ahmadiyya Mosque destruction in Pakistan from 1984-2007.

Another scene of mourning at Mandi Bahauddin.

Destruction of the prayer center at Nankana Sahib, Pakistan, on April 12, 1989.

Gunmen opened fire during dawn (Fajr) prayers on October 30, 2000, in Mong, Punjab, Pakistan.

The Ahmadiyya Mosque in Chak Sikander is destroyed.

All photos on this page : www.thepersecution.org

Africa

Ahmadiyyat was introduced to the African continent when several individuals living in East Africa became Ahmadi Muslims in 1900, during the life of *Hadhrat* Mirza Ghulam Ahmad [as]. In 1997, the *Jama'at* established a mosque in the small country of Swaziland. In 2000, *Hadhrat Khalifatul Masih* IV [rh] announced that Ahmadiyyat had been introduced in every African country. Today, the *Jama'at* continues to contribute to the growth of the continent through important religious, educational and humanitarian services.

BÉNIN

Jama'at established in 1957

A view of the lush landscape of Pendjari National Park, located in northwestern Bénin.

ABOUT BÉNIN

Bénin attained independence from the French in 1960. This small western African nation is 112,000 km^2 with a population of 8.3 million. French is the official language. 43% of the nation is Christian and 24% Muslim. The GDP of Bénin is US $5.4 billion, with a per capita income of US $1,500.

BÉNIN

■Porto-Novo

Edward Bouchet Abdus Salam Institute

A stamp issued by the Republic of Bénin honoring Dr. Abdus Salam and his efforts to create the Edward Bouchert Abdus Salam Institute in Bénin, which promotes educational and scientific ties between Bénin and other nations.

A group photo outside the Ahmadiyya Muslim Mosque in Togouihoue, Bénin.

Ahmadi Muslims in Bénin: Historic Highlights

1957 The Ahmadiyya Muslim Community is established when three Ahmadi Muslim *Da'een* arrive in Bénin from Nigeria.

Jama'at Ahmadiyya, Bénin

1974 On January 27, the foundation stone for the first Ahmadiyya Muslim mosque is laid in Porto Novo, and this mosque is then inaugurated by Missionary M. Ajmal Shahid on August 25.

1981 Mr. Ahmad Shamsheer Sookia arrives in Bénin as the first Ahmadiyya Muslim Missionary for the country.

A group of Ahmadi Muslims in Bénin in the 1980s (exact date unknown). Maulana Ahmad Shamsheer Sookia, the first Ahmadiyya Muslim Missionary to serve the Beninois, is standing in the center of the group (wearing glasses).

1987 Dr. Abdus Salam receives an invitation from the Government of Bénin to visit the country. His visit proves instrumental in the signing of a pact between the International Center for Theoretical Physics in Italy and the Directorate of Advanced Education in Bénin for the advancement of science in the country. As a result of this pact, the Bénin Institute for Mathematics and Physics was created in Bénin in November of 1988.

1993 *Hadhrat Khalifatul Masih IV*[th] experiences a vision, in which he is given news of the expansion of Ahmadiyyat in French-speaking countries.

1999 Extensive efforts are made to convey the message of Islam/Ahmadiyyat in the area, which results in 10,000 new initiations (*ba'aits*) for Bénin this year.

2000 801,000 individuals joining the Ahmadiyya Muslim community.

2001 Over 1.2 million people join the Ahmadiyya Muslim community in Bénin. The year is also marked by the issuance of a new stamp from the Bénin Postal Service in honor of the philanthropic efforts of Dr. Abdus Salam. The stamp features a picture of the Nobel laureate. Commenting on the expansion of Ahmadiyyat in Bénin, *Hadhrat Khalifatul Masih IV*[th] in his UK address said: "There runs an 862 km highway from south to north. It is jointly owned by Niger and Bénin. A 576 kilometer portion belongs to Bénin and the remaining 286 kilometers run through Niger. The Amir of Bénin has informed me that there are 328 cities, towns and villages on both sides of the highway. It is through Allah's grace that Ahmadiyyat has been established in all of them. The number who have offered *Ba'ait* has reached [1.3] million. 328 *Jama'ats* have been established in this region. 228 chiefs and kings have joined the *Jama'at* and Allah granted us 237 mosques along with their Imams."

2002 In December, 50,000 people participate in the *Jalsa Salana* of Bénin. Abdul Ghani Jehangeer is sent as *Huzoor's* envoy to attend the *Jalsa*, which takes place in Toui, a village situated in what is called the 'Department des Collines'. In this 18th *Jalsa Salana*, a great prophecy of the Promised Messiah[as] is realized by the participation of many kings, who arrive on horseback at the *Jalsa* site. *Hadhrat* Ahmad[as] envisioned this in 1869, one hundred thirty-three years before its occurrence.

2004 *Hadhrat Khalifatul Masih V*[aba] travels to Bénin, marking the first time that the *Khalifatul Masih* has visited the nation. During the week of April 4-10, *Huzoor*[aba] visits many cities, towns and villages, including Porto Novo, Parakou, Toui, Alada, and Dassa.

2008 As it stands today, in this historic centenary year of *Khilafate Ahmadiyya*, Bénin has 243 Jama'ats, 251 mosques and 77 mission houses, *Alhumdolillah*. Ten years ago, the number of Ahmadi Muslims in Bénin did not exceed 1,000; now, they number in the millions. As of 2002, 57 kings of various Beninois communities have joined the Ahmadiyya Muslim Community.

"KINGS SHALL SEEK BLESSINGS FROM THY GARMENTS": THE MANIFESTATION OF A DIVINE PROPHECY OF 1869

Kings entering the Jalsa Gah on their horses at the 18th Jalsa of Bénin in 2002.

A strange revelation was vouchsafed to me in Urdu in 1868 or 1869. It happened in the following way: When Molvi Muhammad Hussain Batalvi, who at one time been my fellow student, came back to Batala after finishing his divinity studies, the people of Batala began to disagree with his notions and ideologies and persuaded me seriously to hold a debate with him on the matter of dispute. Yielding to his insistence I accompanied this man at evening time to Molvi Muhammad Hussain and found him in the mosque in the company of his father. On hearing the explanation of Molvi Mohammad Hussain I concluded that there was nothing objectionable, consequently, for the sake of Allah I declined to enter into a debate with him. The same night a revelation came to me from Allah, the Noble in reference to this incidence:

Thy God is well pleased with what thou hast done. He will bless thee greatly so much so that Kings will seek blessings from thy garments. Thereafter in a waking vision (*kashf*) I was shown the Kings who were riding upon horses. As I had adopted an attitude of humility purely for the sake of God and His Messenger, the absolutely Benevolent did not desire to leave me unrewarded."

(*Hadhrat* Mirza Ghulam Ahmad[as] in *Braheen e Ahmadiyya*, Volume IV, pages 520-521, footnote 3).

Hadhrat Khalifatul Masih V [aba] inaugurated Al Mahdi Mosque on April 27, 2008. He delivered a Friday sermon on the subject of mosques. This was the last address on mosques of the first century of Khilafat.

The Building of Mosques: Huzoor's [aba] Sermon in Bénin, April 27, 2008

It is with the grace of Allah, the Exalted, that today we are offering *Jummah Salat* in this mosque of Porto Novo. Allah has enabled us to build this beautiful and large mosque so that a maximum number of people can gather here for his worship. During my last visit here, I had inaugurated this beautiful large mosque of Porto Novo. It is a great blessing of Allah for the Ahmadiyya Community that He is enabling us to build mosques in every region and every city of the world. Mosques are being built remote areas as well as African countries, just as being built in European and Community is making huge building of these mosques. neither has the wealth of any other means. Indeed, we virtue of which the Ahmadis

The Ahmadiyya Community neither has the wealth of oil, nor do we amass wealth by any other means. Indeed, we have the wealth of 'belief' by virtue of which the Ahmadis make sacrifices.

in small villages and towns of large cities of disadvantaged with Allah's grace, they are other Western countries. The sacrifices everywhere in the The Ahmadiyya Community oil, nor do we amass wealth by have the wealth of 'belief' by make sacrifices. You always

should remember that this wealth is to be safeguarded at all times. This is such a limitless treasure that thieves, robbers, and raiders waylay for it everywhere. Neither our nights are safe from these people nor our days. Rather, these robbers run in our blood streams in the shape of Satan. The Holy Prophet (peace and blessings of Allah be on him) alerted us to be safe from the Satan who runs in our veins. Always be mindful that at the time of the birth of Adam, Satan pledged that he would definitely tempt people away from their path. Therefore, always remember that the wealth of belief is such a wealth that its protection is the most difficult of tasks. For other worldly wealth you can make worldly arrangements; put up locks, have guards/sentinels in place. However, this wealth [of belief] is such that for its protection one has to constantly make arrangements for the purity of one's *nafs* (self). For its safety one continually has to endeavor to seek Allah's blessings, because without it, the waylaying Satan is bound to incite man at every step.

Excerpt from the Friday Sermon by Hadhrat Khalifatul Masih V[aba] on April 27, 2008 in Bénin (alislam.org)

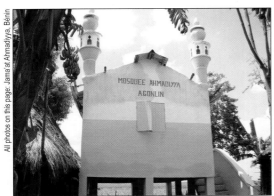

The Ahmadiyya Mosque in Agonlin, Bénin.

The Ahmadiyya Mosque in Togouihoue, Bénin.

The Ahmadiyya Mosque in Lalo, Bénin.

The Ahmadiyya Mosque in Papatia, Bénin.

The Ahmadiyya Mosque in Manigri, Bénin.

The Ahmadiyya Mosque in Oke-Owo, Bénin.

The Ahmadiyya Mosque in Godogossoun, Bénin.

An Arabic inscription of the word "Allah" adorns the Ahmadiyya Mosque in Suya, Bénin.

Highlights of Hadhrat Khalifatul Masih V's[aba] Visit to Bénin: April 4-10, 2004

4 April: Arrival

Huzoor[aba] was welcomed at the airport by the Amir of the Bénin *Jama'at* with his entire *A'amla* (Executive Committee), the King of Porto-Novo, the King of Niger and his eleven member entourage, the acting Foreign Minister of Bénin on behalf of the President of Bénin, twenty-two members of the media and press, and hundreds of members of various Ahmadiyya Muslim *Jama'at* chapters of Bénin.

Various mayors of Bénin and the neighboring country of Burkina Faso decided to embark on a friendly competition to see who would have the best reception for *Huzoor*[aba]. One mayor in Bénin appeared to have outperformed everyone else by personally traveling 450 km — and about five kilometers outside of his own territory — to welcome *Huzoor*[aba]. He also offered a 20,000 m^2 parcel of land to the *Jama'at* for the construction of a large hospital to serve the local community.

5 April

Huzoor[aba] inspected the Ahmadiyya medical facilities in the country.

6 April

Huzoor[aba] was escorted by the two army squad cars from Porto-Novo to Parakou via Alada, where the King and Queen of Parakou welcomed *Huzoor*[aba] at their Palace and expressed their affection and respect to their spiritual Imam. From Alada, Huzoor[aba] traveled to Dassa where the King of Dassa with 41 other lesser kings and chiefs, received *Huzoor Aqdas*[aba] with open arms and deep reverence. Thousands of Ahmadis were lined up on either side of the road to greet *Huzoor*[aba].

7 April

Huzoor[aba] inaugurated Baitul Aafiat mosque in Parakou and also inaugurated a sewing school, which began offering sewing lessons on its four sewing machines. *Huzoor*[aba] donated an additional ten machines to this school and instructed the *Jama'at* to open two more schools in the north. *Huzoor*[aba] also laid the foundation stone for a hospital in Parakou. 393 people traveled from Semere, a town located at a distance of 370 km, to visit Huzoor.[aba] They requested him to accept their *Ba'ait*, which *Huzoor*[aba] graciously accepted. The next stop was Toui, a location 72 km from Porto Novo, where 882 people joined the *Jama'at* and took *Ba'ait* at Huzoor's hand.

8 April

On April 8, the President of Bénin met with *Huzoor*[aba] for 45 minutes and discussed the essential matters of his country. He expressed his deep affection and gratitude for *Huzoor's* visit to Bénin.

9 April

Huzoor[aba] inaugurated Baitul Tauheed Mosque, where he also delivered the Friday sermon, which was televised live via the Muslim Television Ahmadiyya satellite network. The occasion was marked by a commemorative plaque which was unveiled and placed on the outer wall of the Mosque.

On the final day of *Huzoor's* historic tour of Bénin, a large-scale dinner that was attended by the President of Bénin and several dignitaries was arranged in *Huzoor's* honor.

Huzoor[aba] *receives an affectionate welcome at the airport in Bénin.*

Burkina Faso
Jama'at Established in 1986

Mosque Al Mahdi in the capital city of Ouagadougou, Burkina Faso.

ABOUT BURKINA FASO

Formerly known as Upper Volta, Burkina Faso attained independence from France in 1960. Burkina Faso is 274,000 km² with a population of 15 million. French is the official language and about 50% of the population is Muslim. The GDP of Burkina Faso is US $6.9 billion, with a per capita GDP of $1,200.

The Ahmadiyya Muslim mosque in Koudougou, Burkina Faso.

The seed of Ahmadiyyat first was planted in Burkina Faso by Mr. Muhammad Yusuf. He accepted Ahmadiyyat while a student in Ghana. Upon his return to Burkina Faso, he shared this new religion with his father, Muhammad Baru, and brothers, who all embraced Ahmadiyyat. Despite initial opposition from the local villages, the Ahmadiyya Muslim community grew rapidly in the country as more missionaries arrived.

Hadhrat Khalifatul Masih V's [aba] Historic Visit to Burkina Faso in 2004

*H*adhrat Khalifatul Masih V [aba] first visited Burkina Faso during his historic trip in March of 2004. Upon arrival, he was hosted as an official guest of the government and stayed at the Hotel Sofitel in the capital city of Ouagadougou. He was greeted by the President of Burkina Faso, Mr. Blaise Compaore and the Prime Minister, Mr. Paramanga Ernest Yonli.

Huzoor [aba] presided the annual gathering (Jalsa Salana) and his sermon was broadcast live via MTA and the Ahmadiyya radio station in Burkina Faso, *Islamique Radio Ahmadiyya*. 34 dignitaries and officials participated in the Jalsa proceedings, which were attended by over 13,000 people.

Guests from the neighboring countries of Mali and Ivory Coast also attended.

In the days following the Jalsa, *Huzoor* [aba] visited various Humanity First centers, a computer center and a sewing center, where *Huzoor* [aba] donated 20 new sewing machines for students receiving training in sewing and stitching. He also laid the foundation of a new 15-acre primary school near Baitul Tahir in the Dori region.

Huzoor [aba] concluded his historic visit with the inauguration of Masjid Huda in the Kaya region where he was escorted by government officials.

Jama'at Ahmadiyya, Burkina Faso

Huzoor [aba], *during his visit to Burkina Faso in 2004, meets with His Excellency Mr. Blaise Compaoré, the President of Burkina Faso.*

Jama'at Ahmadiyya, Burkina Faso

An Ahmadiyya radio station in Burkina Faso (Radio Islamique Ahmadiyya FM104.1). Right: The radio tower.

JOURNEY OF A LIFETIME:

The story of *Khuddam* from Burkina Faso who traveled hundreds of miles over several days by bicycle to attend Jalsa Salana Ghana

Khuddam from Burkina Faso offer duty at the 2008 Jalsa Salana in Ghana. Visible in the background are rows of hundreds of bicycles by which they traveled.

Hadhrat Khalifatul Masih V[aba], in his Friday Sermon on May 9, 2008, recalled the historical journey of Burkina Faso *Khuddam* led by Abdul Rahman, *Sadr Majlis Khuddamul Ahmadiyya*, Burkina Faso. *Huzoor*[aba] said the Khuddam [from Burkina Faso] who had arrived on bicycles had traveled for seven consecutive days, camping in between. The group had a few *Ansar* of 50-60 age group and two 13-year-olds. Prior to traveling, the *Amir* of Burkina Faso told these two boys that they were too young to make the trip. They were most disheartened and insisted they join. Finally, they were permitted to join. The *Sadr Khuddam* Burkina Faso, Abdur Rahman, had said that they wished to emulate the tremendous sense of sacrifice of the early Muslims at the occasion of the *Khilafat Centenary* and planned the bicycle ride. *Huzoor*[aba] said it is not as if the *Khuddam* had new, strong bicycles; rather, they were old and dilapidated. However, their sincerity for *Khilafat* which the Holy Prophet Muhammad[sa] had prophesised was such that they made the journey. *Huzoor*[aba] said a television correspondent asked one of the bikers from Burkina Faso how had he traveled on such a dilapidated bicycle. He replied that the bicycle was indeed dilapidated, but his faith was strong. *Huzoor*[aba] said this event was broadcast on national television with striking headlines. He noted that these were not born Ahmadis, nor were they of the family of any of the companions of The Promised

Messiah[as]. They lived thousands of miles away in places without electricity, without running water and where there is intense poverty. Yet having joined the Community of the true and ardent devotee of the Holy Prophet Muhammad[sa], they are resolute in their resolve. *Huzoor*[aba] prayed that may Allah increase them in their sincerity.

Amir and Missionaries of Burkina Faso

Nasir Ahmad Sidhu

Muhammad Amin Baloch

Mahmood Nasir Saqib Amir and Missionary-in-Charge

Khalid Mahmood

Hamid Maqsud Atif

Côte d'Ivoire

Jama'at Established in 1961

About Côte d'Ivoire

Côte d'Ivoire (known formerly as the Ivory Coast) attained independence from France in 1960. Côte d'Ivoire is 322,000 km^2 with a population of 18 million. French is the official language and about 40% of the population is Muslim. The GDP of Côte d'Ivoire is US $20 billion, with a per capita income of $1800. It is the world's top producer of cocoa.

CIA World Factbook

Côte d'Ivoire is the world's largest cocoa producer, but many call for labor and other economic reforms in its production.

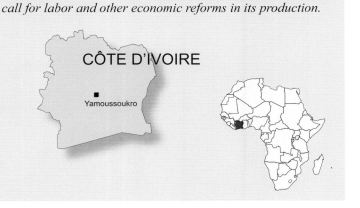

CÔTE D'IVOIRE

Yamoussoukro

Jama'at Ahmadiyya, Côte d'Ivoire

The Ahmadiyya Mosque in Dagara is located in the Dabakala 'department' of the Vallée du Bandama region of Côte d'Ivoire.

Ahmadiyya Mosque, Côte d'Ivoire

Dr. Abdus Salam with a Missionary of Côte d'Ivoire in 1988.

Hadhrat Khalifatul Masih III[rh] consulting with Jama'at members about propagation plans in Côte d'Ivoire.

"The journey via rivers has now come to an end and the time of oceanic travel has begun. For these journeys, Allah's power alone will be the defining force. *Khilafat* has been endowed with those blessings that are destined for the future progress of Islam. To whichever direction the *Khalifa* will face, that will also be the direction of the wind of Allah's grace... in this year alone we have been bestowed with 150,000 *ba'aits* from French-speaking countries. *Alhumdolillah*."

Hadhrat Khalifatul Masih IVth describing his vision relating to the spread of Islam in French-speaking nations; *International Al-Fazl*, August 19, 1994, p. 2.

Hadhrat Mirza Tahir Ahmad, Khalifatul Masih IV[rh], with the Prime Minister of Côte d'Ivoire.

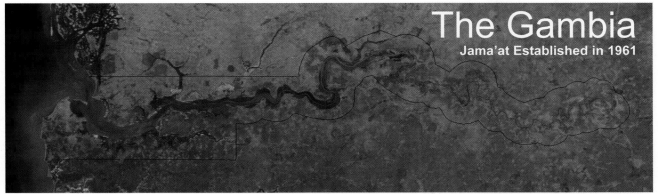

The Gambia
Jama'at Established in 1961

Satellite photograph of the Republic of The Gambia, the smallest country in the African continental mainland. Flowing through the center of the country and emptying into the Atlantic Ocean is the Gambia River.

ABOUT THE GAMBIA

The Gambia attained independence from the British in 1965. This small western African nation is only 11,300 km^2 with a population of 1.7 million. English is the official language and 90% of the nation is Muslim. The GDP of The Gambia is US $379 million, with a per capita income of $800.

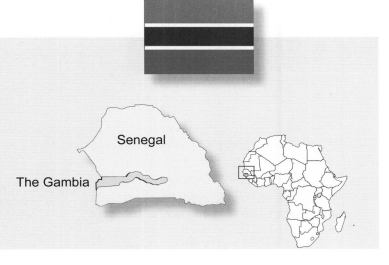

The Ahmadiyya Muslim mosque in Burock, a small village located in the Foli Kansala, which is one of the nine districts in the Western Division of The Gambia.

Ahmadiyya Mosque, Saba, The Gambia.

Hadhrat Mirza Tahir Ahmad, Khalifatul Masih IV^{rh} laying the foundation stone of Baitus Salam Mosque in Talinding Kunjang, The Gambia on January 20, 1988.

The Ahmadiyya mosque in Latrikunda, a locale within Serrekunda, the largest city in The Gambia.

Hadhrat Khalifatul Masih III^{rh} (center) meets with Al-Haj Farimang Mamadi Singateh, the Governor-General of The Gambia, during his visit in May of 1970. Singateh Sahib, pictured standing with his son immediately on Hazoor's left, had the distinction of being the first Ahmadi Muslim to be the Governor General in The Gambia. On Hazoor's far left: Sahibzada Mirza Mubarak Ahmad, In-Charge of Ahmadiyya Muslim Foreign Missions. On Hazoor's right: Respected Mansoora Begum Sahiba, Hazoor's wife; and Respected Aja Basse, Singateh Sahib's wife.

Attendees pose for a group photo during a December, 1966 farewell ceremony marking the departure of Maulana Ghulam Ahmad Baddomalhi, the Amir and Missionary-in-Charge of The Gambia.

Left to Right (Standing): Al-Jah Ibrahima Jikineh, Maulana Ghulam Ahmad Baddomalhi, Al-Haj Farimang Singateh (Governal General of The Gambia), Acting Amir Daud A. Hanif, Mr. Tijan Foon and Mr. Ash Malick. Left to Right (Sitting): Mr. Muhammad Sohna, Mr. Harouna Newland, Mr. Alieu M. Bah, and Muhammad I. Amin.

Hadhrat Khalifatul Masih IV ^{rh} delivers Friday Sermon on January 22, 1988 in which he announced Nusrat Jehan e Nau scheme

Al-Haj Sir Famara Mohammad Singhate, the first Ahmadi Governor-General of The Gambia.

Sidi Mucktar Mydara, the first person to accept Ahmadiyyat from Georgetown MID in The Gambia, 1967.

Do not be upset for God has assured me during my present illness that half a million Christians will be converted to Islam in West Africa. All of them will be educated. That will be a great day for Islam.

— Message of *Hadhrat Hakim Maulvi* Nooruddin, *Khalifatul Masih I* ^{ra}, *Pegham Sulah Newspaper*, March 3, 1914.

Ghana

Jama'at established in 1921

Commemorative stamp issued by the government of Ghana on the occasion of the Khilafat Centenary Celebrations. The theme depicted is wheat cultivation, which Ahmadis pioneered in Ghana through breakthrough experimentation (see Ghana timeline for details).

GHANA KHILAFAT AHMADIYYA CENTENARY 1908-2008

Wheat Grown in Ghana
LOVE FOR ALL HATRED FOR NONE 90GP

ABOUT GHANA

Once a British colony called the Gold Coast, Ghana became the first sub-Saharan country to gain independence in 1957. Ghana is 239,000 km^2 with a population of 23 million. English is the official language, and 69% of the nation is Christian while 16% is Muslim. The GDP of Ghana is US $15 billion, with a per capita income of $1400.

CIA World Factbook

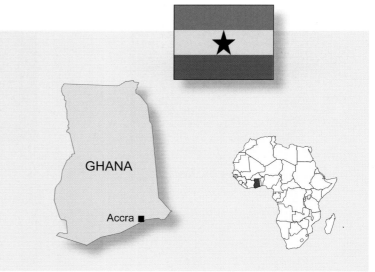

GHANA

Accra ■

The Ahmadiyya Muslim Mosque in Accra, Ghana.

Pioneers of Ahmadiyyat in Ghana: Early Missionaries-in-Charge

Hadhrat Al-Haj Maulana Abdur Raheem Nayyar^ra, 1921-22

Hadhrat Al-Haj Maulana Hakeem Fazl-ur-Rahman, 1922-29, 1933-35

Hadhrat Al-Haj Maulana Nazeer Ahmad Ali, 1929-33, 1936-37, 1946-50

Hadhrat Al-Haj Maulana Nazeer Ahmad Mubashir, 1937-46, 1950-61

Ahmadi Muslims in Ghana: Historic Highlights

1921 Ahmadiyyat is established in Ghana. *Hadhrat* Abdul Rahim Nayyar [ra] becomes the first missionary to Ghana, arriving in March by sea and landing at Saltpond in the Central Region. (Saltpond would be the national headquarters for fifty years until it was moved to Accra in 1978). During his brief time in Ghana, Nayyar Sahib converts thousands to the fold of Ahmadiyyat. The Ahmadi population increases 5 fold in one year.

1922 Missionary Hakeem Fazlur Rahman arrives in Ghana. During his tenure, several secular Ahmadiyya schools are opened.

1950 The first Ahmadiyya secondary school is opened by Maulvi N.A. Mobashir in Kumasi.

1970 *Hadhrat* Khalifatul Masih III [rh] visits Ghana from April 18-26. The Nusrat Jahan Leap Forward Scheme is launched. The scheme saw the opening of six secondary schools throughout Ghana (Asokore, Fomena, Salaga, Essarkyir, Potsin, and Wa). These were fully financed by the Ahmadiyya Mission until the government took over in the 1980s. These schools have produced many important personalities currently holding high positions in both the Jama'at and government of Ghana.

Hadhrat Khalifatul Masih III's [rh] meeting with Dr. Hilla Linman, President of Ghana, in 1970.

As a result of the Nusrat Jahan Scheme, several Ahmadiyya hospitals are established throughout Ghana (Asokore, Kokofu, Techiman, Swedru, Kaleo in Upper West, Daboase and Mim in Brong Ahafo. (Source: 2008 Ghana Souvenir)

Hadhrat Khalifatul Masih III [rh] places a commemorative plaque on the Ahmadiyya Mosque in Mangoase on the occasion of its opening ceremony on April 24, 1970.

1977 *Hadhrat* Mirza Masroor Ahmad [aba] is assigned by *Hadhrat Khalifatul Masih III* [rh] as Missionary to Ghana under the Nusrat Jahan Scheme, where he would serve until 1985.

Sahibzada Mirza Masroor Ahmad [aba] was the founding principal of the Ahmadiyya Secondary School Salaga, a school in the northern region of Ghana, where he served for two years. This school is progressing very well to this day. His success at this school made him the obvious choice for the principal of the Ahmadiyya Secondary School at Essarkyir where he served for another four years. This school is in the central region of Ghana.

Sahibzada Mirza Masroor Ahmad [aba] was appointed as the manager of the Ahmadiyya Agricultural Farm in Depali, in the northern region of Ghana, for 2 years. First experiments had revealed that wheat could not grow in Ghana. But Sahibzada Mirza Masroor Ahmad continued relentlessly. Another Ahmadi Muslim, Mr Qasim Ahmad, joined him in this series of experiments. The efforts of this team of Ahmadi agriculturalists finally paid dividends. The first successful experiment of planting, growing, and nurturing wheat as an economic crop in Ghana was exhibited at an international trade fair and the results were submitted to the Ministry of Agriculture of Ghana. It stands as a great credit to his personal efforts in these experiments that successive presidents of Ghana have commended the Ahmadiyya Muslim community for these highly successful experiments, which revolutionized the country's economy and paved the way for self sufficiency (SOURCE: alislam.org).

Ahmadi Muslims in Ghana: Historic Highlights

1980 *Hadhrat Khalifatul Masih III* [rh] makes his second visit to Ghana.

1984 An Ahmadiyya Homeopathy Clinic is opened by Abdul Wahab Ahmad, Amir and Missionary-In-Charge of Ghana in Kumasi. Since then, two additional clinics have opened and have gained immense popularity, drawing patients from neighboring countries.

1988 *Hadhrat Khalifatul Masih IV* [rh] makes a historic visit to Ghana.

2004 *Hadhrat Khalifatul Masih V* [aba] travels to Ghana for the first time as *khalifa*. During this visit, he lays the foundation and inaugurates several mosques, mission houses, schools and hospitals (A detail of this historic trip is presented separately).

2008 *Huzoor* [aba] embarks on a three-week tour of West Africa to commemorate the *Khilafat* Centenary celebrated by millions of Ahmadis worldwide. On April 17, *Huzoor* [aba] inaugurates the 78th *Jalsa Salana* Ghana and declares Ghana an example to the world.

Hadhrat Khalifatul Masih IV [rh] *with the Ghanian Head of State and Chairman of the P.N.D.C. Government in 1988.*

Maulvi Dr. Abdul Wahab bin Adam, Amir and Missionary-In-Charge of Ghana since 1975.

Hadhrat Khalifatul Masih V [aba] *greets a large Jalsa audience in Ghana in 2004.*

"I have great expectations of Ghana. It is my prayer that may you always march forward. Perhaps these aspirations are because I spent part of my life here."

- *Hadhrat* Mirza Masroor Ahmad [aba] during *Jalsa Salana* Ghana, 2008

Spiritual Connections:
Ahmadis in Ghana and the U.S.

Maulana Ataullah Kaleem, who served for 19 years in Ghana and also was Amir and Missionary-In-Charge, Ghana, presents books to government officials.

Maulana Abdul Malik Khan, who served as Missionary in Ghana from 1961-1964, presents some literature to government officials.

Maulana Ataullah Kaleem later served as the Amir and Missionary-In-Charge of the U.S. Jama'at.

Maulana Abdul Malik Khan seen here in Rabwah after his transfer from Ghana back to Pakistan.

In loving memory of a beloved U.S. khadim: The late Muhaimin Karim of Chicago, USA, is introduced to Hadhrat Khalifatul Masih V ^{aba} by Abdul Wahab Adam, Amir of Ghana.

Nasia Mosque in northern Ghana.

Ahmadiyya Mosque in Pramso, Ghana.

Ahmadiyya Mosque in Salaga, Ghana.

The Nusrat Jahan Mosque in Wa, Ghana.

Ahmadiyya Mosque in Kokobila, Ghana.

Ahmadiyya Mosque in Techiman, Ghana.

On my behalf, and on behalf of the worldwide Ahmadiyya community, I offer hearty congratulations to you and your country. I pray to God for the continued progress and prosperity of your country. My affiliation and relation with your country is not merely superficial; it is based on true sincerity, since about 100,000 citizens of your country are currently Ahmadis and many students of your country are attending Ahmadiyya schools. We hope by the Grace of Allah that our Community will expand in the length and breadth of your country in the years to come at a faster pace, that it will also enhance in every section of activities towards progress and improvements and, as such, play an active role. This is my wish and prayer that Allah may assist you and your country.

A cable telegram from *Hadhrat Khalifatul Masih II*[ra] to
Dr. Kwame Nkrumah, Prime Minister of Ghana in 1957.

Kumasi Central Mosque in Kumasi, Ghana.

Ahmadiyya Muslim Mosque in Abura, Ghana.

Ahmadiyya Mosque in Mangoase, Ghana.

Ahmadiyya Mosque in Daboase, Ghana.

The continent of Africa is most fortunate. The hearts of Africans are full of the light of Allah. On them has poured such a rain of Allah's blessings that is beyond human imagination!

The other city of Ghana is Kumasi. The *Jama'at* has constructed two buildings near this city for the purposes of training *Daeen Ilallah* and for the moral training of new converts. This will help them get trained and then go back in their areas and teach Ahmadiyyat, or the true Islam, to others. The entire expense of the construction of these buildings has been borne by one dedicated Ahmadi. Alongside these buildings is also the Homeopathic Complex. It has a clinic, a laboratory to manufacture homeopathic medications, and a small manufacturing plant for making medication bottles. *Masha'Allah*, this institution is providing a great service to mankind. In different towns and cities of Ghana, opening ceremonies were carried out for mosques, schools, and hospital wards. In short, thirteen mosques were inaugurated during this visit, and a foundation stone was laid down for another two. In addition, either an opening ceremony or a foundation stone were laid down for another seven miscellaneous buildings.

Tamale is another major town situated in the north of Ghana. There is a large population of Muslims in that area. In this town, also, an opening ceremony was held of a large two story mosque building. A few years ago, nobody could have even imagined that such a large mosque could be established in that city and that worshippers would come to it. By the Grace of Allah, a large number of *Ba'aits* have taken place in this area. *Alhumdolillah*. By the Grace of Allah, *Jama'at* Ahmadiyya is expanding rapidly in this area. Here, two individuals who were the drivers of our caravan took the *Ba'ait* and joined *Jama'at* Ahmadiyya. They were so impressed with whatever they saw that they thought they had no choice left but to join *Jama'at* Ahmadiyya. After *Maghrib* and *Isha* prayers, both of them took the *Ba'ait* personally alongside other existing Ahmadis.

— Message from *Hadhrat Khalifatul Masih V*[aba]
during his visit to Ghana in 2004.

Day-to-Day Profile of Huzoor's (aba) Historical Trip to Ghana in 2004

March 17, 2004

Huzoor aba meets with the missionaries and officeholders of the *Jama'at* on a regional and local basis. *Huzoor* aba also visits the botanical gardens in Abora.

March 20, 2004

Huzoor aba visits the Ashante region. and inaugurates the Asokore Hospital and Baitul Habib while en route to Kumasi. *Huzoor* aba inspects Taleem ul Islam School in Kumasi – the first school established in Africa in 1950. *Huzoor* aba unveils a plaque in the central mosque in Kumasi. *Huzoor* aba also visits the Tahir Homeopathic center.

March 16, 2004

Huzoor aba inaugurates a newly built mosque on the premises of the Daboase Hospital. This mosque has four minarets. *Huzoor* aba is greeted by a large gathering at Baitul Aleem in Abora. A large number of members in Salt Pond also welcome *Huzoor* aba.

March 14, 2004

Huzoor aba inspects the Talimul Islam School in Gomoa Poston, an Ahmadiyya Hospital in Agona Swedru, and an Ahmadiyya secondary school in Ekumfi Essarkyir. *Huzoor* aba inaugurates a mosque and the new building of Jamia Ahmadiyya. He also visits the Ahmadiyya Graveyard in Ekrawfo.

March 15, 2004

Huzoor aba meets the President of Ghana, John Kufour. The President affectionately remarks that Ghana was *Huzoor's* aba hometown. Besides visiting Accra Mission House, exhibition halls, auxiliary offices, and the Ahmadiyya press, *Huzoor* aba also attends the reception of the Tema *Jama'at*.

March 18, 2004

The *Jalsa Salana* Ghana commences at *Bustan-e-Ahmad*. *Huzoor* aba arrives at the *Jalsa* site, where President Kufour receives him along with other ministers and dignitaries. *Huzoor* aba delivers the Friday sermon on the topic of moral excellences.

Map locations: Paga, Bolgatanga, Kaleo, Wa, Walewale, Tamale, Salaga, Kokofu, Techiman, Abora, Kumasi, Asokore, Koforidua, Swedru, Accra, Daboase, Potsin, Mangoase, Ekumfi Essarkyir, Saltpond

Source: *International Al-Fazl*

KENYA
Jama'at established in 1900

The lioness shown to the right was photographed in the hot savannah of the Masai Mara Game Reserve. Located in southwestern Kenya, the Mara Masai is one of the most famous game parks in the world, and sections of it are also assigned National Park status.

The Greater Kudu, shown in this postage stamp issued by the Kenyan government in 1966, is one of the many animals that the lions of Kenya prey upon.

ABOUT KENYA

KENYA

■ Nairobi

Kenya attained independence from Britain in 1963. The east African nation is 582,000 km² with a population of 38 million. Swahili and English are the official languages and about 75% of the population is Roman Catholic or Protestant, and 10% Muslim. The GDP of Kenya is US $30 billion, with a per capita income of $1,600.

CIA World Factbook

Ahmadiyya Mosque in Nairobi, Kenya

A circa 1964 photograph showing Mr. Jomo Kenyatta, who was serving as Prime Minister of Kenya at the time, laying a wreath of flowers on the grave of the late Sheikh Amer Abedi, an Ahmadi Muslim who served as a Minister in his cabinet. Standing at the extreme left (holding a walking stick) is Mr. Milton Obote, who was serving as the Prime Minister of Uganda at the time the photograph was taken.

In this photograph, taken circa 1962, Mr. Jomo Kenyatta, who would go on to become Prime Minister and, later, President of Kenya, receives some books about Islam from Sheikh Mubarak Ahmad, the former Chief Ahmadiyya Missionary in East Africa. To the left of Mr. Kenyatta is Mr. Noor ul Haq Anwar, who was serving as Missionary-in-Charge in Kenya at the time. To the right of Sheikh Mubarak Ahmad is an unidentified, locally trained Ahmadi Muslim missionary.

A senior officer of the Kenyan government signs the visitor's book at the Ahmadiyya Mission House in Nairobi, Kenya; circa 1965.

Ahmadiyyat in Kenya: A Brief Timeline

1900 Two companions of the Promised Messiah[as], *Hadhrat* Munshi Mohammad Afzal and *Hadhrat* Mian Abdullah, arrive in Mombassa in 1896. Some additional Ahmadis join them and a *Jama'at of 52 people* is established in East Africa.

Early Ahmadi converts of East Africa in 1901

1928 The Nairobi Counsel gives a 3-4 acre parcel of land to the *Jama'at* to build a mosque. Construction begins in 1929 and is completed in 1931.

1934 *Hadhrat Khalifatul Masih II*[ra] assigns *Maulana* Shaikh Mubarak Ahmad as the first missionary to Kenya, on November 27.

1936 A monthly Ahmadi magazine, *Mapenzi Ya Mungu*, begins (and is still in publication)

1945 Maulana Noorul Haq Anwer arrives as missionary.

1947 Six additional missionaries are assigned in Kenya, including: Mir Ziaullah, Fazal Ilahi Bashir, Syed Waliullah Shah, Inayatullah Khalil, Jalaluddin Qamar and Hakim Mohammad Ibrahim. *Maulana* Mohammad Munawar and Abdul Karim Shirma would later arrive.

1988 *Hadhrat Khalifatul Masih IV*[rh] visits Kenya for one week, marking the first visit of any *khalifa* to the nation.

2005 *Hadhrat Khalifatul Masih V*[aba] visits Kenya and addresses the 40th Jalsa Salana, which is broadcast worldwide on MTA. 7,000 people attended. The Honorable Mudi Awowri, Vice President of Kenya, addresses the *Jalsa* audience and extends his appreciation to the Ahmadiyya Community in Kenya for their work in medical services and in the promotion of peace. He lauds the 68 mosques in the country and personally thanks *Huzoor*[aba] for his visit.

Huzoor[aba] inaugurates Ahmadiyya Hall in Nairobi (a three-story building adjacent to the mosque in Nairobi). He also lays the foundation for mosques in Navaisha and Nukoro, inaugurates a mosque in Banja and a mission house in Eldoret.

Hadhrat Khalifatul Masih V's [aba] Historic Visit to Kenya in 2005

Members of Majlis Atfal ul Ahmadiyya, Kenya, (young boys' group) recite poems inside the Jalsa site to greet Hadhrat Khalifatul Masih V[aba] during his arrival on the occasion of the 40th Jalsa Salana (Annual Gathering) of the Ahmadiyya Muslim Community in Kenya. The Jalsa took place in April of 2005.

Mapanzi ko Ote, Usi Chuki Mtu.

Hadhrat Khalifatul Masih V[aba] is welcomed by Malis Khuddamul Ahmadiyya Kenya to the Jalsa site at Parklands Primary school in Nairobi, Kenya in April, 2005.

Lesotho
Jama'at established in 1999

Although small in size and landlocked within the larger country of South Africa, Lesotho is unique in being the only independent nation with all of its territory residing at an elevation greater than 1,000 meters above sea level. As such it is often known as the "Mountain Kingdom."

ABOUT LESOTHO

Basutoland was renamed the Kingdom of Lesotho upon independence from the UK in 1966. Landlocked within the Republic of South Africa, Lesotho is only 30,000 km^2 with a population of 2.1 million. English is the official language, and Christianity is the predominant religion. The GDP of Lesotho is US $1.6 billion, with a per capita income of $1,500.

CIA World Factbook

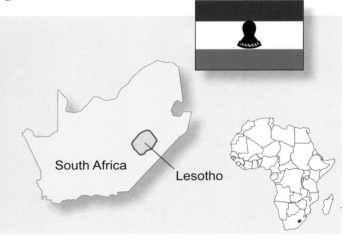

Jama'at Ahmadiyya, South Africa

See our entry for Swaziland to learn more about the history of the *Jama'at* in this country.

Baitul Mahdi Mosque, located in Lesotho.

LIBERIA
Jama'at established in 1956

A hazy sun over the tallest point in Liberia, in Pademal Lofa County.

Kevin McNulty

ABOUT LIBERIA

Freed slaves from the U.S. during the 19th century settled in present day Liberia. It is 111,000 km^2 with a population of 3.3 million. English is the official language. 40% of the nation is Christian and 20% is Muslim. The GDP of Liberia is US $732 million, with a per capita income of $500.

CIA World Factbook

Monrovia

LIBERIA

Jama'at Ahmadiyya, Liberia

Arshad M. Khan

This mosque, which was graciously named Baitul Mujeeb Mosque by Hadhrat Khalifatul Masih IV^{rh}, was inaugurated by Mr. Muhammad Akram Bajwah, the Amir & Missionary-in-Charge of Liberia, on July 7, 2000. This inauguration marked the celebration of the mosque's reconstruction after it suffered fire damage in 1996 during the First Liberian Civil War. It was originally built in 1986, and is located in Monrovia. The double-story building also includes a mission house.

Mr. Mubarak Ahmed Saqi delivers a speech on Islam from Radio Liberia. Date unknown.

Mr. Muhammad Akram Bajwah, Amir and Missionary-in-Charge, Liberia.

Mr. Muhammad J. Annan, Naib Amir of Liberia.

Hadhrat Khalifatul Masih III[rh] Visits Liberia

Hadhrat Khalifatul Masih III[rh] and President Tubman in the Executive Mansion on April 29, 1970.

Hadhrat Khalifatul Masih III[rh] replying to the welcome address given by President Tubman, during the State Banquet held in Huzoor's[aba] honor at the Chief Executive Mansion on April 30, 1970.

Hadhrat Khalifatul Masih IV[rh] Visits Liberia

Hadhrat Khalifatul Masih IV[rh] meets with Dr. Harry F. Momba, Vice President of Liberia.

Liberian Ahmadis bid farewell to Hadhrat Khalifatul Masih IV[rh].

Ahmadi Muslims Break New Ground in Liberia

Jama'at Ahmadiyya, Liberia

Jama'at Ahmadiyya, Liberia

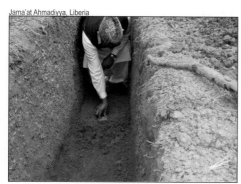

Muhammad Akram Bajwah Sahib, Amir Jama'at Liberia, lays the foundation of Tubmanburg Mosque on September 8, 2007.

Collective prayers after the foundation laying of a mosque in Tubmanburg, Liberia

Spreading Ahmadiyyat in Liberia

Mr Javaid Iqbal Langah, Central Missionary, Bomi County, Liberia

Mr Hadji Ismael Conneh, Local Missionary, Tewor District of Grand Cape Mount County, Liberia

Dr. Abdul Haleem Arain, Sadr Majlis Ansarullah and Doctor-in-Charge, Ahmadiyya Muslim Clinic, Monrovia

Dr Tahir Ahmed Mirza, Doctor-in-Charge, Ahmadiyya Muslim Clinic Tubmanburg City, Bomi County

Mr. Mansoor Ahmad Chaudhry, Principal, Shah Taj Ahmadiyya Elementary & Junior High School, Tweh Farm, Bushrod Island Monrovia

Mr Muhammad Zakkria, New Central Missionary, Grand Cape Mount County, Liberia

Mr Muhammad Ahsan Ahmad, Sadr Majlis Khuddamul Ahmadiyya, Liberia

Individual photos courtesy of Ahmadiyya Jama'at, Liberia

Ahmadi Muslims in Liberia: Historic Highlights

1917 A college professor in Liberia requests for more information about Ahmadiyyat from the London office of the *Jama'at*.

1952 Maulana Siddique Amritsari visits Liberia and spends one month learning about the country.

1956 In January, Sufi Muhammad Ishaq establishes the first Ahmadiyya mission in Liberia.

1959 The Honorable Dag Hammarskjold visits the Ahmadiyya Mission House during his tour of Liberia while serving as the second Secretary-General of the United Nations. There, he was introduced by Maulana Siddique *Sahib*, who presented him with a copy of the book *Ahmadiyyat, The True Islam*. The Honorable Secretary-General sent a note expressing his appreciation to the Ahmadiyya Community in Liberia.

1960

M. L. Wysinger, online.

Empress Waizero Menen and Emperor Haile Selassie.

Maulana Siddique challenged the Reverend Billy Graham to an open debate regarding accusations Mr. Graham leveled against the Holy Qur'an. An Egyptian ambassador and an American press reporter support this challenge and demand that the Reverend come forward to face it.

On December 1 of this year, His Imperial Majesty Haile Selassie I, the Emperor of Ethiopia (formerly known as Abyssinia), visits the Mission House in Liberia, where he is welcomed by the Ahmadiyya Community and presents with the Holy Qur'an. The king declares that he is the 63rd monarch descending directly from the progeny of King Negus of Abyssinia, who gave shelter to Muslims in the time of the Prophet Mohammad[sa].

1964 Mubarak Ahmed Saqi informs the President of Liberia, William V. S. Tubman, that Friday is a holy day for Muslims and requests that a leave from work for Friday prayers should be officially granted to all Muslims. This request was accepted by the President and was announced throughout the country.

1967 A building to serve as a mission house is purchased in Liberia.

1970 On April 29, *Hadhrat Khalifatul Masih III*[rh] makes his first visit to Liberia, and meets with President Tubman. *Huzoor* also addresses the press and attends a reception dinner held by the the Ahmadiyya Community in his honor. President Tubman made the following remrks: "It is a great privilege to have the spiritual king of the present age among us – one whose prayer is always heard. Politicians and statesmen have lost the ability to cope with the situation in the world today. They have fumbled, sinned and are frustrated with the deteriorating situation." He added, "It is an honor indeed to welcome the Caliph, one of the greatest leaders of Islam, who has missionaries all over the world." The President also announced that he would grant 150 acres of land to the Ahmadiyya Muslim Mission in Liberia for the construction of schools and clinics.

1973 Missionary Ch. Rashiduddin remains the President of Pakistan Forum of Liberia for two years to promote the image of Pakistan in Liberia.

1974 The first Ahmadiyya Junior High School is founded in Sanoyea. Also during this year, *Hadhrat Khalifatul Masih III*[rh] sends his special Eid Greetings to Liberia – reported by *The Liberian Star* on December 24, 1974. A summary of the *Khalifa's* message is read by Ch. Rashiduddin at the *Eid* gathering.

1976 In September, the Minister of Education, Mr. Advertus A. Hoff, inaugurates the Ahmadiyya school at Sanoyea, and in November, Missionary Ch. Rashiduddin addresses a Pakistan Celebration at the school.

1979 On March 13, *Maulana* Ataul Karim Shahid welcomes the Archbishop of Canterbury to Liberia and reminds him to hold a dialogue with Ahmadi Muslims. This was Archbishop's first tour to Africa.

Ahmadi Muslims in Liberia: Historic Highlights

1981
In November, an Ahmadiyya Mission House is founded and the construction of its two-story building is completed in February of 1982.

1984
On January 24, the construction of an Ahmadiyya mosque begins in Monrovia, and is inaugurated on June 1, 1984 with *Taravee* prayers led my *Maulana* Abdul Shukoor.

1988
Hadhrat Khalifatul Masih IV[rh] reaches Liberia on January 31, 1988. In addition to a large number of Ahmadis, the Education Minister of Liberia receives *Huzoor* [rh] at the airport. National TV Liberia presents a full coverage of his arrival, and interviewes him at the VIP lounge. On the morning of February 1, *Huzoor* [rh] meets the President of Liberia and addresses a press conference. Later that evening, he attends a reception held in his honor, which is attended by the Vice President of Liberia, several Ambassadors, scholars, and dignitaries of this country. On February 2, he addresses the *Majlis-e-A'amla* (Executive Body) of the Liberian *Jama'at*.

Jama'at Ahmadiyya, Karachi, Pakistan

Dr. Samuel Kanyon Doe, the President of Liberia, receives Hadhrat Khalifatul Masih IV [rh] *at the State House in Liberia.*

Jama'at Ahmadiyya, Liberia

A Jama'at delegation meets with His Excellency Joseph Boakai, the Vice-President of Liberia on Sep 18, 2006.

Jama'at Ahmadiyya, Liberia

The Honorable Kabinneh Jann'eh, Associate Justice of the Supreme Court of Liberia, addresses the Jalsa Salana gathering in Liberia on December 23, 2006.

Ahmadi Muslims in Liberia: Historic Highlights

1996 An Ahmadiyya elementary and junior high school is established in Monrovia by the approval of *Hadhrat Khalifatul Masih IV*[rh], who gives the school the name "Shah Taj Ahmadiyya"

1999 The *Jama'at* purchases a 12-acre parcel of land in Po-River, named Ahmed-e-Abad by *Huzoor*[rh]. This is the future site for headquarters of *Jama'at* Ahmadiyya Liberia. The foundation is laid in 2007. The mosque is being built in celebration of *Khilafat Jubilee.*

Jama'at Ahmadiyya, Liberia

The Ahmadiyya Muslim Mission House in Gohn Town, Grand Cape Mount County, Liberia

2000 Baitul Mujeeb in Monrovia, which was burnt during the Liberian Civil War in 1996, is rebuilt. The opening ceremony on July 7 is attended by the wife of the President of Liberia.

An Ahmadiyya Muslim mosque and mission house is inaugurated in Teh Town, Farwula District, Grande Cape Mount County.

Two young Ahmadis from Liberia are sent to Jamia Ahmadiyya Ghana for missionary training: Hadji Ismael Conneh and Hassan Jenekai. They completed their training and returned to Liberia in 2004. Conneh is presently serving the *Jama'at*. Jenekai passed away in March, 2007.

2001 After 13 years, the annual *Jalsa Salana* resumes in Liberia.

A mosque and mission house is built in Lyean Town, Dewoin District, Bomi County.

2004 Humanity First is established in Liberia and has played an active part in humanitarian relief. A computer school is later established in 2007.

2005 A mosque is established in Gohn Town, Tewor District, Grand Cape Mount County. The mosque was constructed by *Majlis Khuddam-ul-Ahmadiyya,* Liberia.

The first *Khuddamul Ahmadiyya* magazine, *Al Khidmat,* is published.

2007 Construction is completed on a mission house, principal's residence, doctor's residence and clinic in Tubmanburg. The foundation stone of an Ahmadiyya mosque is laid later that year. The bricks are given by *Hadhrat Khalifatul Masih V*[aba] with his prayers.

2008 The Ahmadiyya Central Library is being prepared in Monrovia, and is due for inauguration in 2008.

Jama'at Ahmadiyya, Liberia

The Ahmadiyya Muslim Mission House and Mosque in Teh Town, Cape Mount County, Liberia.

MADAGASCAR
Jama'at established in 1980s

Arshad M. Khan

A stamp from Madagascar (formerly known as Malagasy), celebrating the invention of the telephone by Alexander Graham Bell.

A trio of Ring-Tailed Lemurs sit in a protective huddle. Lemurs are native only to the island nations of Madagascar and nearby Comoros and have been listed as an endangered species.

ABOUT MADAGASCAR

The island nation of Madagascar attained independence from the French in 1960. Located in the Indian Ocean off the coast of southern Africa, Madagascar is 587,000 km^2 with a population of 20 million. English and French are the official languages. 7% of the nation is Muslim. The GDP of Madagascar is US $7 billion, with a per capita income of $1,000.

CIA World Factbook

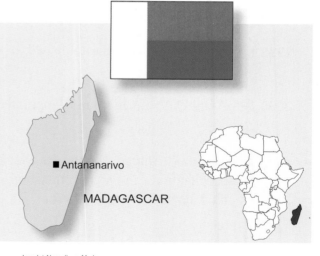

■Antananarivo

MADAGASCAR

Jama'at Ahmadiyya, Madagascar

A view of Baitun Nasir, which is located in Andranomadio, Madagascar.

Jama'at Ahmadiyya, Madagascar

The Ahmadiyya Muslim Community mission house in Madagascar.

Ahmadi Muslims in Madagascar: Historic Highlights

1970s Ch. Bashir Ahmad travels frequently while on his duty in the Naval ship and conveys the message of Ahmadiyyat to the residents of Madagascar. A few peoples accept Ahmadiyyat through his efforts.

1980s Later Mauritian misionaries travel to Madagascar and invite people to Islam and a Jama'at is formed.

1992 Mozaffar Ahmed Soodhun visits the Diego region of Madagascar to spread the message of Ahmadiyyat per the instructions of *Hadhrat Khalifatul Masih IV*[rh].

1995 Siddique Ahmed Munawar visits Madagascar as the second central missionary for three months.

1996 Siddique A. Munawar permanently establishes residence as a missionary to Madagascar.

1997 Under the supervision of *Hadhrat Khalifatul Masih IV*[rh], the *Jama'at* is officially registered in Madagascar as '*L'association Musulmane Ahmadiyya de Madagascar*.' During Siddique Munawar's tenure as missionary, two additional *Jama'ats* are established in Antananarivo and Mahajanga. The first *Jalsa Salana* is held.

1998 A primary school is established in Antananarivo.

2000 Ataul Qayyum Joomun is appointed Missionary-in-Charge of Madagascar.

2001 Mashood Ahmed Toor visits Madagascar for three months and completes a successful propagation campaign in the southwest province of Mankara. Since then, eight mosques have been constructed there.

2002 Muzaffar Ahmed Soodhum becomes Missionary-in-Charge of Madagascar.

2004 Muhammad Iqbal becomes Missionary-in-Charge and starts a spiritual training class in Antananarivo.

2006 Under the direction of *Hadhrat Khalifatul Masih V*[aba], Muhammad Iqbal organizes a *Muwalimeen* Class (missionary training). Twenty participants are sent to six Madagascar provinces resulting in the establishment of 20 missions and 38 prayer centers. The first Ansar and Khuddam *Ijtema'at* (spiritual retreat) are held in the Diego and Manakara provinces.

2007 The first *Lajna Ijtema* is held.

Mauritius
Jama'at established in 1913

"Dost thou not see that Allah sends down water from the sky, and We bring forth therewith fruits of different colors; and among the mountains are streaks, white and red, of diverse hues and others raven black" (Qur'an, 35:28)

Hadhrat Khalifatul Masih V [aba] taking a photo of the world-famous colored earths of Chamarel in southwest Mauritius (2005). These hills are particularly unsual; created by volcanic rocks that cooled at different temperatures, the earths form beautiful patterns of color in the exposed hillsides. When the grains of colored sand are mixed together, they eventually settle into separate layers.

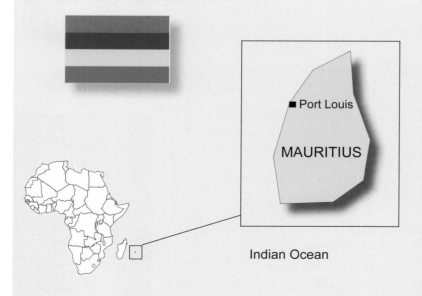

Port Louis

MAURITIUS

Indian Ocean

ABOUT MAURITIUS

Known to Arab sailors as early as the 10th century, Mauritius was first explored by the Portuguese in 1505, and eventually attained independence from the British in 1968. Situated in the Indian Ocean near southern Africa, Mauritius is only 2000 km² with a population over 1.2 million. Over 80% of the inhabitants speak Creole. 48% are Hindu, 24% Roman Catholic and 17% Muslim. The GDP is US $ 7 billion, with a per capital income of $ 11,900.

Ahmadi Muslims in Mauritius: Historic Highlights

1912 Noor Mohammad Noroya becomes the first Mauritian to accept Ahmadiyyat. Noroya was the publisher of a French newspaper called *Islamism* and sent a copy of his publication to Abdullah Koilum of the U.K., who himself was the publisher of *The Crescent*. Koilum would, in turn, establish a communication with the *Review of Religions* and thus Ahmadiyyat was introduced. *Islamism* printed *Hadhrat* Ahmad's [as] claims and even news of his sad demise. It was through this correspondence that Noroya embraced Ahmadiyyat.

1913 Mohammad Azim Sultan Ghaus accepts Ahmadiyyat through the *tabligh* of Noor Mohammad Noroya.

Hadhrat Sufi Ghulam Mohammad[rh], *first Missionary to Mauritius*

1915 *Hadhrat Khalifatul Masih II*[rh], in response to the *Jama'at's* request, sends Sufi Ghulam Mohammad[ra] as the first missionary to Mauritius. He stayed in Mauritius for 12 years. The first mission in Rose-Hill is established.

1923 The first mosque, Dar-us-Salam, is constructed in Rose-Hill.

Hadhrat Hafiz Obaidullah Shaheed[ra] becomes Missionary of Mauritius. He would later pass away tragically at the young age of 32, thus becoming the first Indian Ahmadi to achieve the status of martyrdom. *Hadhrat Khalifatul Masih II*[ra] gave a glowing tribute in his Friday Sermon on December 7, 1923: "*Maulvi* Obaidullah was a fellow countryman. He proved with his exemplary conduct what it really means to offer a lifetime for the *Jama'at* as a missionary and then hold on to this promise with great steadfastness." *Hadhrat* Khalifatul Masih V[aba] inaugurated a guest house in Qadian that has been named Sarae Obadullah after Hafiz Obaidullah Shaheed.

Hafiz Obaidullah Shaheed, Missionary to Mauritius in 1923

1928 *Hadhrat* Hafiz Jamal Ahmad[ra] becomes the third missionary of Mauritius. He was the companion of *Hadhrat* Ahmad[as] and a *Hafiz-e-Qur'an* (one who commits the entire text of the Qur'an to memory). He established the Rizwan Mosque in St. Pierre.

1944 Masjid Mubarak in Montagne Blanche is established.

1958 Noor Mosque in Pailles is constructed.

Hadhrat Hafiz Jamal Ahmad[ra], *Missionary to Mauritius in 1928.*

1975 *Hadhrat* Mirza Wasim Ahmad lays the foundation of Nusrat Mosque in Quarte Bornes, and *Masjid* Baitul Zikr is built in Rose-Hill.

1988 *Hadhrat Khalifatul Masih IV*[rh] makes his first visit to Mauritius. *Masjid* Baitus Salam is constructed in New Grove, and Masjid Tahir is built in Quatier Militaire.

1993 *Hadhrat Khalifatul Masih IV*[rh] makes his second visit to Mauritius and meets with the Mauritian Prime Minister.

2001 Masjid Uthman in Stanley is inaugurated by *Hadhrat* Mirza Wasim Ahmad, and Masjid Nasir is constructed in Curepipe.

Hadhrat Khalifatul Masih IV[rh] *lays the foundation for a mosque during his visit in 1993.*

The Mosques of Mauritius

Dar-us-Salam, the central mosque in Rosehill, was built in 1923 and renovated in 1963. Extensions for offices were created in 2000.

Masjid Mubarak in Montagne Blanche was built in 1944 and renovated in 1961 into a concrete structure. This was financed by local Ahmadis.

Masjid Bait-us-Salam in New Grove. Hadhrat Khalifatul Masih IV [rh] laid the foundation in 1988 and inaugurated it in 1993. The land was donated by M. Abdul Rahman Bhugeloo.

Masjid Tahir in Quartier Millitaire. The foundation stone was laid by Hadhrat Khalifatul Masih IV^{rh} in 1988 during his first visit.

The mosque in Casernes was inaugurated by Hadhrat Mirza Wasim Ahmad in 2001. Rashid Joolfoo offered the land, and Shams Tajoo financed the construction.

Fazal Mosque in Phoenix was built in the 1950s with the donation of Ghulam Subhan Auckloo on behalf of his father.

Masjid Uthman in Stanley was built in 2000 and inaugurated by Hadhrat Mirza Wasim Ahmad in 2001. Land was offered by Salima Sookia and construction financed by Shams Taujoo on behalf of his family.

Rizwan Mosque, St. Pierre. Built in the late 1920's by Hafiz Jamal Ahmad^{ra}, it was renovated in 1958 and reconstructed in 1994. Hadhrat Khalifatul Masih V^{aba} inaugurated this mosque in 2005.

Umar Mosque in Triolet. Built in 1944, the land was donated by Mrs. Zulekha Soodhun. Due to cyclone damage foundations were raised again by M. Ismail Munir in 1971 and rebuilt by Ahmad Doomun.

Hadhrat Khalifatul Masih V [aba]: Historic Visit to Mauritius, 2005

Huzoor [aba] Greeted at the Airport in Mauritius

Huzoor [aba] with M. Amin Jowahir, Amir of Mauritius

Huzoor [aba] with a local delegate of Nasirat.

Huzoor [aba] with the Jama'at

Huzoor [aba] with various Missionaries currently in Mauritius including, from the left: Maulana Basharat Naweed (Naib Ameer), Maulana Shamsher Sookia, M. Amin Jowahir (Amir Mauritius), Hadhur [aba] Maulana Muzafar Soodhun, Abdul Majid Tahir and another missionary.

Huzoor [aba] with Waqfe Nau Children

Hadhrat Khalifatul Masih V [aba]: Historic Visit to Mauritius, 2005

Huzoor [aba] at the 44th Jalsa Salana Mauritius

Huzoor [aba] delivering a speech during the 44th Annual Jalsa Salana

Huzoor [aba] addressing Lajna

Huzoor [aba] concluding the Jalsa with silent prayers.

Huzoor [aba] with the President and Vice President of Mauritius

Above: Huzoor [aba] with Amir Mauritius and the Vice President of Mauritius, Mr. M Xavier-luc Duval. Right: Huzoor [aba] presenting a gift to the President of Mauritius, Sir Aneerood Jugnauth.

Huzoor[aba] enjoying his time in Mauritius

Huzoor [aba] *with Hadhrat Begum Sahiba at the botanical gardens in Mauritius. It is the third largest botanical garden in the world.*

Huzoor[aba] *enjoying a joke with the Amir of Mauritius*

"I shall cause Thy message to reach the corners of the the earth."

(The Promised Messiah[as]*)*

Huzoor[aba] *with the Ahmadi delegate in front of "Bout du monde" in Mauritius, which translates to "Corner of the World"*

Huzoor's [aba] visit to Rodrigues Island

Nasirat and Atfal of Rodrigues Island welcoming Huzoor [aba]

Rodrigues is a small island (109 km²) in the middle of the Indian Ocean, approximately 560 km east of (and politically a region of) Mauritius. *Huzoor* [aba], during his visit to Mauritius in late 2005 and early 2006, made a special visit to Rodrigues to meet with local Ahmadis.

Masjid Mahmood in Rodrigues Island

Huzoor [aba] with M. Fazl Muslun and M. Ameen Jowahir, Amir of Mauritius

Huzoor [aba] during the foundation laying of Masjid Mahmood

NIGER
Jama'at established in 1956

A Saharan dune sea in East Niger. A dune sea (or erg) is a large, relatively flat area of desert covered with wind-swept sand with little to no vegetation cover.

Holger Reineccius

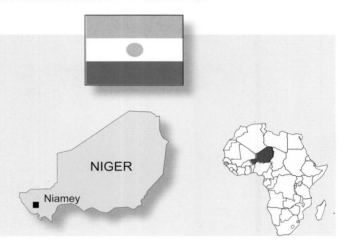

ABOUT NIGER

Niger attained independence from the French in 1960. The desert nation is 1.3 million km^2 with a population of over 13 million. French is the official language and 80% of the nation is Muslim. The GDP of Niger is US $4 billion, with a per capita income of $700.

CIA World Factbook

NIGER

Niamey

Masjid Mahmood, Doubo, Niamay Region, Niger inaugurated on August 31, 2007.

Noor Mosque Algada, Marawi Region, Niger

*Shakir Muslim,
Missionary, Niger*

*Akbar Ahmad Tahir,
Missionary-in-Charge
Niger*

*Fakhrul Islam,
Missionary, Niger*

I saw in a vision that I am sailing downstream a river in a small boat. I am alone. It suddenly occurs to me that I must proceed to the mouth of the river, where I am to meet someone important. I do not know this person. As the boat takes me down the river, I sense that someone has tried coming here before, but to no avail. The rapids are quite rocky and the waters both treacherous and uncertain. But I am not scared at all and I calmly pass by. I see many people standing at the river bank witnessing the entire scene. Before, the boat had been traveling at a high speed due to river current; but now, upon entering the ocean, its speed declines. Now in front of me, I see a small ship anchored in the ocean. I have the feeling that the person I have to meet is on that ship. Using my hands as oars, I push the waves back so that the boat moves forward. I spin the boat and approach the stern, or back of the ship. I see a few people, one of whom asks me to wait. The person who asks me to wait, attempts to contact someone by phone or a similar device. My feeling is that he is trying to contact the same person whom I am trying to meet. A lady approaches the person on the phone, and in French, tells him to stop calling him. She says he will install the machine himself and catch the fish. At this moment I ask the woman, "Does this important person speak French?"

A vision of *Hadhrat* Mirza Tahir Ahmad [rh] interpreted as Divine direction towards propagation in French-speaking countries. Source: Naseer Qamar, Editor, *International Al-Fazl*, July 1993.

NIGERIA
Jama'at established in 1916

This beautifully colored fish is a cichlid, a type of fish found throughout Africa. This specific cichlid is a female member of the genus Pelvicachromis taeniatus, also known as the "Nigerian red."

Gerard Delany

ABOUT NIGERIA

Nigeria attained independence from the British in 1960. This western African nation is 923,000 km² with a population of 138 million. English is the official language, and 50% of the nation is Muslim. The GDP of Nigeria is US $ 127 billion, with a per capita income of $ 4200.

CIA World Factbook

Jama'at Ahmadiyya, Nigeria

A view of the Central Mosque of the Ahmadiyya Muslim Community in Sabo, Ilaro Town, Ogun State, Nigeria.

All photos on this page: Jama'at Ahmadiyya, Nigeria

Masjid Mubarak in Abuja, Nigeria was inaugurated on April 29, 2008, by Hadhrat Khalifatul Masih V ^{aba} on the occasion of Khilafat Centennary Jalsa Celebration. This is the last mosque inaugurated by Huzoor ^{aba} in the first century of Khilafat.

Jama'at Ahmadiyya, Nigeria

Tahir Mosque in Ojokoro, Nigeria. The foundation was laid by Hadhrat Khalifatul Masih IV ^{rh} in 1988.

The Ahmadiyya Muslim mosque located in Orita, which is also in Ilaro Town, Ogun State, Nigeria.

Jama'at Ahmadiyya, Nigeria

Jama'at Ahmadiyya, Nigeria

Dr. Mashud A. Fashola, Amir of the Ahmadiyya Muslim Community, Nigeria

Mr. Zikrullah Ayyuba, Naib Amir and Missionary, Lagos

Jama'at Ahmadiyya, Nigeria

Jama'at Ahmadiyya, Nigeria

Jama'at Ahmadiyya, Nigeria

Mr. Mahmud Ahmad, Missionary serving Kwara State, Nigeria

Mr. Abdul Haq Nayyar, Missionary-in-Charge, Nigeria

Hafiz Muslihuddin Opayemi, Director, Hafiz Class, Ilaro Town, Ogun State, Nigeria

Ahmadiyyat in Nigeria

1970: Hadhrat Khalifatul Masih III [rh]

Right: A view of the minaret of the Ahmadiyya Muslim Mosque in Ijebu-Ode, Nigeria, on the occasion of its inauguration by Hadhrat Khalifatul Masih III [rh]. Above: A glimpse of the crowd of guests attending the inauguration event as seen from the top of the minaret.

Hadhrat Khalifatul Masih III [rh] addressing attendees of a press conference held in the Federal Palace Hotel in Lagos, Nigeria.

1988: Hadhrat Khalifatul Masih IV [rh]

Hadhrat Khalifatul Masih IV [rh] enjoys a moment with a Nigerian child; Below: Huzoor [rh] with Khuddam in Nigeria

Hadhrat Khalifatul Masih IV [rh] addressing a Jalsa in Nigeria

Ahmadiyyat in Nigeria

2004: Hadhrat Khalifatul Masih V [aba]

Hadhrat Khalifatul Masih V [aba] offers prayers on the occasion of the formal opening of the Owode Mosque in Ogun State, Nigeria.

Huzoor [aba] stands among members of Nasirat ul Ahmadiyya (young girls' auxiliary), Nigeria.

2008: Hadhrat Khalifatul Masih V [aba]

Scenes from the 58th Jalsa Salana Nigeria held in May of 2008 in Hadeeqa-e-Ahmad, Nigeria. During Huzoor's [aba] historic 2008 West African Tour, he inaugurated several mosques in Nigeria and met with many dignitaries and high government officials.

Ahmadiyyat in Nigeria

The seed of Ahmadiyyat was planted in Nigeria in 1916 and has grown into a predominant religious and social institution in the country. The Jama'at now has branches in over one thousand towns and villages throughout Nigeria.

The first Islamic primary school was established by the Ahmadiyya community in 1922, and now hundreds of primary and secondary Jama'at institutions are in operation. The first Muslim weekly newspaper, *The Truth*, also is credited to the Jama'at. The Holy Qur'an has been translated into several Nigerian dialects, including Yoruba, Hausa and Igo. Work almost is complete on the translation into Etsako and Tiv. The Ahmadiyya community has also contributed significantly to healthcare in the country, with the establishment of several hospitals and clinics and leads the way in healthcare delivery in Nigeria.

The Jama'at has a post-secondary Missionary Training Center (Jami'a Ahmadiyya) based in Ilaro, Ogun State, from where the Jama'at Missionaries are trained and turned out on a yearly basis. Another remarkable achievement of the Jama'at is its Madrasatul Tahfizul Qur'an (Qur'an Memorization Class) at Ilaro, Ogun State, where young Children are being trained to commit the whole of Holy Quran to memory. More than ninety of such Hufaz have been produced from the class within just nine years of its establishment, while the fourth set of seventy-three is now in session.

Khilafat has been an integral part of the rich history of Ahmadiyyat in Nigeria, and the Jama'at has been blessed with several visits by various Khulafa, including *Hadhrat Khalifatul Masih III*[th] in 1970, *Hadhrat Khalifatul Masih IV*[th] in 1988 and the present Khalifa, *Hadhrat* Mirza Masroor Ahmad[aba] in 2004.

In May of 2008, *Hadhrat Khalifatul Masih V*[aba] made a return visit to Nigeria as part of a historic West African Tour to launch worldwide centenary celebrations of Khilafat. Notable milestones during the Nigerian leg of his trip included: the opening of a new x-ray unit at the Al-Apapa Ahmadiyya General Hospital in Apapa, Nigeria; the inauguration of Baitur Raheem Mosque in Ibadan, Nigeria; inspection of the Raqeem Ahmadiyya printing press in Lagos; a meeting with a senior Judge in the Nigerian high court; an official visit with the Emir (head of state) of Borgu; the foundation laying of the Hediza Memorial Islamic Center; the inauguration of the Mubarak Mosque in the Nigerian capital, Abuja; and finally, Huzoor's[aba] presiding of the 58th Jalsa Salana Nigeria at Hadeeqat-e-Ahmad (the official Jalsa site) near Lagos which was attended by several thousand people and covered by the national media.

Jalsa Salana Nigeria, 2008

Sierra Leone

Jama'at established in 1937

Toke Beach, Sierra Leone

ABOUT SIERRA LEONE

Sierra Leone attained independence from the British in 1961. This western African nation is 71,000 km^2 with a population of 6.3 million. English is the official language, and 60% of the nation is Muslim. The GDP of Sierra Leone is US $ 1.5 billion, with a per capita income of $ 800.

CIA World Factbook

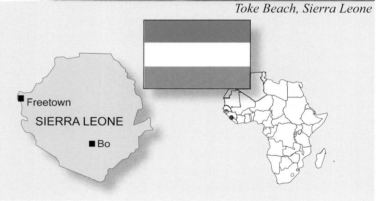

Freetown

SIERRA LEONE

Bo

Jama'at Ahmadiyya, Sierra Leone

The Ahmadiyya Muslim Mosque in Gbonkobana, Sierra Leone.

*Ahmadiyya Muslim Mosque
in Gbendembu, Sierra Leone.*

*The Ahmadiyya Muslim Mosque
in Kailahun, Sierra Leone.*

*The Ahmadiyya Muslim Mosque
in Makeni, Sierra Leone.*

The Ahmadiyya Muslim Mosque in Bo, Sierra Leone.

Al-Haj Maulana Nasir Ahmad Ali, who first served as a missionary in Ghana, arrived in Sierra Leone in 1937. The first Ahmadi convert was Pa Musa Gabba. Since then the Sierra Leone Jama'at has seen exponential growth and incredible progress. There are now 345 mosques, 12 central missionaries, and 80 local missionaries and teachers. 175 Ahmadiyya primary schools and 41 secondary schools have been established. On February 28, 2007, Jama'at Sierra Leone introduced Ahmadiyya Muslim Radio in the country.

Sierra Leone was blessed with the visits of *Hadhrat Khalifatul Masih III*rh in 1970 and *Hadhrat Khalifatul Masih IV*rh in 1988. *Hadhrat* Mirza Masroor Ahmad aba recently assigned another 7 missionaries to the growing West African nation.

*Al-Haj Maulana
Nazir Ahmad Ali*

Seated (at left) is Al-Haj Missionary Nazir Ahmad Ali. Standing (center) is Chaudhry Abdul Haq Anwar Nangli. Seated (at right) is Mohammad Siddique Amritsari, the Missionary-in-Charge, Sierra Leone.

Ahmadiyyat in Sierra Leone

1970: Hadhrat Khalifatul Masih III [rh]

Hadhrat Khalifatul Masih III [rh] meets with Sir Banja Tejan-Sie , the then Acting Governor General of Sierra Leone (center) on May 6, 1970. To the right of the Mr. Tejan-Sie is Sahibzada Mirza Mubarak Ahmad [ra], Head of the Ahmadiyya Muslim Foreign Missions Office.

Hadhrat Khalifatul Masih III [rh] delivers the Friday sermon on the occasion of the formal opening of the Ahmadiyya Muslim Mosque in Leicester Village, Sierra Leone, on May 8, 1970.

Hadhrat Khalifatul Masih III [rh] watches as Hadhrat Begum Sahiba participates in laying the foundation for the Ahmadiyya Muslim Mosque in Bo, Sierra Leone on May 10, 1970.

Ahmadiyyat in Sierra Leone

1988: Hadhrat Khalifatul Masih IV [rh]

Hadhrat Khalifatul Masih IV [rh] alights from the Presidential Helicopter at Freetown, Sierra Leone. The helicopter was at Huzoor's disposal during his entire tour of the country.

Huzoor [rh] addresses a reception held in his honor at Hotel Cape Sierra on January 25, 1988. At Huzoor's left is Mr. Musa Kabir, Minister for Religious Affairs, Sierra Leone, who was representing the President of Sierra Leone.

Huzoor [rh] is made honorary Paramount Chief of the Yoni Chiefdom in Sierra Leone's central Tonkolili District, on the occasion of his visit to the country in 1988. In this picture, Huzoor [rh] is standing for the ceremonial wearing of the Paramount Chief's robe.

Huzoor [rh] conducts the Bai'at (Initiation) Ceremony of young students studying at the Ahmadiyya Secondary School in Freetown, Sierra Leone, on January 27, 1988.

Huzoor [rh] addresses the police force of the city of Bo, Sierra Leone, upon the invitation of Chief Police Officer, Mr. S. K. Forbs (standing next to Huzoor [rh]).

Glimpses of the 46th Jalsa Salana
Bo, Sierra Leone

Mr. Lutfur Rahman Mahmood, the Special Representative of Jama'at Ahmadiyya Headquarters, leads Friday prayers, marking the opening of the Jalsa. His Excellency Al-Haj Ahmad Tijan Kabbah, who served as Sierra Leone's President from 1996-1997 and 1998-2007, is praying directly behind him. At President Kabbah's right is Vice President Solomon Berewa (tenure: 2002-2007), followed by Mr. Saeed ur Rahman, the Ameer and Missionary in Charge of Sierra Leone.

President Kabbah presides at the first session of Jalsa Salana, Sierra Leone. Mr. Saeed ur Rahman sits at President Kabbah's immediate right, followed by Mr. Lutfur Rahman Mahmood. At the President's left sits Vice President Berewa, followed by the Deputy Ameer II of Jama'at Ahmadiyya, Sierra Leone.

A view of the ladies' audience in attendance at the Jalsa Salana in Bo, Sierra Leone.

A number of special guests attended the Jalsa, including Paramount Chiefs from various Chiefdoms in Sierra Leone, as well as Members of Parliament.

South Africa

Jama'at established in 1946

A view of the lighthouse at Cape Agulhas, South Africa. Contrary to popular opinion, it is Cape Agulhas and not the Cape of Good Hope, which marks the most southern geographic point of the African continent.

ABOUT SOUTH AFRICA

Once a Dutch colony, South Africa eventually gained independence from British rule in 1910 after the Boer Wars. South Africa is 1.2 million km^2 with a population of 44 million. There are various African tribal dialects spoken in addition to English. The GDP of South Africa is US $274 billion, with a per capita income of $10,600.

CIA World Factbook

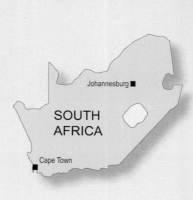

Jama'at Ahmadiyya, South Africa

Baitul Awwal Mosque is located in Cape Town, South Africa.

Jama'at Ahmadiyya, South Africa

Mr. Zaheer Ahmad, the Amir and Missionary-in-Charge of the Ahmadiyya community in South Africa

Swaziland
Jama'at established in 1997

Mantenga Falls, Swaziland

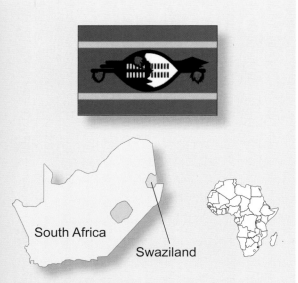

South Africa

Swaziland

ABOUT SWAZILAND

Swaziland attained independence from the British in 1968. It is only 17,000 km^2 with a population of 1.1 million. English is the official language and 10% of the nation is Muslim. The GDP of Swaziland is US $2.7 billion, with a per capita income of $4,800.

CIA World Factbook

Baitul Hadi Mosque, located in Hiatikulu, Swaziland.

Ahmadiyyat in Swaziland and Lesotho
by Abbas Bin Suleiman and Dawood Sadique Arthur

The first rays of the message of Ahmadiyyat touched Swaziland in 1997 and Lesotho in 1999. This was in accordance to the instructions of the immediate past supreme Head of the worldwide Ahmadiyya Muslim *Jama'at*, *Hadhrat* Mirza Tahir Ahmad [rh], who called for establishing Ahmadiyyat in four countries; namely Botswana, Namibia, Lesotho and Swaziland. Under the direction of the former South African National President Mr. Rashid Yahya, Mr. Ijaz Ahmad Chaudhry and Dr. Hamad Asim, together with their families, visited Swaziland for this noble cause and in that trip toured Mbabane and Manzini cities, distributed leaflets and pamphlets, and also made contacts with some prominent personalities to give them the message of Ahmadiyyat.

In 1999, Mr. Rashid Yahya allocated Swaziland/ Botswana to the Johannesburg *Jama'at* and Lesotho/ Namibia to the Cape Town *Jama'at*. Mr. Ijaz Ahmad Chaudhry was made in charge of Swaziland and responsible for the establishment of Ahmadiyyat in Swaziland.

To carry out an effective *Tablighi* programme Mr. Abdul Latif Bennet, Dr Aleem Khan, and Mr. Tahir Vilakati, led by Mr. Ijaz Ahmad Chaudhry, paid a five day working visit to Swaziland, wherein they traveled approximately all over the country, and in some cases, they traveled kilometers upon kilometers on foot due to lack of motorable roads, all in an effort to meet chiefs, opinion leaders and other personalities so as to introduce the message of Ahmadiyyat to the people of Swaziland. These meetings were very fruitful as 32 people were converted along with their chief. This marked an important point for the establishment of Ahmadiyyat in Swaziland.

Mr. Dawood Sadique Arthur, Ahmadiyya Missionary for Lesotho, speaks at the South African Jalsa Salana.

In 2002, Abbas bin Suleiman from Ghana was posted as resident missionary in Swaziland, and Dawood Sadique Arthur was appointed resident missionary in Lesotho. In Swaziland, several *ba'aits* have been made and the whole family of the chief has taken the *bai'at* and presently, his eldest son, Mr. Ntokozo Salim Dlamini, is the *Jama'at* President.

Jama'at Ahmadiyya, South Africa

Respected Abbas Bin Suleiman, Ahmadiyya Missionary to Swaziland.

In Swaziland, *Jama'ats* have been estabilshed in Hiatikulu, Manzini, Mantabeni and Mbelebeleni. The 32 converts in 1999 have grown to over 250 members presently. Now, under the able leadership and supervision of the present South Africa National President and Missionary-in-Charge, Mr. Zaheer Ahmad, the Swaziland *Jama'at* is growing from strength to strength. In late 2005, under his guidelines, the first ever Ahmadiyya Mosque in Swaziland and the only mosque in that region of Swaziland was constructed in Hiatikulu, our very first *Jama'at* in Swaziland. The commissioning ceremony of this mosque took place on January 7, 2006. About 20 people from South Africa led by the National President joined the locals for this historic ceremony. *Hadhrat Khalifatul Masih V* [aba] has graciously named this mosque Baitul Hadi.

In Lesotho, approval was received to construct a mosque in Thaba-Bosiu. This began on March 21, 2005, with the foundation being laid by Dawood Sadique Arthur. In February of 2006, the mosque was finally completed and named Baitul Mahdi by *Hadhrat Khalifatul Masih V* [aba].

The Ahmadiyya Muslim community in Lesotho has grown gradually from 25 members to 350 in 7 local *Jama'ats*.

Tanzania
Jama'at established in 1934

Mount Kilimanjaro (Kilima Njaro or "shining mountain" in Swahili), the highest point in Africa, is the tallest free-standing mountain on the Earth's land surface, rising about 4,600 meters (15,000 feet) above the surrounding plain.

Arshad M. Khan

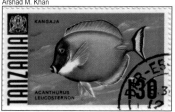

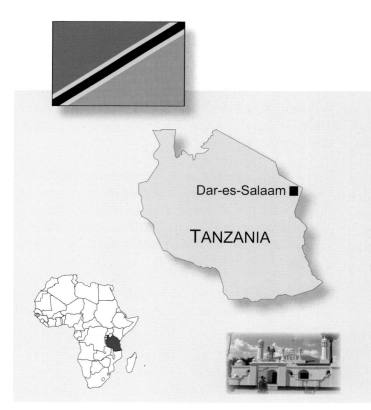

ABOUT TANZANIA

After achieving independence from the British in the early 1960s, Tanganyika and Zanzibar merged to form the nation Tanzania in 1964. Tanzania is approximately 945,000 km² (twice the size of California) and a population exceeding 40 million. Kishwahili (a form of Swahili) is the official language. About 35% of Tanzanians are Muslim and 30% Christian. The GDP of Tanzania is US $14 billion, with a per capital GDP of $1,100.

CIA World Factbook

A Brief Introduction to the Ahmadiyya Muslim Community in Tanzania

Hadhrat Khalifatul Masih II[ra] once stated "Tanganyika (Tanzania) is our country." Indeed, the subsequent history of Ahmadiyya in Tanzania amply has vindicated his words.

Ahmadiyyat first entered into East Africa during the blessed period of the Promised Messiah[as]. There was a revolt in Zanzibar under Sultan Majid, and the Sultan asked for military help from the colonial power in Great Britain. A number of soldiers were sent to Zanzibar, including a few Ahmadi soldiers. These soldiers preached the truth about Ahmadiyyat during their service in Zanzibar. Some time later, Ahmadi clerks, doctors, and accountants were sent to Zanzibar for preaching. Among them were the devoted companions of the Promised Messiah[as]. These companions not only preached by word of mouth, but also distributed literature produced by the *Jama'at*.

After the partition of Africa, colonial powers decided to cease the slave trade and encourage legitimate trade. To this end, the British decided to build a railway line from Mombasa to Kampala. Some companions of the Promised Messiah[as] came to work on the rail line from Mombasa to Kampala. While engaged in building the railway line, they began preaching. As the word of Ahmadiyyat spread, *Hadhrat Khalifatul Masih II*[ra] sent *Maulana* Sheikh Mubarak Ahmad as the first missionary to Tanzania.

In 1934, Ahmadiyya officially was registered in Tanzania and headquartered in Tabora, where Sheikh Mubarak Ahmad taught religion at the government school. He immediately began the project of translating the Holy Qur'an into Kiswahili in 1936 and completed this noble endeavor in 1953. The translation was highly recommended and the poet laureate of Kiswahili, Shaaban Robert, hailed the translation as the "Mother of Kiswahili."

In 1936, the Ahmadiyya Community published a newspaper called "Mapenzi ya Mungu" ("the love of God"). Sheikh Mubarak Ahmad also instituted the first ever English language Muslim newspaper: "East African Times." In 1940, he started the first Muslim Primary School in the country. In 1947, the mosque popularly known as the "Taj Mahal of East Africa" was inaugurated and given the name *"Masjid Fazal"* by *Hadhrat Khalifatul Masih II*[ra]. A number of mosques have been built since then, adding beauty to many towns. The Ahmadiyya Community now has two mosques in Dar es Salaam: Masjid Salaam and Kitonga Ahmadiyya Mosque. Other mosques include Tanga Ihsani Mosque, Mtwara Baitul-Karim, and Songea Furkan Mosque.

The Ahmadiyya community is now flourishing in Tanzania. The *Jama'at* has produced illustrious Kiswahili poets, including Sheikh Kaluta Amri Abedi, Malik Mbungiro, Khamisi Wamwera, Kainuza Mbambwa, Ramadhani Shamte, and many others. The Ahmadiyya Community also was involved in the struggle for Tanzania's independence and Mohammed Iqbal Dar, an Ahmadi, is credited with coining the name "Tanzania."

Masjid Fazal in Tabora was the first Ahmadiyya mosque in Tanzania, inaugurated in 1947.

Maulana Shaikh Mubarak Ahmad, First Missionary to Tanzania.

Masjid Baitul Hamid in Dodoma, Tanzania.

Tahir Mahmood Chaudhry, Missionary-in-Charge, Tanzania.

Masjid Salam, Dar es Salaam, Tanzania.

Uganda
Jama'at established in 1935

A view of the Nile River in Uganda. The Nile flows through 9 African countries. It has two main tributaries, the White and Blue Nile. The White Nile, shown here, flows through Uganda, Sudan and Egypt. The Blue Nile starts in Ethiopia and joins the White Nile in Sudan as it courses northward to Egypt and empties into the Mediterranean Sea.

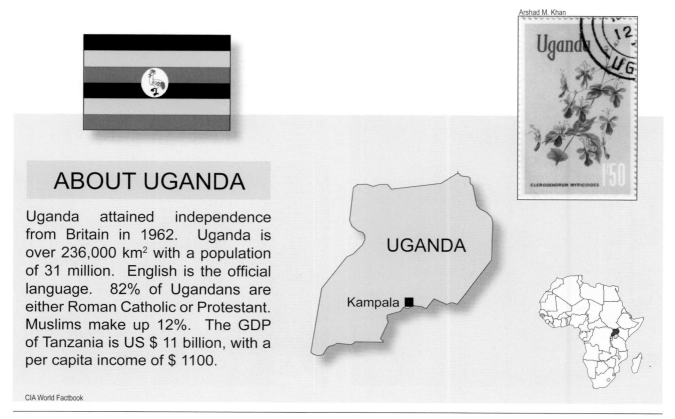

ABOUT UGANDA

Uganda attained independence from Britain in 1962. Uganda is over 236,000 km^2 with a population of 31 million. English is the official language. 82% of Ugandans are either Roman Catholic or Protestant. Muslims make up 12%. The GDP of Tanzania is US $ 11 billion, with a per capita income of $ 1100.

UGANDA

Kampala

All captions on this page: Jama'at Ahmadiyya, Uganda

Ahmadiyya Central Mosque in Kampala, Uganda

Left: The Ahmadiyya Muslim Mosque in Iganga, Uganda. Below: Mirza Mahmud Ahmad, Amir of Uganda, inaugurates the mosque in Iganga

Ahmadiyyat in Uganda

The Ahmadiyya Muslim Community in Uganda has grown rapidly since its inception in 1935. Maulana Shaikh Mubarak Ahmad was sent by Hadhrat Khalifatul Masih II to Uganda as the first missionary. The Central Ahmadiyya Mosque in Uganda was established in the capitol city of Kambala. The first brick laid was sent from Qadian, India, and *Hadhrat* Chaudhry Zafrullah Khan[ra] conducted the inauguration ceremony.

The first Khalifa to visit Uganda was *Hadhrat Khalifatul Masih IV*[rh] in 1988. There are now thirteen missionaries in Uganda, as well as 26 instructors, a physician and a high school headmaster. The Ahmadiyya Community has a strong presence in Uganda, with several mosques, high schools, elementary schools and a hospital in Mbale which has a full-functioning maternity ward and modern radiology technology.

The Holy Qur'an has been translated into the local Ugandan language. There are several mosques and schools under construction, and the central mosque is undergoing expansion. *Hadhrat Khalifatul Masih V*[aba], during a historic tour of Africa in May of 2005, visited Ghana and met with several government officials including the President of Uganda, Mr. Yoweri Museven.

Jama'at Ahmadiyya, Uganda

Maulana Inayatullah Zahidi, Amir and Missionary-in-Charge, Uganda

Jama'at Ahmadiyya, Uganda

From Right to Left: Ch. Hamidullah, Wakil-e-A'la, Mr. Kasirivu Atwoki, Minister of Lands in Uganda, and Mirza Mahmood Ahmed, Amir of Uganda.

Hadhrat Khalifatul Masih V's [aba] Historic Visit to Uganda in 2005

Huzoor [aba] raising the Ahmadiyya flag at the Uganda Jalsa

Huzoor [aba] addressing a press conference.

Hadhrat Khalifatul Masih V [aba] lays the foundation for the Ahmadiyya Muslim Mosque in Iganga, Uganda.

Hadhrat Khalifatul Masih V's [aba] Historic Visit to Uganda in 2005

Huzoor [aba] laying the foundation for an Ahmadiyya Hospital in Mbale, Uganda.

Hadhrat Khalifatul Masih V [aba] speaking with the Ugandan Minister of Information at a banquet.

Hadhrat Khalifatul Masih V [aba] with his entourage at the Uganda Equator marker.

Asia

Ahmadiyyat originated on the Asian continent in 1889, with the birth of the *Jama'at* taking place in Qadian, India (its permanent headquarters). Following the partition of India and Pakistan, the *Jama'at* also migrated and established the town of Rabwah in Pakistan. In 2008, Ahmadiyyat is in most Asian countries, but unfortunately also is the target of persecution almost exclusively on this continent alone.

MOSQUES

116

Bangladesh

Jama'at established in 1912

In 1947, East Bengal became East Pakistan after the partition of India. East Pakistan eventually seceded from West Pakistan in 1971 and became Bangladesh. Bangladesh comprises a total area of 144,000 km^2. Bangla is the official language, and the predominant religion (88%) is Islam. One third of the country floods annually during the monsoon season, hampering economic development. The GDP of Bangladesh is US $71 billion, with a per capita income of US $ 600.

Islam
on the horizon

Jama'at Ahmadiyya, Bangladesh

1904

Yaqub Ali Munshi Sahib from Khudra Brahmanbaria (near Talshohor) is the oldest living Bangali Ahmadi (105 years old)

Hadhrat Janab Ahmad Kabir Noor Muhammed of Chittagong accepts Ahmadiyyat at the hands of the Promised Messiah [as], becoming the first Ahmadi Bengali

1906

Raisuddin Khan of Nagergaon embraces Ahmadiyyat in Qadian at the hands of the Promised Messiah[as]. His wife, Azizatunnesa Begum, also accepts Ahmadiyyat through a written letter of initiation sent to the Promised Messiah [as].

Through the work of Maulana Syed Abdul Wahed, Ahmadiyyat is officially established in Bangladesh under the Khilafat of Hadhrat Khalifatul Masih I[ra] and headquarters are located in Brahman Baria.

1912

ahmadiyyat *in* bangladesh

1917

The first Bangla magazine in Bangladesh, The Ahmadi, is started. It would later become a fortnightly magainze in 1938

First National Annual Gathering (Jalsa Salana) takes place

Jama'at Ahmadiyya, Bangladesh

Mubasher Rahman, National Amir, Bangladesh

1925

Jama'at Ahmadiyya, Bangladesh

Abdul Awwal Khan Chowdhury, Missionary In Charge, Bangladesh

1963

With a very low-profile beginning almost a century ago, Jama'at Ahmadiyya Bangladesh now has 103 chapters across the country, and Ahmadies reside in 425 cities and villages. There are 65 missionaries, a full-fledge MTA studio in Dhaka, and Jamia Ahmadiyya Bangladesh.

Twelve Ahmadis have given their lives as martyrs in Bangladesh

2008

Clockwise from top left: Members in front of the recently inaugurated Maharajpur Mosque in the Natore District; an Ahmadi mosque in Khulna; members in front of Galim Gazi Mosque in Betal, Kishoregonj; members in the recently inaugurated Madaratek Mosque in Dhaka.

Jama'at

snapshots

Bangladesh

Jama'at Ahmadiyya, U.S.A.

Hazrat Khalifatul Masih II^ra, quoted in Ahmadiyya Bulletin, 1925.

spiritual insight

'O my Brothers! I have expressed repeatedly, Bangladesh has some of the most potential to spread the message of Ahmadiyyat across the world. Allah has showered His mercy upon you in such a way that the people of this country are humble and simple by nature; at the same time, they are intelligent and thirsty for knowledge. When these two qualities combine in a nation, then they will definitely prosper. Especially when it is observed that Islam has made its deep impact on this land after Punjab, then no doubt can remain in this matter. I always feel a special attraction of love and affection towards the Bengali nation.'

Jama'at Ahmadiyya, Bangladesh

Darrut-Tabligh, Dhaka, Bangladesh

Cambodia

Jama'at established in 2001

Sunrise at Angkor Wat, Cambodia's famous landmark, which served as the state temple and capital city in the 12th century. The main towers are also featured in the Cambodian flag. Angkor Wat is a UNESCO World Heritage Site.

Reproduced under GFDL Licensing. User: Oxag. Wikimedia Commons.

life after khmer

This Southeast Asian country borders the Gulf of Thailand and is situated between Thailand, Vietnam and Laos. Cambodia has gone through many occupations after the 13th century when the rule of the Angkor Empire came to an end. In 1863, the country was placed under French protection and became part of French Indochina in 1887. Following Japanese occupation in World War II, the Kingdom of Cambodia gained full independence from France in 1953. Of the 14 million inhabitants of the country, 90% identify themselves as Khmer, and 5% as Vietnamese. The vast majority of the people (95%) are Theravada Buddhists.

jama'at ahmadiyya cambodia

Mr. Ahmad bin Sholey, National President, Ahmadiyya Community, Cambodia

At-Taqwa Mosque, located in Cambodia.

A few Cambodian Ahamdis stand in front of Baitul Awwal Mosque.

missionaries

Maulana Abdussattar Rauf, Current Missionary-In-Charge, Ahmadiyya Community, Cambodia

Missionary Fajar Ayub, Cambodia

Missionary Mujib Ahmad, Cambodia

Missionary Ihsan Salim, Cambodia

2001

SEP 01 50 Cambodians in Comwong Kafoor accept Ahmadiyyat, creating the first Jama'at in the country. *Hadhrat Khalifatul Masih IV [rh]* approves construction of a new mosque, with financial support from Indonesia, Malaysia, and Singapore.

Jama'at Ahmadiyya, Cambodia

FEB 03 Al-Taqwa Mosque, named by *Hadhrat Khaliftul Masih IV [rh],* is inaugurated, in a ceremony attended by the Assistant Prime Minister and Members of Parliament. Governor Compung Chanang calls the community "Samakoom," or "excellent organization."

2003

ahmadiyyat in cambodia

2005

Jama'at Ahmadiyya, Cambodia

MAR 05 The Khanna Koko chapter is established in Compong Chanang, where 825 members from 15 chapters attend the 2nd Annual Jalsa Salana Cambodia, more than tripling the attendance of the inaugural convention.

APR 07 Members congregate for the 4th Annual Jalsa Salana Cambodia.

In 2001, Ahmadiyyat is introduced in a small village Minchey, 70 km from Phom Penh. All 252 residents accept Ahmadiyyat. Nooruddin Mosque is built and is inaugurated on March 14, 2004 (International *Al-Fazl*)

2007

India

Wikimedia Commons

Humayun's Tomb, located in New Delhi, was constructed in the 16th century in a Mugal architectural style. It's mausoleum blueprint served as the basis for the Taj Mahal in Agra. In 1993, UNESCO labeled it a World Heritage Site.

Srinagar

NEW DELHI ■

Agra ●

Mumbai ●

about india

Perched between Burma and Pakistan and bordering the Arabian Sea and Bay of Bengal, India is the seventh largest country in the world, at roughly one-third the size of the United States, and the second most populous, with 1.14 billion inhabitants. Nonviolent resistance to British colonialism led by Mohandas Gandhi and Jawaharlal Nehru helped India gain independence in 1947. Once at the center of naturical trade routes, India remains one of the fastest growing economies in the world, with twin successes in agriculture and information technology. Twenty-one langauges are spoken throughout the land, with Hindi as the primary tongue. Over three-quarters of India's population follows Hinduism, with minority pockets of Muslims and other sects. India holds the distinction as the second most culturally, linguistically, and genetically diverse geographical region after the entire African continent. Qadian, the permanent headquarter of Ahmadiyya Muslim Community is located in India.

Kashmir

Jama'at Ahmadiyya, India

*Masjid Ahmadiyya
Sri Nagar, Kashmir,
India*

missionaries

Abdul Salam Taak,
Amir, Sri Nagar

Dr. Abdul Hamid, Naib Amir
Naib Amir, Sri Nagar

Maulana Ghulam Nabi Nyaz
Sri Nagar

Jama'at Ahmadiyya, India

Syed Bashir Ahmad, Provincial Amir, Jharkand, welcoming Huzoor[aba] at the airport during his visit to India.

Jharkand

Ahmadiyya Masjid in Simliya Ranchi, Jharkand, India

Andhra

Masjid Noor.

Ahmadiyya Muslim Mission, Ahmedabad, Gujrat.

Pradesh

Masjid Jamay, built in 2003.

West Bengal

Ahmadiyya Muslim Mission, Melapalayam.

Ahmadiyya Muslim Mission, Sattankukam.

A LETTER FROM HUZOOR [rh]

To: Mr. Mohd. Mashreque Ali Sahib

...it gives me immense pleasure that the responsibilities which I entrusted to you are being discharged ably. I pray that Allah may graciously grant you the fulfillment of your noble desires...

From: Hazrat Mirza Tahir Ahmad
17 Aug 95

All photos on this page: Jama'at Ahmadiyya, India

Ahmadiyya Muslim Mission, Soorankudy.

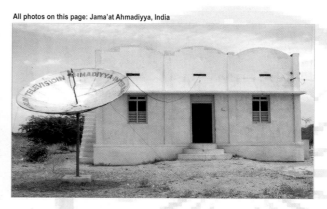

Ahmadiyya Muslim Mission, Virdhunagar.

Indonesia

Jama'at established in 1925

This volcano, named Galunggung, rises 2,168 m above sea level and is located in western Java, Indonesia. It first erupted in 1822 and then in 1894. The photo shows a spectacular view of lightning strikes during a third eruption on December 3, 1982. A fourth eruption occurred in 1984.

Data: USGS. Photo: R. Hadian / USGS

land of many blends

The former Dutch colony of Indonesia, later to be controlled by Japan, declared its independence after Japan's surrender in World War II. Located in Southeast Asia, it is the world's largest archipelago, situated between the Indian Ocean and the Pacific Ocean. Of its 17,508 islands, only 6,000 are inhabited. Together, it is slightly less than three times the size of Texas. Today, it is home to the world's largest Muslim population, with 86% of the people practicing Islam. Indonesia is home to over 300 ethnic groups, each with cultural differences developed over centuries with Indian, Arabic, Chinese, Malay, and European influences. Indonesia's debt has been declining steadily, its foreign exchange reserves are at an all-time high of over US$50 billion, and its stock market has been one of the three best performers in the world in 2006 and 2007.

Jama'at Ahmadiyya Indonesia

'Mubalighin Square' includes residences for Jama'at Missionaries and their families.

A view of Nasir Mosque in Indonesia.

All photos on this page: Jama'at Ahmadiyya, Indonesia

The An-Noor Mosque in Indonesia.

The Jama'at Ahmadiyya Indonesia Guest Quarters and Mission House.

JAMA'AT INDONESIA: revisited

Abdul Mukhlis Ahmad
+ Muharraim Awwaluddin

An historic group photo of Hadhrat Khalifatul Masih II [ra] with Maulana Rahmat Ali (sitting at the extreme left) and Indonesian students studying at Qadian, India, among which were Abubakar Ayyub, Zaini Dahlan, Ahmad Nurdin, and Abdul Wahid.

The Ahmadiyya Muslim *Jama'at* in Indonesia was established in 1925, when *Hadhrat* Maulana Rahmat Ali arrived in Tapak Tuan city, in the Aceh province of Indonesia, as the first missionary to the country. He was sent by *Hadhrat* Khalifatul Masih II [ra], in response to a request by Indonesian students who were studying Ahmadiyyat at that time in Qadian, India, for purposes of bringing back their knowledge to aid propogation efforts in Indonesia. After this time, several missionaries were sent from India including: Malik Aziz Ahmad Khan, Sayyid Syah Muhammad Al-Jailani, Imam ud Din, Mian Abdul Hayee, Mirza Muhammad Idris, Muhammad Sadiq Sumatri, Mirza Rafi Ahmad and Mahmud Ahmad Cheema.

Young Indonesian men who had finished their studies in Qadian were also sent as missionaries to Indonesia, including: Zaini Dahlan, Abubakar Ayyub, Ahmad Nuruddin, Abdul Wahid, Saleh A Nahdi, Sufi Zafar Ahmad, Sayuti Aziz Ahmad, Abdul Basit, Ahmad Hidayatullah, Hasan Basri, Khairuddin Barus, and Abdus Sattar Ra'uf. Abdual Wahid, H.A. is recorded in the history of Ahmadiyyat as the first foreign missionary. *Jama'at* Ahmadiyya Indonesia also has local missionaries who have graduated from Jamia Ahmadiyya Indonesia. Presently, *Jama'at* Indonesia has a total of 200 missionaries and more than 300 local chapters. It also has sent missionaries to neighboring countries such as Malaysia, Phillipines, Singapore, Thailand, Papua New Guinea and Cambodia. In June through July of 2000, the Indonesian *Jama'at* was blessed with the historic visit of *Hadhrat* Khalifatul Masih IV, Mirza Tahir Ahmad [rh]. On that occasion, a dialogue was held in Jakarta with religious dignitaries; at another occasion a homeopathic seminar was held in Sari San Pacific Hotel in Jakarta, which was attended by doctors and paramedics. In Yogyakarta, *Huzoor* [rh] also was the keynote speaker for the 'International Seminar for the Revitalization of Islam in the Modern Age'. A historic

occasion took place in Parung, the *Jama'at* center within Indonesia, where a *Jalsa* was held and was attended by almost 20,000 Ahmadi Muslims, in addition to a regional *Jalsa* which was also held in the presence of *Huzoor* [rh]. When, upon his return to London, someone asked *Huzoor* [rh] of his impressions about Indonesia, whereupon he spontaneously answered, 'Our *Jama'at*'. During these blessed occasions, three Friday sermons delivered by *Huzoor* [rh] and the proceedings of the International Seminar in Yogyakarta were telecast live via satellite. The visit of *Huzoor* [rh] was covered widely by the national press, both electronically as well as in newspapers. *Huzoor* [rh] urged Jama'at members to acquire more land to establish a center for the Indonesian *Jama'at*. Indonesia. Today, *Jama'at* Ahmadiyya Indonesia has as many as 385 mosques, 174 mission houses and 36 schools. ∎

Hadhrat Khalifatul Masih IV [rh] attends 'The International Seminar for the Revitalization of Islam in the Modern Age', which was held in Yogyakarta, Indonesia, on June 24, 2000.

Maulana Abdul Basit Wahid, Amir Jama'at Indonesia.

Group Photo of Hadhrat Khalifatul Masih II^{ra} with Molvi Rahmat Ali, the first Missionary to Indonesia.

Maulana H. Sayuthi Ahmad Aziez, Missionary-in-Charge, Indonesia.

A glimse of Jalsa Salana, Jama'at Indonesia.

Hadhrat Khalifatul Masih IV^{tba} meets with the President of Indonesia

Students of Urdu class.

Central Jama'at Officials Visit Indonesia

The Late Hadhrat Mirza Waseem Ahmad, former Amir Jama'at, Qadian, is photographed here emerging from the Jalsa Hall at Manislor, Indonesia, on July 2, 1991.

Chaudhry Hamidullah Sahib, Vakilul 'Ala from Rabwah, Pakistan headquarters is speaking in Parung, Indonesia, while Zafrullah Pontoh, a Missionary, translates.

Sahibzada Mirza Mubarak Ahmad, Vakilul 'Ala (standing in center) meets with Jama'at members during his visit to Indonesia in 1981. Here, he his photographed speaking with Al-Haj Hadi Iman Sudita (second from left) and Marah Hanafi (far left).

The Vakilut Tabshir (right) is engaged here in a lively discussion with Ahmad Supardi, Sadr Majlis Khuddamul Ahmadiyya, Indonesia (at left).

Israel

Jama'at established in 1925

Slightly smaller than the size of the state of New Jersey, Israel borders the Mediterranean Sea and sits between Egypt and Lebanon. In 1947, the United Nations approved the partition of the Mandate of Palestine into two states, one Jewish and one non-Jewish Arab, and on May 1948, the Jewish provisional government declared Israel's independence. There are 242 Israeli settlements and civilian land use sites in the West Bank, 42 in the Israeli-occupied Golan Heights and 29 in East Jerusalem. Roughly seven million people live in Israel, of which 76.4% are Jewish, 16% Muslim. With a technologically advanced market economy, it depends on imports of crude oil, grains, raw materials and military equipment. Despite limited natural resources, it has intensively developed its agricultural and industrial sectors, cut diamonds, high-technology equipment, and agricultural products as its main exports.

Mahmoud Mosque in Al-Kababir

Jama'at Ahmadiyya, Israel

Jama'at Ahmadiyya, Israel

Muhammad Sharif Odeh, Amir Jama'at Israel (right), with Mr. Abdul Mumen Tahir, Head of Arabic Desk in London, hositing a flag at Jalsa Salana Israel.

Jama'at Ahmadiyya, Israel

Dignitaries of different faiths at Tabligh Center during Jalsa Salana, Israel. In all black with his back to the camera is the Mayor of Haifa City; government officials include the first two persons at the right and the last on the left.

Mahmoud Mosque overlooking the Mediterranean Sea in Al-Kababir, during sunset.

A group photograph, circa 1964, showing members of the Ahmadiyya Jama'at, Haifa, Israel. In the center (seated) is Chaudhry Mohammad Sharif, one of the Ahmadiyya Missionaries serving the region.

Japan
Jama'at established in 1935

Freer and Sackler Galleries

"Boy at Mount Fuji," a painting by Katsushika Hokusai (1760-1849)

land of rising sun
once devoid of true Islam
now accepts Ahmad

Japan is the tenth largest populated country in the world with an estimated 128 million people densely occupying about one-quarter of the total land. Consisting of 3,000 islands located betwen the North Pacific Ocean and the Sea of Japan, the remaining three-quarters of the country is forested, mountainous, and unsuitable for agricultural, industrial, or residential use. The large majority of Japan observes both Shinto and Buddhist religions (84%), and the remaining 16% is comprised of other religions, including Christianity. Japan boasts a high per capita GDP of US $33,800, with 4.6% of the work force in agriculture, 27.8% in industry, and 67.7% in services. Even after the devastating aftermath of the second World War, Japan has reemerged as the third largest economy after the U.S. and China.

Above: *Anees Ahmad,*
Missionary-In-Charge,
Japan.

Right:
Ahmadiyya Mission
House in Nagoya, Japan

Left: Hadhrat Khalifatul Masih IV rh arriving in Japan. Right: Huzoor rh eating dinner with Japanese
government officials.

Hadhrat Khalifatul Masih V [aba] looks at an exhibit at the Hiroshima Peace Memorial Museum in Japan.

Spiritual Reflections

On Monday, August 6th and Thursday, August 9th, 1945, the United States of America authorized nuclear attacks on the Japanese cities of Hiroshima and Nagasaki, respectively. On August 10, *Hadhrat Khalifatul Masih II* [ra] wrote a letter of protest to then U.S. President, Harry Truman. In Hiroshima, the immediate blast killed 70,000 Japanese, and subsequent radiation increased the death toll to roughly 200,000. *Hadhrat Khalifatul Masih V* [aba], while in Japan, made it a point to visit the Hiroshima Peace Memorial Museum and pray for the victims.

Background: AskMaps

Hadhrat Khalifatul Masih V [aba] examines a model map of Hirsoshima at the time of the bombing.

Hadhrat Khalifatul Masih V ^{aba} leads prayers after a lecture session at Tokyo University.

Hadhrat Khalifatul Masih V ^{aba} speaks with an Ahmedi Professor of Tokyo University.

Hadhrat Khalifatul Masih IV ^{rh} seated with some Jama'at members in Japan.

ahmadiyyat *in* japan

1905 — Hadhrat Ahmad [as] proclaims: "If I would receive Divine instructions (about Japan), without even knowing the language, I would immediately proceed there."

1904 — Hadhrat Ahmad [as] receives revelation: "an Eastern power, and the insecure Korea." Two years later, Japan overtakes Korea.

1935 — Sufi Abdul Ghafoor arrives as the first Ahmadi missionary in Japan.

1945 — Hadhrat Musleh Maud [ra] sees in vision Japan as a spiritually dying state that will draw towards Ahmadiyyat like birds to the call of Abraham.

1958 — first accepted by Mohammad Owais Kobayashi.

1963 — Sahibzada Mirza Mubarak Ahmad, Wakil ut Tabshir, visits and establishes Darul Tabligh Tokyo.

1981 — Hadhrat Khalifatul Masih III [rh] establishes first mission house in Nagoya.

1989 — Hadhrat Khalifatul Masih IV [rh] tours from July 24-30.

2006 — Hadhrat Khaliftul Masih V [aba] tours for a week in May.

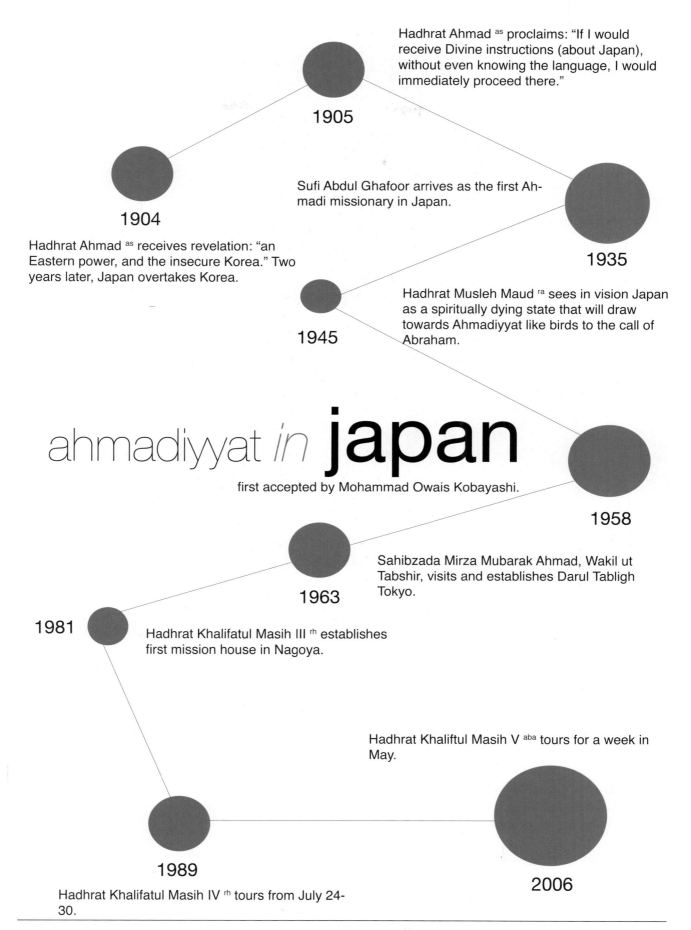

A Russian Soyuz rocket lifts off from Baikonur Cosmodrome, Kazakhstan, at 11:06 p.m. EDT on Oct. 13, 2004. The Baikonur Cosmodrome is the world's largest space launch facility.

Launch Data: NASA / Photo: NASA and Bill Ingalls

Kazakhstan

Jama'at established in 1991

energy & growth

The natives of Kazakhstan are a mix of Turkic and Mongol nomadic tribes who migrated into the region in the 13th century. Situated northwest of China and west of the Ural River, Kazakhstan recently declared independence in 1991. The Republic of Kazakhstan's economy is larger than all the other Central Asian states combined, largely due to its vast natural resources, including petroleum, natural gas, coal, and iron ore, and newfound political stability. The 15 million people living in Kazakhstan speak many languages and practice a variety of religions, but the predominant language is Kazakh, with nearly one-half practicing Islam. Kazakhstan carries a wanting per capita GDP of US$10,400, with 13.8% of the population living below the poverty line.

A view of the Ahmadiyya Muslim Mission House in Almaty.

Another view of the Ahmadiyya Muslim Mission House in Almaty.

missionaries in kazakhstan

Syed Hasan Tahir Bukhari,
Missionary In Charge, Kazakhstan

Rufat Jan Tukamov,
Local Missionary, Kazakhstan

first jalsa salana kazakhstan 2007

A happy gathering posing outside on the occasion of Jalsa Salana Kazakhstan.

Malaysia

Jama'at established in 1935

Bait-us-Salam Mosque, Kuala Lumpur, Malaysia

pushing ahead

Members of the Malaysian Jama'at, shown here in Singapore, on the occasion of Jalsa Salana.

Malaysia consists of thirteen states and three federal territories in Southeast Asia. It is home to over 25 million people, with one-half of these Malaysian natives, roughly one-quarter Chinese, and the remaining a combination of various ethnic groups; the majority of residents practice Islam. The country is working on resolving environmental issues including air and water pollution, deforestation, smoke and haze. From 1981 to 2003, under the leadership of Prime Minister Mahathir bin Mohammad, Malaysia successfuly diversified its economy by expanding into manufacturing, services, and tourism.

Myanmar
Jama'at established in 1935

The lotus flower is a sacred symbol of the Buddhist tradition. It is shown here in silent protest of the turbulent country of Myanmar, which has stripped many of their fundamental rights to free speech, religion and peaceful assembly. As Ahmadi Muslims, we denounce religious persecution in all shapes and forms.

a tumultuous past

The Union of Myanmar, formerly known as Burma, was conquered by Britain over a period of 62 years (1824-1886) and incorporated into its Indian Empire; it gained independence from the Commonwealth in 1948. The country of approximately 48 million people is situated in Southeast Asia, bordering the Andaman Sea and the Bay of Bengal, between Bangladesh and Thailand. The country's natural resources include petroleum, timber, tin, zinc, and copper. It is currently working on resolving environmental issues stretching from deforestation and industrial pollution to inadequate sanitation and wastewater treatment.

Members congregate during 35th Jalsa Salana, Myanmar. Central envoy Mubarak Muslehuddin Ahmad is seen at the center

The first Ahmadiyya Muslim mosque established in Myanmar, Rangoon Mosque was the name given to this building by Hadhrat Khalifatul Masih II^{ra}.

Mohammad Salik, Missionary-In-Charge Myanmar since 1996.

Ch. Hameedullah, Wakil e A'ala is being greeted by a Burmese devout Ahmadi in 1986.

An Ahmadiyya Muslim mosque established in Mawlamyaing, which is the third largest city in Myanmar.

Philippines

Jama'at established in 1985

Jama'at Ahmadiyya Philippines

The Ahmadiyya Muslim Mission House in the Philippines.

In 1935, Philippines became a self-governing commonwealth after nearly four decades of U.S. occupation following the 1898 Spanish-American War. After a decade under Japanese control, the Republic of the Philippines finally secured its independence on July 4, 1946. Situated between the Philippine and South China Seas, Philippines, an archipelgao of over 7,000 islands, is home to 93 million people, with over three-quarters professing the Roman Catholic faith. It is favorably situated near many of Southeast Asia's main water bodies, facilitating trade but leaving the mainland vulnerable to cyclones and tsunamis. Eight major dialects of Filipino permeate the vernacular, with Tagalog-based Filipino the official language. Its major crops include sugarcane, coconuts, rice, corn, bananas, and pineapples.

ahmadiyyat in philippines: a brief history

1985 Jama'at is established on August 23.

1989 A few Jama'at members meet Hadhrat Khalifatul Masih IV [rh] when he visits Singapore.

1999 On April 11, Missionary Sibthe Ahmad Hasan is assigned President and Missionary In-Charge of Jama'at Ahmadiyya Philippines. Headquarters are now in Zamboanga City.

2005 Jama'at Mission moves to the capital city of Manila.

2006 Hadhrat Khaliftaul Masih V [aba] visits Signapore and addresses an audience from the Philippines Jama'at Amila. The Jama'at currently has six mosques, five mission houses, five local missionaries, and a national missioanry; it is organized in nine chapters across the country.

Russia
Jama'at established in 1924

The Palace Square, St. Petersburg, Russia

Toshio's Russia Photo Gallery. Online.

A NEW DAWN

Russia, along with 14 other indepedent republics, emerged out of the dismantling of the Union of Soviet Socialist Republics (USSR) in August 1991. Since then, it has struggled to fashion a democratic political system and market economy from the dregs of an expired Communistic framework. Situated in Northern Asia, bordering the Arctic Ocean, between Europe and the North Pacific Ocean, Russia has broad plains with low hills west of the Urals, vast coniferous forests, and tundra in Siberia. It also has uplands and mountains along the southern boarder regions. Russia's 140 million people mainly speak Russian and some other minority languages; nearly 20% practice Russian Orthodox and 10-15% practice Islam.

Hadhrat Maulana Zahoor Hussein, the first Ahmadiyya Muslim Missionary sent to Russia on July 14, 1924.

A group of Russian Ahmadis are shown here meeting with Hadhrat Khalifatul Masih IV [rh] in 2002. Missionaries Mr. Ristam Hammad Wali and Mr. Khalid Ahmad (holding Huzoor's hand) are standing behind Huzoor [rh].

Some Russian Ahmadis with Nawab Mansoor Ahmad Khan (standing in the center in white dress).

Ahmadiyya Mission House in St. Petersburg

missionaries

Jama'at Ahmadiyya, Russia

Hafiz Saeed-ur-Rahman,
Kazan Tatarstan

Mr. Khalid Ahmad,
Moscow

Mr. Ristam Hammad Wali,
Moscow

Tolstoy & Ahmadiyyat

Leo Tolstoy (9 September 1828 – 20 November 1910), one of Russia's most celebrated authors and philosophers, is among the greatest minds of the nineteenth century. In his final years, Tolstoy kept correspondence with Mufti Muhammad Sadiq^{ra}, the first Ahmadi missionary in the United States, on the message of the Promised Messiah.^{as}

Hadhrat Mufti Muhammad Sadiq^{ra} wrote:

Your Highness! I read your religious views in the recently published British Encyclopaedia vol.33. I am glad that real gems can be found bowing to the manifestation of the true deity even in the darkness created by the concept of Trinity in Europe and America. Your thoughts about true 'well being' and prayer are exactly the same as of a true Muslim believer. I completely agree with you that Jesus Christ was a spiritual teacher but to consider him god or to worship him like a god, is the greatest disbelief. Furthermore, I wish to inform you with great pleasure that the discovery of the tomb of Jesus proves substantially that he died a natural death. The tomb has been discovered in Kashmir. This research has been publicised by Hadhrat Mirza Ghulam Ahmad(a s), the greatest protector of the unity of God, and to whom the Lord Almighty has given the title of the Promised Messiah because he is replete in his love for the one true God. Allah appointed him, as a person from God, an inspirer and a reformer of the age and G o d 's true messenger. God will bless all those who will believe in this prophet. Whosoever will deny him, will face God's wrath. I am sending you in a separate packet, a picture of this holy person from God along with the picture of the tomb of Jesus. On receiving your reply, I would be glad to send you more books. I remain your well wisher.

Mufti Muhammad Sadiq of Qadian, 28 April 1903.

Leo Tolstoy is famous for his realistic fiction in War and Peace *and* Anna Karenina.

Leo Tolstoy replied:

Dear friend! Your letter along with Mirza Ghulam Ahmad's picture and a sample of the magazine *Review of Religions* has been received. To engage in the proof of the death of Christ or in the investigation of his tomb is a futile effort because an intelligent man can never believe that Jesus is still alive. We need reasoned religious teaching, and if Mr. Mirza presents a new reasonable proposition then I am ready to benefit from it. In the specimen number, I approved very much two articles, 'How to get rid of the Bondage of Sin' and 'The Life to Come', especially the second. The idea is very profound and very true. I am most thankful to you for sending me this and am also grateful for your letter.

Yours Sincerely,

Tolstoy, from Russia. 5th June 1903.

(Zikre Habib pp 399-401 published Qadian, First Edition, December 1936)

Singapore

Jama'at established in 1935

A view of the Singapore skyline at night.

gem *of the* malay

Singapore, made up of 63 islands, was founded as a British trading colony in 1819. It joined the Malaysian Federation in 1963 but gained its independence two years later. Nestled in the heart of Southeast Asia between Malaysia and Indonesia, Singapore boasts strong international trading links and the world's busiest port. Of its 4.6 million residents, over three-quarters are of Chinese background, with the remaining of Malaysian or Indian descent. Singapore promotes freedom of religion, with Buddhism as the predominant sect. Throughout the year, the country goes through two monsoon seasons, the Northeastern (December to March) and Southwestern, which bring tropical, hot, humid, and rainy weather.

Taha Mosque, located in Singapore.

Hadhrat Khalifatul Masih V [aba] lays the foundation stone of a two-story mission house.

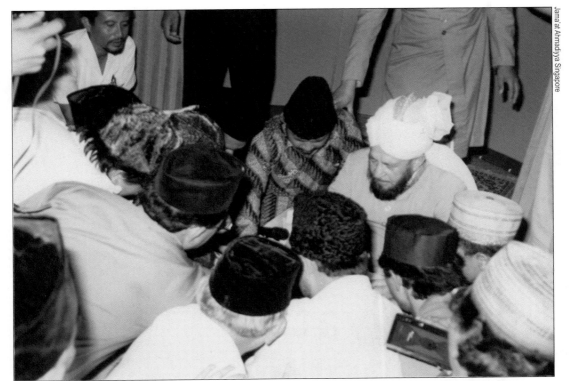

Hadhrat Khalifatul Masih IV ^{rh} performing a Bai'at (Initiation) Ceremony in Singapore.

Hadhrat Khalifatul Masih V ^{aba} addressing attendees of Jalsa Salana, Singapore, which was held at Taha Mosque in 2006.

Jama'at Ahmadiyya Singapore

1935 Ahmadiyyat established in Singapore. Enduring persecution and threats, Ghulam Hussain Ayaz arrives as the first missionary in May.

1938 Haji Jaffar becomes the first Ahmadi convert in Singapore.

1949 Maulana Muhammad Sadiq stays for eight years as missionary in Singapore. He would return in 1958 for an additional year.

Hadhrat Khalifatul Masih IV [rh] conducting a Question & Answer Session (Majlis-e-Irfan) in Singapore.

ahmadiyyat *in* singapore

1989 Hadhrat Khalifatul Masih IV [rh] vsists Singapore in his first-ever Asian tour. He states in his Friday sermon:

"I am foresseing signs that armies upon armies of people are about to entre the fold of Islam in a very short time. In the far East Allah has opened new avenues for the victory of Islam." (Al-Fazl, 15 Oct 1983)

2006 Though only staying for two days in April, Hadhrat Khalifatul Masih V [aba] accomplishes numerous tasks on his first trip to Singapore, including: laying the foundation stone for a two-story mission house; delivering a Friday sermon; meeting with Jama'at members; speaking with Waqfeen-e-Nau; and meeting with Amila members from local and regional Jama'ats.

Jama'at Ahmadiyya Singapore

156 ASIA | Singapore

Sri Lanka

Jama'at established in 1915

A lush tea field in Sri Lanka. The largest tea producer in the world, Sri Lanka exports nearly 300,000 metric tons of tea per year.

turning a new leaf

Ceylon, later named Democratic Socialist Republic of Sri Lanka in 1972, gained its independence from Britain in 1948. Since then, peace among the differing political parties is wanting. Scores of people have died in ethnic conflict and, despite a ceasefire treaty between the government and the Liberation Tigers of Tamil Eelam, violence continues. Since the mid-1980s, thousands of Tamil civilians have sought refuge in the West, shrinking the country's population of 21 million. Three-quarters of the country identify with the Sinhalese and over two-thirds are practicing Buddhists.

A group photo, taken in 1929, of members with Dr. Mufti Muhammad Sadiq [ra] (seated, second from left). Maulana A. P. Ibrahim is also seated (second from right).

A view of the Fazl Mosque in Negombo, Sri Lanka

Bait ul Hamd in Colombo serves as the national headquarters of Jama'at Sri Lanka

1907 — Abdul Aziz requests Bai'at in a letter to The Promised Messiah [as], becoming the first Ahmadi Muslim in Ceylon. In December, he publishes an article on Ahmadiyyat in Muslim Guardian.

1915 — Hadhrat Sufi Ghulam Mohammad [ra] spends three months in Ceylon en route to Mauritius. He addressed the Young Literacy Association, resulting in new converts and the country's first Jama'at.

A.P. Ibrahim is the first central missionary on the island; ten people accept Ahmadiyyat and establish a branch in Nagomo.

Jama'at Ahmadiyya Sri Lanka

1920 — A center is established in Slave Island.

1923

ahmadiyyat *in* sri lanka

1932 — First Ahmadiyya mosque is built.

1937 — B. Abdullah establishes a Jama'at in Gampola.

1948 — Mohammad Ismail Munir arrives as Missionary-In-Charge and Amir. 5,000 copies of The Philosophy of the Teachings of Islam are translated into Sinhalese.

1952 — Ceylon gains independence from Britain and become a sovereign nation

Jama'at Ahmadiyya Sri Lanka

1978 — Muhammad Umar arrives as missionary. Rasheed Ahmad is martyred in Nagoma.

1983 — Professor Abdus Salam visits and addresses a Jama'at gathering.

1985 — Hadhrat Khalifatul Masih IV [ra] visits Sri Lanka for the first time.

Thailand

Jama'at established in 1986

The Bangkok Superhighway

HDRW-Tarun, Google Picasa

about thailand

Known as Siam until 1939, Thailand is the only Southeast Asian country to successfully resist European colonization. A bloodless revolution in 1932 led to a constitutional monarchy. Bordering the Andaman Sea and the Gulf of Thailand, Thailand is home to 65 million people. Three-quarters of these residents identify themselves as Thai, and a minority as Chinese. The official language is Thai, with English as the secondary language. Almost all of its inhabitants (95%) follow Buddhist teachings.

Jama'at Ahmadiyya Thailand

Ahmadiyya Mission House, located in Bangkok.

Jama'at Ahmadiyya Thailand

A delegation of Thai Ahmadies meets with Hadhrat Khalifatul Masih V [aba] at the 2006 Jalsa Salana, in Singapore. At Huzoor's immediate right stands Uung Kurnia (President & Missionary of Thailand Jama'at); next, Muallim Jumakhan (serving the local area); finally, Hafiz Imran Ahmad (General Secretary). A Nau Mobay (new initiant) stands at Huzoor's left.

Thai Ahmadis meeting with Hadhrat Khalifatul Masih V [aba]. On Huzoor's immediate right stands Muallim Jumakhan, followed by Mrs. Novitalia Nurlaeli (Lajna Finance Secretary and wife of Muallim Jumakhan), and finally, Dr. Surayya (Sadr Lajna Imaillah, Jama'at Thailand). At Huzoor's immediate left stands Hafiz Imran Ahmad (General Secretary), then Uung Kurnia (President of Thailand Jama'at), Siti Hazrah (wife of Uung Kurnia), and Mrs. Juwairiah, a Nau Mobay (new initiant).

Glimpses of Jalsa Salana, Thailand (2005-2007)

Uung Kurnia, President of Jama'at Thailand, offering some remarks during the 3rd Annual Jalsa Salana, Thailand.

Uung Kurnia, President of Jama'at Thailand, welomes guests to the Jalsa Salana.

Members congregate during the 4th Annual Jalsa Salana, Thailand.

Reaching the Corners of the Earth

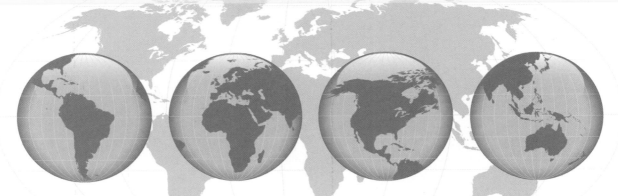

In 1898, *Hadhrat* Mirza Ghulam Ahmad[as], the Promised Messiah and *Mahdi*, received the following glad tiding from Allah in a revelation in the Urdu language (as translated into English):

"I shall cause Thy Message to reach the corners of the earth."

This relevation saw its literal fulfillment during the lifetime of the Promised Messiah[as]. The message of Ahmadiyyat spread to countless individuals across the corners of the world, including Australia, East Africa, Libya, U.K., Arabia, Sri Lanka, Afghanistan, Bengal, India, Burma, Syria the United States.

Hadhrat Khalifatul Masih IVth once pointed out that the most important word in the revelation is "I", meaning that it is Allah who will make this message reach the corners of the earth. He continued to describe how Allah blessed the *Jama'at* to transmit the Promised Messiah's[as] message via Muslim Television Ahmadiyya (MTA). Little human strategy or effort was put in to be blessed with such a bounty of immense impact and utility.

During his tour to the Far East in 2006, *Hadhrat Khalifatul Masih V*[aba] shared another aspect of Promised Messiah's[as] revelation:

"This is a great favor and blessings of Allah that today I am addressing this Friday Sermon from that area and country of the world, which is considered the last corner of the world. From this perspective, we are experiencing the fulfillment of the promises made to the Promised Messiah[as] as manifested in another way -- first *Hadhrat* Ahmad's[as] message reached the corner of the world through MTA, and now it is being spread from a corner of the world to the world over . . . At the occasion of *Jalsa Salana* Qadian, the Eid sermon and other addresses were transmitted from Qadian, and today, Allah has provided us the means to transmit from the corner of the world the message of the Promised Messiah[as] as to the rest of the world. This is Allah's grace that we are able to see this bounty of Allah.

On April 26, 2006, *Huzoor*[aba] visited the Fiji Islands and set a new milestone in the history of Ahmadiyyat. On this day, he addressed the world live though Muslim Television Ahmadiya (MTA). Eleven satellites broadcasted the sermon. Owing to the special geographical position of Fiji, being situated near the International Date Line, *Huzoor*[aba]'s Friday sermon was literally the first sermon broadcasted that day in the whole world.

The Expansion of Ahmadiyya Muslim Community Worldwide (1889-2008)

• During the lifetime of *Hadhrat* Promised Messiah[as] 1889-1908
    India, Afghanistan, Bengal, Ceylon, Burma, Australia, Libya, Kenya, Arabia, England, USA, and Syria

• During the life of *Hadhrat Khalifatul Masih I*[ra], the *Jama'at* expanded into these countries:
    China, Egypt, Hong Kong, Tanzania, Mauritius and New Zealand
    The message reached to 18 countries by 1914

• During the life of *Hadhrat Khalifatul Masih II*[ra], the *Jama'at* expanded into these countries:

Africa:
    Ghana, Nigeria, Liberia, Malta, Togo,Morocco, Tunisia, Ivory Coast, Gambia, Abbysinia, Sierra Leone,
    Uganda, Gambia, Ivory Coast, South Africa, Zanzibar

Asia:
    Borneo, Brunei, Egypt, Fiji Islands, Iran, Iraq, Israel, Japan, Java, Jordon, Kuwait, Lebanon, Malaysia,
    Muscat, Pakistan, Palestine, Philippines, Qatar, Russia, Singapore, Sumatra, Turkey, U.A.E, and Yemen
Europe:
    Albania, Austria, Germany, Holland, Hungary, Italy, Poland, Spain, Switzerland, Yugoslavia

The Americas:
    Argentina, Guyana, Suriname, Trinidad & Tobago

    Total reached to 75 countries in 1965

• During the life of *Hadhrat Khalifatul Masih III*[rh], the *Jama'at* expanded into these countries:
    Belgium, Bénin, Canada, Denmark, France, Iceland, Madagascar, Mali, Norway, Papua New Guinea,
    Senegal, Sudan, Sweden
    Total reached to 91 countries

• During the period of *Hadhrat Khalifatul Masih IV*[rh], the *Jama'at* expanded into these countries:
    1985   Burundi, Mauritania, Mozambique, Rwanda
    1986   Burkina Faso, Bhutan, Brazil, Caribas, Nepal, Tuvalu, Western Samoa
                Rodriguez Island, Yugosalavia, Zanzibar
    1987   Congo, Finland, Nuaru, Portugal
    1988   Gabon, Maldive Islands, Solomon Islands, South Korea, Tonga
    1990   Marshall Island, Mexico, Micronesia, Tokelau
    1991-2   Belarus, Chuukis, Guam, Lithuania, Monglia, New Caledonia
    1993   Columbia, Hungary, Tataristan, Ukraine, Uzbekistan
    1994   Albania, Bulgaria,Chad,Cape Verde, Khazakistan, Norfolk Island, Romania
    1995   Cambodia, Equatorial Guinea, Grenada, Jamaica, Laos, Macedonia,Vietnam
    1996-7   Bosnia and Herzegovina, Croatia, El Salvador, Slovenia
    1998-9   Czech Republic, Ecuador, Lesotho, Myoti Island, Nicaragua, Slovakia Republic
    2000-2   Andorra, Azerbaijan, Botswana, Central African Republic, Cypress, Djibouti, Eritrea,
                Kosovo, Malta, Moldova, Monaco, Namibia, Sao Tome & Principe, Swaziland, Venezuela,
                Western Sahara
    Total reached to 175 countries

• During the period of *Hadhrat Khalifatul Masih V*[aba], the *Jama'at* expanded into these countries:
    Antigua, Bermuda, Bolivia, Cuba, Estonia, French Guyana, Guadeloupe, Gibraltar, Haiti, Martinique,
    St. Lucia, St. Kitts, St. Martin. The number of countries where Ahmadiyyat has been introduced and a
    Jama'at established is **189** as of 2008.
    Source: *Tarikh e Ahmadiyyat, Al-Fazl International, and various Tabshir publications.*

Hadhrat Mirza Ghulam Ahmad (1835-1908) The Promised Messiah and Mahdi[as]

"I shall cause thy message to reach the corners of the earth."

(Revelation to The Promised Messiah [as], 1898)

Hadhrat Al-Ha
Hakeem Maulv
Nooruddin
Khalifatul Mas
(1908 - 1914)

Hadhrat Mirza
Bashiruddin
Mahmood Ahmad
Khalifatul Masih II [ra]
(1914 - 1965)

Hadhrat Mirza
Nasir Ahmad
Khalifatul Masih III [rh]
(1965 - 1982)

Hadhrat Mirza
Tahir Ahmad
Khalifatul Masih IV [rh]
(1982 - 2003)

Hadhrat Mirza
Masoor Ahmad
Khalifatul Masih V [aba]
(2003 - Present)

Europe

Ahmadiyyat was introduced to the European continent in 1907, when, in response to *Hadhrat* Mirza Ghulam Ahmad's [as] messages to Europe, a German woman, Mrs. Carolyn, began corresponding with him. A century later, Ahmadiyyat is now in most European countries, including the newly formed country of Kosovo, which achieved independence in early 2008.

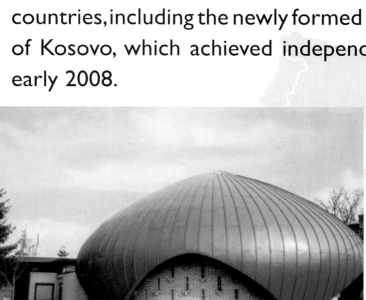

Photos clockwise from upper left: Jama'at Ahmadiyya, The Netherlands; Jama'at Ahmadiyya, Denmark; Jama'at Ahmadiyya, Denmark; Jama'at Ahmadiyya, Belgium; Jama'at Ahmadiyya, Denmark; United Nations Mission in Kosovo.

Petr Kratochvil

ALBANIA
Jama'at established circa 1934

A view of the shoreline residences of the coastal city of Sarandë, Albania. A popular tourist location, Sarandë lies along the Ionian Sea in the Mediterranean (see map below, right).

ABOUT ALBANIA

Located in southeastern Europe, the Republic of Albania borders the Adriatic and Ionian Seas to the west, and Montenegro, Serbia, Macedonia and Greece to the north, east and south. A republic since 1920, Albania was invaded by the Axis Powers during World War II, after which it came under Communist control until the 1990s. Currently, the country exists as a parliamentary democracy but remains, at the time of this writing, outside of European Union membership. The country has a population of about 3.6 million people, an estimated 70% of whom are Muslim, 20% Albanian Orthodox, and 10% Roman Catholic. A relatively poor country, Albania has a per capita GDP of US $6,500.

Data: CIA World Factbook 2007, wikipedia.org. Map: CIA World Factbook / Arshad M. Khan

A sunlit view of Baitul Awwal Mosque, located in Tirana, Albania. The mosque was built in 2005.

Located in the capital city of Tirana, the Darul Falah Mission House serves the Albanian Ahmadi Muslim Jama'at.

A happy international crossroads at Jalsa Salana U.K., 2007. From left to right: Respected Munir Hamid, Naib Amir U.S.A., Mr. Mubarak Tanvir of Jama'at U.S.A. (Philadelphia chapter), and Mr. Shahid Ahmad Butt, the Missionary for Jama'at Ahmadiyya, Albania.

Ahmadi Muslims in Albania: Historic Highlights

compiled by Mr. Shahid Ahmad Butt, Ahmadiyya Missionary serving the Albanian Jama'at

1934-5 Missionary Mohammad Din arrives in Albania and begins conveying Ahmadiyya Muslim teachings to the local community. A few families become Ahmadi Muslims, but soon he is deported from the country due to his religious beliefs.

1939 Italy, as a member of the Axis Powers during World War II, invades Albania on April 7.

1944 Albanian nationalist groups successfully throw out invading Italian and German occupants. Soon, however, the nation comes under Communist rule.

1967 A total ban on all religious activities is imposed. Mosques are destroyed or converted to cultural or community centers. This state of affairs continues until the widespread fall of Communism in 1990.

1990 For the first time in nearly five decades, a democratic society comes into being and religious freedoms are afforded to Albanian citizens. *Hadhrat Khalifatul Masih IV*[rh] immediately initiates the preparation of Ahmadiyya *Jama'at* literature in the Albanian language.

1990-4 Maulana Mohammad Zakariyya was appointed to undertake the task of preparing the necessary literature and to translate the Holy Qur'an into the Albanian language. An extensive distribution of literature and frequent visits of *Waqifeene Arzi* (temporary devotees) allows the *Jama'at* to grow.

1995 The Ahmadiyya Muslim Community formally is registered within the country.

1997 A serious economic slump within the country results in civil war in Albania. With local tensions escalating, many families flee the country and go to Germany.

1999 During the Kosovo conflict, many Ahmadi Muslim families flee to Germany. *Jama'at* Ahmadiyya Germany demonstrates the true spirit of hospitality by giving safe refuge to these migrating Ahmadis. A series of *Mulaqaat* (meetings with *Huzoor*[rh]), accompanied by question & answer sessions, helps create a renewed sense of spiritualism among Albanian Ahmadis.

2000 A 33,676 m² parcel of land is purchased in the Albanian capital city of Tirana, and the construction of a mission house begins immediately. Construction of Baitul Awwal mosque also commences on the same plot. Mr. Sajid Ahmad Nasim undertakes the noble task of building these structures.

2003 The three-story Mission House finally is completed, and includes a library, lecture halls, meeting rooms, computer facilities, and guest accommodations. *Hadhrat Khalifatul Masih IV*[rh] names this Mission House Darul Falah. On May 16, Friday prayers are offered for the first time at the newly completed Baitul Awwal.

2005 Two missionaries from Qadian, Mr. Shahid Ahmad Butt and Mr. Samad Ghauri, arrive in Albania and begin formally learning the Albanian language while actively serving the Ahmadiyya Muslim Community.

2007 On May 20, the first *Jalsa Salana* (Annual Gathering) of *Jama'at* Ahmadiyya Albania is held and 138 Albanians participate, along with delegates from Germany, the United Kingdom, and other European *Jama'ats*.

Missionaries Shahid Ahmad Butt (left) and Samad Ghauri (right).

Jama'at Ahmadiyya Albania

A group photo of Albanian Jama'at members with guests in front of Baitul Awwal Mosque. The guests include the Amir of Jama'at Germany (standing, fifth from the right). Standing in the center of the group (with white cap and dark, buttoned suit coat) is Missionary Samad Ahmad Ghauri. Missionary Shahid Ahmad Butt is sitting (second from left).

A glimpse of the first Jalsa Salana of Jama'at Ahmadiyya Albania, which was held on May 20, 2007.

AUSTRIA
Jama'at established circa 1936
www.ahmadiyya.at

Alicia Michalik

A nighttime view of the beautiful Nibelungenbrücke Bridge in the city of Linz, Austria. This bridge crosses the Danube, the European Union's longest river, which also flows through the capital city of Vienna.

ABOUT AUSTRIA

The Republic of Austria is located in central Europe, and its current borders encompass what was left after the collapse of the Austro-Hungarian Empire at the end of World War I. Its borders were redrawn as a result of the Treaty of Saint-Germain-en-Laye in 1919. The country was annexed by the Nazi Germany in 1938 and liberated in 1945. Austria declared itself to be "permanently neutral" in 1955. Of the over 8 million people living in Austria today, 74% are Roman Catholic, 5% are Protestant and about 4% are Muslim. Austria has been a member of the European Union since 1995.

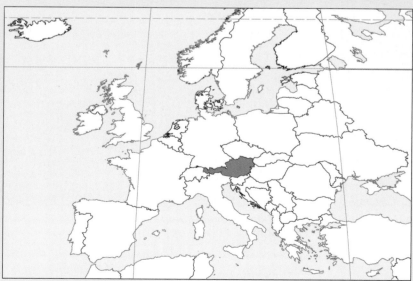

Data: CIA World Factbook 2008, wikipedia.org. Map: CIA World Factbook / Arshad M. Khan

Majlis Khuddamul Ahmadiyya, Karachi, Pakistan

Shaikh Nasir Ahmad, the Ahmadi Missionary serving Switzerland, delivers a lecture about Islam in Austria, circa 1962.

Arshad M. Khan

Austrian postage stamp showcasing Almsee, a beautiful lake located in Upper Austria (see map on previous page).

Jama'at Ahmadiyya, Austria

The Ahmadiyya Mission House in Vienna, Austria.

Jama'at Ahmadiyya, Austria

Hadhrat Khalifatul Masih V ^{aba} meeting with Mr. Qazi Shafiq Ahmad, Amir of Jama'at Austria (shown at left), and Mr. Mohammad Wahab, General Secretary, Jama'at Austria (shown at right).

Jama'at Ahmadiyya, Austria

Mr. Munir Ahmad Munawar, the Ahmadi Missionary serving in Austria. Behind him is a view of the gardens and palace of Schönbrunn, one of the most significant cultural landmarks of Vienna and a UNESCO World Heritage Site.

BELGIUM

Jama'at established circa 1982
www.ahmadiyya.be

Photo: Roswitha Schacht. Data: FAO, United Nations. www.chocolate-history.co.uk.

Although Belgium is the second largest exporter of chocolate products in the world, it ranks first in the luxury chocolate market. In particular, Belgian pralines, shown here, are the most popular luxury chocolate confection and are produced by the hundreds of thousands of metric tons each year.

ABOUT BELGIUM

Located in northwestern Europe between France and the Netherlands, the Kingdom of Belgium is a nexus for diverse cultures and linguistic traditions. Belgium's 10.5 million inhabitants include those in the Dutch-speaking Flemish region to the north (60% of the population), and those in the French-speaking Walloon region to the south (31%).

Belgium gained independence from the Netherlands in 1830 and was occupied by Germany during both World Wars. Most Belgians are Roman Catholic (75%) or Protestants (25%). A founding member of the European Union and host of the EU's headquarters, the per capita GDP of Belgium is US $33,000.

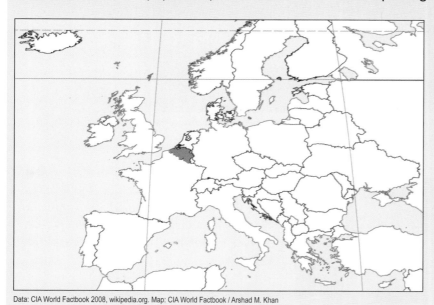

Data: CIA World Factbook 2008, wikipedia.org. Map: CIA World Factbook / Arshad M. Khan

Darul Tabligh Aziz Mission House, located in Antwerp, Belgium.

Baitur Raheem in Hasselt, Belgium.

www.alislam.org

Baitus Salam Mission House is located in Dilbeek, a town just outside the capital city of Brussels, Belgium.

Left: Mr. Hamad Mehmood Shah, Amir of the Belgian Jama'at. Right: Mr. Naseer Ahmad Shahid, Missionary-in-Charge, Belgium.

A Brief Introduction to the Ahmadiyya Muslim Community in Belgium

The first presence of Ahmadiyyat in Belgium was manifest in 1956 when a Belgian family by the name of Van Den Broek embraced Ahmadiyyat through information they obtained from the Ahmadiyya Muslim Community in Holland. Officially, the first missionary to Belgium was Mr. Saleh Mohammad Khan, who was appointed to serve Belgium in 1982.

Today, through the Grace of Allah, the Ahmadiyya Muslim Community has three mission houses in Belgium. Belgium's first mosque, Baitus Salam, was purchased in 1985. It is situated in Dilbeek, a town outside Brussels, the capital city of Belgium. Baitus Salam, which was inaugurated by *Hadhrat Khalifatul Masih IV*[rh], can accommodate 250 people.

In 2000, a second mosque, named Darul Tabligh Aziz, was purchased in Antwerp. Antwerp is the second largest city in Belgium and the second largest seaport in Europe. This mosque was purchased to meet the expanding needs of the Belgian *Jama'at* and maintains a capacity of 500 worshipers. Darul Tabligh Aziz also was blessed with the presence of *Hadhrat Khalifatul Masih IV*[rh], who performed its inauguration ceremony. A third structure, a mission house called Baitur Rahim, was established in the city of Hasselt and can hold 150 worshippers. It too, was blessed by *Huzoor's* inauguration. Now, by the Grace of Allah, the *Jama'at* exists in more than twelve cities in Belgium.

Belgium's monthly magazine, *As-Salam*, is published regularly in Urdu, Dutch, and French. In 2007, the Belgium *Jama'at* created a website: http://www.ahmadiyya.be.

Today, the Belgian *Jama'at* numbers over 1,150 members. The *Jama'at* consists of members from Belgium, Pakistan, Bangladesh and various countries in Africa. Belgian Ahmadis participate earnestly in the *Tehrik-e-Jadid*, *Waqfe-e-Jadid*, and *Waqfeen-e-Nau* programs of the *Jama'at*.

Jama'at Ahmadiyya, United Kingdom

An aerial view of Baitus Salam Mission House located in Dilbeek, Belgium.

Huzoor's Visits to Belgium (2004, 2006)

Nasirat holding both Belgian and Ahmadiyya Jama'at flags await the arrival of Hadhrat Khalifatul Masih V ^{aba} on the occasion of the 12th Annual Jalsa Salana Belgium. The Jalsa was held from September 10-12, 2004.

Photo / Data: www.alislam.org

Hadhrat Khalifatul Masih V ^{aba} presides over the final session of Jalsa Salana, Belgium, on June 4, 2006. Mr. Ray Mazhar Ahmad is at the podium reciting a poem.

Jama'at Ahmadiyya, Belgium

Jama'at Ahmadiyya, Belgium

Hadhrat Khalifatul Masih V ^{aba} leads Jama'at members in silent prayers in front of Baitus Salam Mission House during his visit to Belgium in 2006.

Hadhrat Khalifatul Masih V ^{aba} enjoys a moment of reflection during his visit to Belgium in 2006.

BOSNIA AND HERZEGOVINA

Jama'at established in 1996
www.ahmadija.ba

The Rimski Most (Roman Bridge), located in Ilidža (see map below), Bosnia and Herzegovina, was built over the Bosna River by 16th century Ottoman architects using the stones from the remains of the old Roman town, Aquae Sulphurae.

ABOUT BOSNIA AND HERZEGOVINA

Bosnia and Herzegovina declared independence from Yugoslavia in 1992. Located in Southeastern Europe, Bosnia and Herzegovina is 51,000 km² with a population of 4.6 million. Bosnian, Croatian and Serbian languages are spoken, and 40% of the country is Muslim. The GDP of Bosnia and Herzegovina is US $14.2 billion with a per capita income of $6,600.

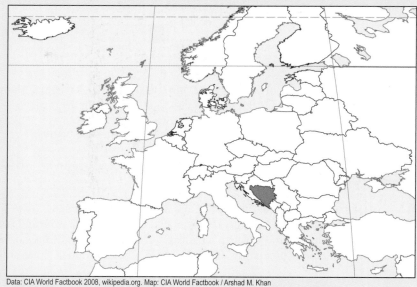

Banja Luka
Srebenica
Sarajevo · Ilidža
Mostar

Data: CIA World Factbook 2008, wikipedia.org. Map: CIA World Factbook / Arshad M. Khan

The Ahmadiyya Mission House located in the city of Sarajevo, Bosnia and Herzegovina.

Ahmadi Muslims in Bosnia and Herzegovina: Historic Highlights

1937 Missionary Muhammad Din arrives in Eastern Europe, and partly because of looming tensions related to World War II, returns home.

1992 On April 6, Bosnia declares its independence, but soon experiences an economic crisis. In addition, severe bloodshed results in 200,000 Muslims being killed, with thousands migrating to western European countries as refugees. The Ahmadiyya Muslim Community extends a helping hand to these displaced people and supports the safe shelter of a large number of Bosnians at various locations.

1996 With the violence largely over, Missionary Wasim Ahmad arrives in Bosnia in September of this year. He rents a small house in the city of Tuzla and begins his preaching efforts.

1997 This year, the Mission House moves to the capital city of Sarajevo, and missionary activities resume. Many individuals join the Ahmadiyya community, and a need is felt to build a mosque/mission in the area.

2002 After an extensive search, a parcel of land is purchased and construction of the new mosque begins.

2003 The new Mission House opens on March 1. The new facilities include two prayer halls, a library, living quarters for the missionary, and other *Jama'at* offices.

2008 As of this year, the *Jama'at* is organized in four cities in Bosnia and Herzegovina, with the *Jama'at* headquarters in Sarajevo. The new Ahmadi converts are very active members of the *Jama'at* and are assisting in the translation of *Jama'at* literature into the Bosnian language. About one dozen of the books written by the founder of the Ahmadiyya Muslim Community, *Hadhrat* Mirza Ghulam Ahmad [as], are now available in the Bosnian language.

BULGARIA

Jama'at established circa 1992

The famous Rocks of Belogradchik, located in northwestern Bulgaria, are of considerable scientific interest because several periods of the region's geologic history are represented in these formations. The Belogradchik formation is under consideration for status as a UNESCO World Heritage Site.

ABOUT BULGARIA

Gaining independence from the Ottoman Empire in 1908, Bulgaria found itself defeated during both World Wars. Communist control ensued, and Bulgaria became an ally of the Soviet Union following World War II. Communist rule ended in 1990 with the first free elections in the country since 1931. Today, Bulgaria's nearly 8 million inhabitants live in a democratic, constitutional republic that has since joined the European Union (in 2007). Approximately 83% of the population belongs to the Bulgarian Orthodox Church, and about 12% are Muslim. The per capita GDP of the country is US $11,904.

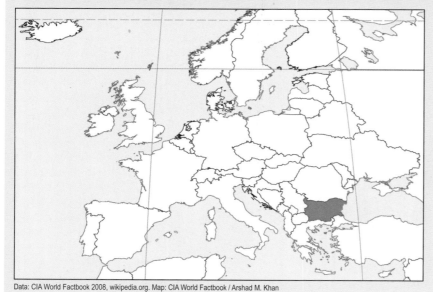

Data: CIA World Factbook 2008, wikipedia.org. Map: CIA World Factbook / Arshad M. Khan

A group of Bulgarian Ahmadis meet with Hadhrat Khalifatul Masih V [aba] in Germany, on the occasion of Jalsa Salana in 2005.

A group photo of some Bulgarian Ahmadis.

The foundations for a Bulgarian *Jama'at* were established in 1992 when a Bulgarian native joined the Ahmadiyya Muslim Community in Germany through the efforts of Mr. Sheikh Shaukat and Dr. Abdul Ghaffar, the Ahmadiyya Muslim Missionary serving Germany. Later that year, Dr. Ghaffar visited Bulgaria, where he met many people who spoke the Turkish language. Thus, using his skills in Turkish, and with the hard work and the prayers of *Hadhrat Khalifatul Masih IV* [rh], Dr. Ghaffar was successful in converting many local people and forming a *Jama'at* in Bulgaria. Some time later, Mr. Shujaud Din Ryhan, along with his wife and three children, emigrated to Bulgaria. Following the instructions of *Hadhrat Khalifatul Masih IV* [rh], they decided to remain in Bulgaria to help build an Ahmadiyya Muslim *Jama'at* there.

After the *Jama'at* was formed in the country to maintain the strength Rifat Jahan Ara (the President Bulgaria) worked diligently Bulgarian language, but also and children about Islam.

A Brief History of the Ahmadiyya Muslim Community in Bulgaria by Tahir Ahmad, Ahmadiyya Muslim Missionary serving Bulgaria

Bulgaria, Dr. Ghaffar frequently visited and activity of the *Jama'at*. Mrs. of the *Lajna Imaillah* for not only to master the to teach Bulgarian women

In 1999, *Hadhrat Khalifatul* approval for two Ahmadiyya Rabwah, Pakistan, to Bulgaria, the Bulgarian language. As a result,

Masih IV [rh] granted his Missionaries to be sent from where they were assigned to learn Missionary Ashraf Zia (who now serves as the National President of the Ahmadiyya Muslim Community in Bulgaria) and Missionary Tahir Ahmad were sent to Bulgaria. Both have now completed, by the Grace of Allah, M.A. degrees in the Bulgarian language and have recently gained admission to doctorate programs as well.

Over 400 individuals are now members of the Bulgarian Ahmadiyya Muslim Community, only eight of whom are of Pakistani origin, with most of the remainder being native to Bulgaria. Each year, a large number of Bulgarian Ahmadi Muslims participate in the *Jalsa Salana* (Annual Gathering) of *Jama'at* Ahmadiyya Germany. A major challenge that remains for the Bulgarian *Jama'at* is to register successfully with the Bulgarian Government as a religious organization, a process that has been delayed largely because of unreasonable pressures exerted by intolerant Muslim clerics.

DENMARK
Jama'at established 1959

The famous Kronborg Castle in Denmark. Also known as "Hamlet's Castle" because of its fame as the inspired setting for Shakespeare's Hamlet, *Kronborg was designated in 2000 as a UNESCO World Heritage Site.*

ABOUT DENMARK

Denmark became a monarchy in 1849 and joined the European Union in 1973. Situated on a peninsula north of Germany (Jutland), Denmark is 43,000 km^2 with a population of 5.5 million. Dutch is the official language. 95% of the population is Evangelical Lutheran, and 2% Muslim. The GDP of Denmark is US $311 billion with a per capita income of $37,400.

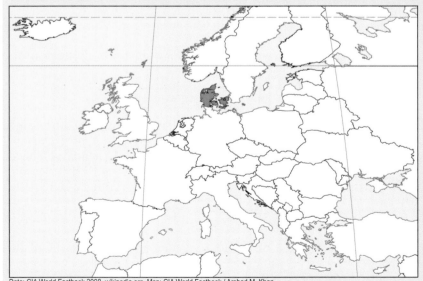

Data: CIA World Factbook 2008, wikipedia.org. Map: CIA World Factbook / Arshad M. Khan

Ahmadi Muslims in Denmark: Historic Highlights

1959 The mission is established formally on March 25, under the guidance of the Ahmadiyya Muslim Community of Germany, and is headed by Mr. Syed Kamal Yusuf, the Regional Missionary for Scandinavia.

1961 In October Mirza Mubarak Ahmad, Secretary of the Ahmadiyya Muslim Foreign Missions office, visits Denmark and instructs Syed Kamal Yusuf to acquire land for the construction of a mosque. Mr. Ahmad also holds a press conference to inform the media of this project.

1964 Syeda Umme Mateen, *Sadr Lajna Imaillah* (President of the Ahmadiyya Ladies' Auxiliary) for Pakistan, addresses the *Jalsa Salana* (Annual Gathering) on December 27. In her address, she appeals to the *Lajna* members to donate money for the construction of a mosque in Europe as a way to express their gratitude for the successful completion of 50 years for the second *Khalifa*. Copenhagen, Denmark, she further states, is the proposed site for this mosque, which has been purchased by Syed Masood Ahmad. *Lajna* members respond enthusiastically to this appeal.

1966 Mirza Mubarak Ahmad lays the foundation for Nusrat Jahan Mosque in Copenhagen on May 6. Extensive media coverage of the event is given, with editorials also printed in Danish newspapers. Chaudhry Muhammad Zafrullah Khan[ra] leads Friday prayers at the mosque site.

1967 On July 21, *Hadhrat Khalifatul Masih III*[rh] inaugurates the Nusrat Jahan Mosque and leads the first Friday prayers inside the mosque. He then delivers an address in English which describes the purpose of mosques and their great significance in Islam. Among the guests are members of the Danish Missionary Society who are conducting research on the Ahmadiyya Muslim Community. Several Danish newspapers cover the event, including *Valby Bladet, Kristeligt Dagblad, Aktuelt* and *Lollands Tidende.* The year also is marked by the translation of the Holy Qur'an into the Danish language by Mr. Abdus Salam Madsen, a devout Danish Ahmadi Muslim.

1982 *Hadhrat Khalifatul Masih IV*[rh] performs a tour of Scandinavian countries in July. He is welcomed by Syed Kamal Yusuf, Hamid Karim, Noor Ahmad Bustad, and many members of the *Jama'at* at the Oslo airport. On August 1, *Huzoor*[rh] holds a rejuvenation of *Ba'ait* (Initiation Ceremony) and speaks about the meaning and concept of *Ba'ait*. After staying in Norway and Sweden, *Huzoor*[rh] arrives in Denmark on August 11. *Huzoor*[rh] addresses a session at the Nusrat Jahan Mosque and responds to questions from attendees. Prominent newspapers cover the visit.

2005 On September 6, 2005, *Hadhrat Khalifatul Masih V*[aba] visits Denmark on his way to participating in the *Jalsa Salana* of the Scandanavian countries for the very first time. *Huzoor*[aba] is very warmly greeted upon his arrival at the Nusrat Jahan Mosque. His arrival is covered by national television; a national newspaper, *Jyllands-Posten,* also interviews *Huzoor*[aba] at the mosque. The entire interview also is televised on the evening news.

"The time is not distant but near when you will percieve hosts of angels descending on the hearts of people in Asia, Europe and America. So watch for the sign. If the angels do not descend, if you see no evident effect or influence of their coming down, if you do not find an extraordinary movement in human hearts in the direction of truth, you would be free to take it that no one had really come from Allah. But in case all these things come to pass, then you should desist from denial, so that in the sight of Lord, you should not be held to be a rebellious people."

— Hadhrat Mirza Ghulam Ahmad[as]
The founder of the Ahmadiyya Muslim Community

Nusrat Jahan Mosque is located in Copenhagen, Denmark.

Imam Kamal Yusuf, seen here inside Nusrat Jahan Mosque.

Far left: Mr. Naimatullah Basharat, the Amir and Missionary-in-Charge serving Denmark. Immediate left: Usman Sahib, a Missionary serving Denmark.

Imam Kamal Yusuf, the first Ahmadi Muslim Missionary to Denmark (the first missionary to all of Scandinavia), is shown here with school children.

Sahibzada Mirza Mubarak Ahmad lays the foundation of Nusrat Jahan Mosque in Copenhagen on May 6, 1966. The foundation stone, which was a brick from Mubarak Mosque in Qadian, India, was blessed by Hadhrat Mirza Bashiruddin Mahmud Ahmad, Khalifatul Masih II ra, just a few months before his death in November of 1965.

Hadhrat Khalifatul Masih III ^{rh} in the home town of Abdus Salam Madsen, the first Danish Ahmadi.

Hadhrat Khalifatul Masih III ^{rh} reads his opening address on the occasion of the inauguration of Nusrat Jahan Mosque in Denmark in 1967.

Hadhrat Khalifatul Masih III ^{rh} is standing outside Nusrat Jahan Mosque. At far left is Haji Nuh Svend Hansen, and at far right is Kamal Ahmad Krogh, both of whom are Danish Ahmadis.

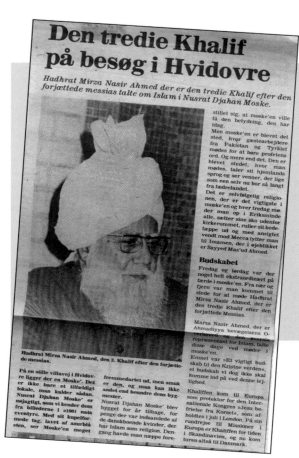

Above: Hadhrat Khalifatul Masih III[rh] is featured in a Danish newspaper on the occasion of his visit in August, 1978.

AHMADIYYAT IN THE DANISH PRESS

THE EARLY PRESS ON AHMADIYYAT

These Ahmadis are more serious people than other Muslims. They particularly do not agree with the rest of the Muslims on the point of Jihad with the sword. According to them, the Quranic verse which means there should be no compulsion in matters concerned with religion is conclusive of the point.

Kristeligt Dagblad, Copenhagen, December 15, 1958

Hadhrat Khalifatul Masih IV[rh] Visits Denmark, 1982

Left: Hadhrat Khalifatul Masih IV[rh] speaks with members of the Danish Jama'at during his visit in 1982. Above: Press coverage of the visit.

Hadhrat Khalifatul Masih V [aba] Visits Denmark

Hadhrat Khalifatul Masih V [aba] is seen signing a guest book at Nusrat Jehan Mosque in 2005.

Hadhrat Khalifatul Masih V [aba] inside Nusrat Jehan Mosque, during his first visit to Denmark in 2005.

Jama'at Ahmadiyya Denmark Holds a Reception in Honor of Hadhrat Khalifatul Masih V [aba] in Copenhagen
(September 7, 2005 at the Radisson SAS Hotel)

The Danish Government Welcomes Huzoor [aba]

After the address of the Missionary-in-charge, the Danish Minister for Refugees, Immigration and Integration Affairs, Mrs. Rikke Hvilshøj, welcomed Huzoor [aba] on behalf of the Government of Denmark. The Minister described the opportunity to address the head of the Ahmadiyya movement and the *Jama'at* of Denmark as a great honor. She stated that her country, as well as the whole world, looked to the common values that could transform the disorder and unrest of the current environment into a peaceful society. The Minister said that the good society of Denmark owes its goodness only to the democratic values held in this country. She said that she herself has lived in many Islamic countries and knows from firsthand experience that there are many difficulties that come in the way of leaving one's native country and migrating to another. She said people who migrate to Denmark are faced with a similar situation. The good values, whether derived from one's religion or from a secular culture, have many common modalities and, as such, create a common ground for all to come together upon. The Minister stated her happiness in seeing the flag of Denmark flying at the Ahmadiyya Mosque. She continued by describing the unique character of *Jama'at* Ahmadiyya in that it always busied itself in engaging in dialogue with the people and religions of other countries. She stated that there could never be peace and respect for each other without dialogue. Dialogue is the most important need of our time.

Summary of the Address by Hadhrat Khalifatul Masih V [aba]

Jama'at Ahmadiyya, Denmark

Hadhrat Khalifatul Masih V [aba] addressing a reception held in his honor.

Addressing the reception's attendees, Huzoor [aba] stated that the real teachings of Islam are found in the Holy Qur'an and are exemplified through the life of the Holy Prophet [sa]. The founder of Ahmadiyya *Jama'at*, *Hadhrat* Mirza Ghulam Ahmad [as], was raised in this age as the Promised Messiah to revive the pure teachings of the Holy Qur'an and their practice by the Holy Prophet [sa].

Huzoor [aba] said that the one of the factors that adds to the unrest and chaos of the world today is mutual distrust among nations. The Western world thinks ill of the East, and the East thinks ill of the West. A small minority of self-proclaimed religious figures and politicians, living in both the East and the West, are making the whole world suffer through their actions. It is not fair to hold one nation or one religion as being responsible for the world's chaos. Instead, there are many contributing religions and countries that are involved in creating disorder and restlessness.

Huzoor [aba] said that Allah desires humankind to come

towards Him by worshiping Him, fulfilling the rights of His creations, feeding the hungry, helping the poor and the needy, being forgiving, patient, respectful, and cooperative with one another, refraining from speaking ill of others, and treating others with fairness and justice. He further stated that Allah has addressed the Muslims through the Qur'an and has told them that they are the best nation ever to be raised on the face of this earth as a benefit to mankind. They therefore are tasked with the objective to do good for others as well as to prevent the committing of bad deeds.

Huzoor [aba] said that a person who is engrossed in bad things should be counseled and made to understand fully what is expected of him; but in doing so, force should never be used under any circumstances. Huzoor [aba] said that the teaching of the Holy Qur'an is that if somebody is killed for no apparent fault, the sin is equivilent to the killing of humankind as a whole. Huzoor [aba] said that no individual or group of persons has the right to take the law into their own hand. But today, in sharp contrast to the Qur'an's teachings, there are Muslims as well as Christians from all over the world involved in unjustifiable crimes. The reason for this is that they have forgotten God and therefore have lost control over themselves. Patience has been replaced with distrust and intolerance of others. Huzoor [aba] said that today suicide attacks are taking the lives of many innocent people. These acts are all very wrong and have absolutely nothing to do with the teachings of Islam. Similarly, the indiscriminate air bombing by Western powers also is very cruel.

> Huzoor [aba] said that today, suicide attacks are taking the lives of many innocent people. These acts are all very wrong, and have absolutely nothing to do with the teachings of Islam. Similarly, the indiscriminate air bombing by Western powers is also very cruel.

Huzoor [aba] said that today, by the Grace of Allah, Jama'at Ahmadiyya is the only Jama'at sending the message of peace and love all over the world. The central message of Jama'at Ahmadiyya is to worship and love God. Without practicing this message there never can be unity and brotherhood among humankind. When a person develops a relationship with God, the power and ability to serve humankind with zeal and enthusiasm is bestowed upon him or her.

Huzoor [aba] said that while the Ahmadiyya Jama'at is relatively small, it has been fortunate to serve many of the poorest nations by creating and supporting institutions of education, endeavoring to find ways to make drinking water more accessible to the masses, and by providing medical facilities and expertise in regions of need. It is indeed by the Grace of Allah that the Ahmadiyya Jama'at has been privileged to serve those in need. He further stated that the members of Jama'at Ahmadiyya, who now live in 180 countries of the world, strive to stay away from creating disorder and lawlessness, but rather they abide by the laws of the land and are faithful and peaceful citizens of their respective countries. They, in fact, are an example for others to follow.

Huzoor [aba] reiterated the teachings of Hadhrat Masih Maoud [as] about peace and love, good deeds, Taqwa (fear of Allah), and service to humanity. He said this is the real Islamic teaching that Jama'at Ahmadiyya always follows and seeks to spread to others.

(Originally published in the Urdu language in Al Fazl International, October 14-20, 2005, pages 13-14).

FRANCE
Jama'at established in 1946
www.ahmadiyya.fr

Joachim Bor

The Place Stanislas, a portion of which is seen here illuminated at night, is a major public pedestrian park and architectural landmark. Located in Nancy, France, the park and surrounding buildings have been listed as a UNESCO World Heritage site.

ABOUT FRANCE

France, which has had a presidential-parliamentary government since 1958, has a total are of 643,000 km². 88% of the 64 million inhabitants are Roman Catholic, with another 5-10% Muslim. French is the official language. The GDP of France is US $2.5 trillion with a per capita income of US $33,800.

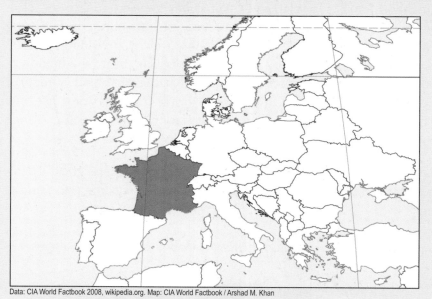

Data: CIA World Factbook 2008, wikipedia.org. Map: CIA World Factbook / Arshad M. Khan

Amour pour Tous, Haine pour Personne

Jama'at Ahmadiyya, France

Hadhrat Khalifatul Masih IV [rh] is received by Jama'at members during his first tour of France as Khalifa.

Amir Rehman

Hadhrat Khalifatul Masih IV [rh] with Mr. Lutfur Rehman Naz, the first Amir of Jama'at France, on the occasion of Huzoor's visit in 1983.

Jama'at Ahmadiyya, France

Hadhrat Khalifatul Masih IV [rh] hoists the French flag in front of Baitus Salam, the Jama'at Mission House in Paris, on the occasion of the Centennial celebrations of the Ahmadiyya Muslim Community in 1989.

Amir Rehman

Mr. Lutfur Rehman Naz, who then was Amir Jama'at France, receives Dr. Abdus Salam at the Paris airport.

Mubarak Mosque and Mission House in France.

An evening view of the recently constructed buildings.

One of the main prayer rooms of Mubarak Mosque.

Jalsa Salana, France

Hadhrat Khalifatul Masih V[aba] addressing the Jama'at on the occasion of the 13th Jalsa Salana (Annual Gathering) in France, which was held on December 27, 2004.

Hadhrat Khalifatul Masih V[aba] performing the Ba'ait (Initiation) ceremony for individuals newly joining the Ahmadiyya Muslim Community. This particular ceremony took place during the 13th Jalsa Salana held in France.

Missionary Hafeez Ehssan Secundar serves Jama'at Ahmadiyya, France.

Mr. Ashfaq Rabbani, the Amir of Jama'at Ahmadiyya, France.

Hadhrat Khalifatul Masih V [aba] conducts a children's class during his visit to France in 2004.

Hadhrat Khalifatul Masih V [aba] Visits Versailles

During his December, 2004 tour of France, Hadhrat Khalifatul Masih V [aba] visited the famous Palace at Versailles. Here, he is accompanied by a young Tifl and Imam Ataul Mujeeb Rashid, Missionary-in-Charge, UK.

Ahmadiyya Mosques Around the World **195**

GERMANY

Jama'at established in 1923
www.ahmadiyya.de

Filled with parks and public gathering places, the city of Hamburg is a popular site for visitors. In its large park known as 'Planten und Blomen' (literally, 'Plants and Flowers'), visitors can watch the 'water ballet' during summer nights, in which water jets and a dazzling light show keep time with classical music.

ABOUT GERMANY

Germany, the second most populous European nation, reunified in 1990 in the post-Cold War era. Spanning 357,000 km², Germany has a population of 82 million, of which 34% are Protestant, 34% Roman Catholic and 4 % Muslims. German is the official language. The GDP is US $3.3 trillion with a per capita income of US $34,400.

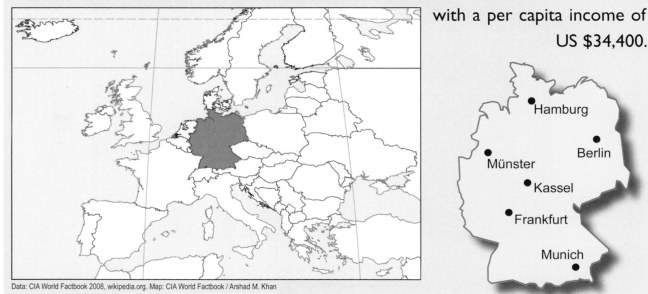

Hamburg
Berlin
Münster
Kassel
Frankfurt
Munich

Data: CIA World Factbook 2008, wikipedia.org. Map: CIA World Factbook / Arshad M. Khan

Maulana Mubarak Ali, the first missionary sent to Germany (1922 - 1924)

Mr. Abdullah Wagishauser, Amir, Jama'at Germany

Maulana Haider Ali Zafar, Missionary-in-Charge serving Jama'at Ahmadiyya Germany

Hamburg

A glimpse of the foundation-laying ceremony of Hamburg Mosque in 1957.

Message from Hadhrat Khalifatul Masih II [ra]: May Allah enable the German nation to accept Islam. Just as they are European leaders in the material world, so may they be spiritual leaders in the same respect.

Hamburg

Liebe für alle, Hass für keinen

The Fazle Omar Mosque, built in Hamburg, is the first mosque constructed by the Ahmadiyya Muslim Community in Germany.

A glimpse of the inauguration ceremony of the Fazle Omar Mosque, in Hamburg, Germany. The ceremony took place behind the mosque. Among those seated at the head table are Chaudhry Muhammad Zafrullah Khan^{ra} and Sahibzada Mirza Mubarak Ahmad.

Circa 1966. Chaudhry Abdul Latif, the Ahmadiyya Missionary in Charge, delivers the Eidul Adhea sermon in the Fazle Omar Mosque.

Hadhrat Khalifatul Masih V ^{aba} reads the list of individuals who made early contributions for the construction of Fazle Omar Mosque, the first Ahmadiyya Mosque in Germany.

Hadhrat Khalifatul Masih V ^{aba} plants a tree during his visit to Hamburg in 2005.

Hadhrat Khalifatul Masih V ^{aba} enjoys a moment of relaxation playing cricket during an outing with the Hamburg Jama'at in 2005.

The Holy Prophet ^{sa} and Mosques

For him who makes his ablution at home and then walks to one of the Houses of Allah to discharge the obligation imposed on him by Allah, one single step of his towards the Mosque wipes out a sin, and another step raises his status. (*Sahih Muslim*)

Frankfurt am Main

Sir Chaudhry Muhammad Zafrullah Khan [ra], who served as President of the United Nations General Assembly and also as the Chief Justice at the International Court at the Hague, is seen here addressing attendees of the inauguration ceremony for Nuur Mosque in Frankfurt, Germany. The function was televised throughout the country.

Left: A pre-1965 photo (exact date not obtainable) taken on the occasion of Eidul Adhea ceremonies at Nuur Mosque in Franfurt, Germany. Standing in the foreground, from left to right: Mr. Mahmood Ismail Czoelsch, Maulana Fazal Ilahi Anwari, Chaudhry Mahmood Ahmad Cheema, and Mr. Harmut Henze, a German Ahmadi Muslim. Above: A more recent view of Nuur Mosque in Frankfurt, Germany.

Mr. Muhammad Ali, the U.S. heavyweight boxing champion, offers prayers at the Nuur Mosque in Frankfurt, Germany. Seated at prayer to his right is Chaudhry Abdul Lateef, Missionary In Charge, Germany. At Mr. Ali's left is Mr. Fazal Ilahi Anwari, who was the Ahmadiyya Missionary serving Frankfurt. Although the exact date of this photo is not known, it may have been at Friday prayers on September 9, 1966, a day before Mr. Ali successfully was to defend his heavyweight boxing title against Mr. Karl Mildenberger in Frankfurt.

Several years ago, when I just completed my education at Oxford University and the Germans had lost the war, I saw a vision that in the center of the map of Germany was inscribed "There is none worthy of worship except Allah and Muhamad is His Messenger" It was a strange phenomenon but I was pleased with it.

— *Hadhrat* Mirza Nasir Ahmad [rh] (*Khalid*, May 1983, p. 276)

An enthusiastic gathering of Nasirat (young Ahmadi Muslim girls' group) waving German flags as they greet Hadhrat Khalifatul Masih V [aba] on the occasion of his arrival in Frankfurt in 2005. A few days later, Huzoor [aba] would deliver the Friday sermon to open the 2005 Jalsa Salana, which was held in Mannheim, Germany.

Towards the Construction of 100 Mosques:
A Pioneering Plan for Ahmadi Muslims in Germany

In 1989, *Hadhrat Khalifatul Masih IV*[rh] announced a plan to make one hundred mosques in Germany:

"It is my desire that Germany be the first European country where Jama'at Ahmadiyya be blessed with the ability to construct one hundred Mosques." (Final address, Jalsa Salana Germany, 1989)

In 2006, *Hadhrat Khalifatul Masih V*[aba] continued this goal further and addressed the Jama'at as follows:

"This target that has been assigned to you, so try your best to achieve it. Every year, instead of constructing ten new Mosques you can [for] now construct five new Mosques… I want to tell you that for the construction of Mosques, we will not take loans from banks. Instead, Mosques will be constructed [through financial] sacrifices that will be presented for the sake Allah's pleasure and with purity of heart, Insha'allah. Thus, we put all our trust in Allah. Make your pledges for the construction of Mosques every year, and also fulfill them every year. I am addressing men women, and children of the Jama'at." (Friday sermon, June 16, 2006, Hadhrat Khalifatul Masih V[aba]*)*

Fazle Omar Mosque	Nuur Mosque	Baitul Shukoor	Ham'd Mosque	Basharat Mosque
1957	1959	1985	1997	1999
Baitul Momin	Habib Mosque	Nasir Mosque	Tahir Mosque	Nuurud Din Mosque
1999	1999	1999	2000	2000
Aziz Mosque	Jame-a Mosque	Sami Mosque	Aleem Mosque	Baitul Huda
2000	2000	2001	2001	2001
Muqeet Mosque	Mahmood Mosque	Bashir Mosque	Nasir Mosque	Anwaar Mosque
2003	2004	2004	2004	2006
Khadija Mosque	Qamar Mosque	Mannheim Mosque	Lübeck Mosque *under construction*	Neuwied Mosque *under construction*
2006	2006	2007	2007	2007

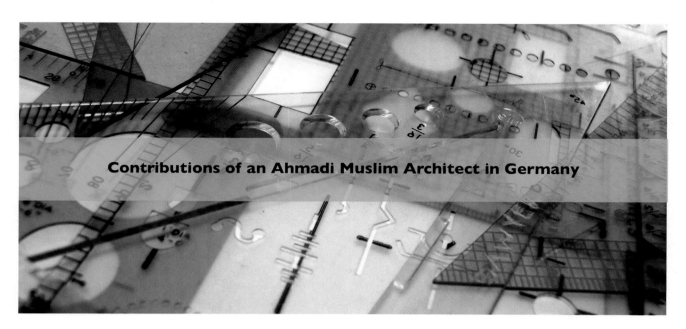

Contributions of an Ahmadi Muslim Architect in Germany

Mrs. Mobashira Ilyas, a German-born Ahmadi Muslim, bears the distinction of designing three Ahmadiyya Muslim Mosques in Germany. She graduated from Darmstadt University of Technology (TU Darmstadt) with a Master's degree in Architecture, and began her services for the *Jama'at* during her graduate studies. The mosques she designed include Nasir Mosque in Stuhr/Bremen, the Jame-a Mosque, and now, Khadija Mosque. Thus, she has set a new standard for services rendered to the *Jama'at* by Ahmadi women. For these architectural projects, she had the honor of being guided directly by *Hadhrat Khalifatul Masih V* [aba].

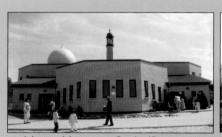

Nasir Mosque, Stuhr/Bremen	*Jame-a Mosque, Offenbach*	*Khadijah Mosque, Berlin*
Building base area: 257.11 m²	Building base area: 422.51 m²	Building base area: 257.11 m²
Mosque area: 128.00 m²	Mosque area: 533.45 m²	Mosque area: 128.00 m²
Building capacity: 221	Building capacity: 889	Building capacity: 221

Whoever builds a House of Allah in this world, Allah will prepare for that person a house in Paradise.

— *Hadith* of the Holy Prophet [sa]

Photo of Rulers: Jane M. Sawyer. Photos / Data of Mosques: Jama'at Ahmadiyya, Germany

Münster

Baitul Momin Mosque, located in Münster, Germany. The foundation of this mosque was laid by Hadhrat Khalifatul Masih IV ^{rh} in 2000, and its construction was completed in 2003.

Hadhrat Khalifatul Masih IV ^{rh} offers prayers on the occasion of the foundation ceremony for Baitul Momin Mosque on August 31, 2000, in Münster. Mr. Abdullah Wagishauser, the Amir of Jama'at Germany, stands at Huzoor's right.

Hadhrat Khalifatul Masih IV ^{rh} reviews the architectural drawings of Baitul Momin during his visit to Münster on August 31, 2000.

Jama'at Ahmadiyya, Germany

Hadhrat Khalifatul Masih V [aba] meets members of the German Jama'at while visiting Münster in 2007.

The flash of the camera brightens the reflective strips on the weatherproof sport jacket of Mr. Abdullah Wagishauser, the Amir Jama'at, Germany, as he poses with Khuddam in a group photo outside Baitul Momin. Hours later, Hadhrat Khalifatul Masih V [aba] arrives at the mosque, which is decorated with signs of welcome for the special January 2007 occasion.

Jama'at Ahmadiyya, Germany

Jama'at Ahmadiyya, Germany

Hadhrat Khalifatul Masih V [aba] offers silent prayers outside Baitul Momin Mosque in January, 2007.

Ahmadiyya Mosques Around the World **205**

Koblenz

A view of Tahir Mosque in Koblenz, Germany. The foundation of this mosque was laid in December, 2002, and it was inaugurated in May, 2004, by Hadhrat Khalifatul Masih V[aba].

A young Tifl welcomes Hadhrat Khalifatul Masih V[aba] with a bouquet of flowers at the opening of Tahir Mosque in May, 2004.

Hadhrat Khalifatul Masih V[aba] plants a sapling at the Koblenz mosque grounds on May 25, 2004.

Würzburg

Jama'at Ahmadiyya, Germany

Baitul Aleem Mosque in Würzburg.

Würzburg, Germany is famous not only for its cathedrals, but also for its reputation as a center of learning. Indeed, no less than thirteen of its citizens have been recipients of the Nobel Prize, and approximately one-third of the city's 150,000 inhabitants are students. For Ahmadi Muslims, this town also is special because the first European to contact *Hadhrat* Mirza Ghulam Ahmad [as], the founder of the Ahmadiyya Muslim Community, hailed from this small city. Specifically, a woman named Carolyn wrote to *Hadhrat* Ahmad [as]: "*I will be glad if you could write me back a few words of advice. Could I be of any help to you in this part of the world?*" (*Badar*, March 14, 1907).

Hadhrat Khalifatul Masih V [aba] visited this town and inaugurated Baitul Aleem Mosque on August 31, 2005 ('*Aleem*' means 'All-knowing' and appropriately reminds those in this intellectual city that God alone possesses all knowledge). The area of the mosque property is 2700 m^2 while the covered area is 400 m^2 and has a capacity of 360 worshippers. Baitul Aleem has many distinctive features, including a solar energy-based system to help perform the heating and cooling of its facilities, and a tall minaret which is illuminated at night. This mosque also is noteworthy in that the various permits and approvals for its construction were obtained easily. *Hadhrat Khalifatul Masih V* [aba], in his inaugural address for the mosque, said: *Allah says eat and drink but do not overdo either, this is also related to the mosques; when we come here we should not indulge in worldly affairs. Rather, our main objective should be to worship Allah. Populating mosques should be our focus. Therefore, those who live in this area have the responsibility to keep this mosque occupied.*"

Commenting about the minaret of the mosque he said: *This is the first minaret in this area that has arrangements of being lit. If it is merely for show, it has no use, but if the purpose is symbolic and to provide light then it is useful, as the light will emanate from it. Whenever you will come to mosque, this light would remind you that we will not be stagnant at a figure of 180 (the number of Ahmadis in Würzburg). We have to introduce this message to people all around us and demonstrate with our actions and example that this is what Islam is all about: to enlighten one's awareness of salvation and nearness to Allah.*" (From the *International Al-Fazl*, September 16, 2005).

Bremen

A view of Nasir Mosque, located in Bremen, Germany. The foundation of this mosque was laid in November, 2001, and it was inaugurated in May, 2004.

Members of Lajna Imaillah and Nasiratul Ahmadiyya greet Hadhrat Khalifatul Masih V aba upon his arrival at Nasir Mosque in Bremen.

Huzoor takes a tour around the grounds of Nasir Mosque during his visit on May 18, 2004.

Hadhrat Khalifatul Masih V aba addresses the Jama'at at the opening Nasir Mosque.

Darmstadt

Nuurud Din Mosque was inaugurated in May of 2004 in Darmstadt , Germany by Hadhrat Khalifatul Masih V ^{aba}.

Hadhrat Khalifatul Masih V ^{aba} sits among Darmstadt Jama'at members at the opening of Nuurud Din Mosque.

Kassel

2005 - Foundation Ceremony

Hadhrat Khalifatul Masih V [aba] lays the foundation stone for Mahmood Mosque in Kassel, Germany, on August 31, 2005.

2007 - Inauguration Ceremony

Although the day of the inauguration ceremony was overcast and rainy, young Atfal and Nasirat energetically wave vividly colored German flags in anticipation of Huzoor's arrival.

A red-uniformed Tifl on traffic duty is blessed with a rare vantage point, as he watches Huzoor unveil a plaque commemorating the opening of Mahmood Mosque in Kassel, on September 4, 2007. The occasion happily coincides with a return of clear skies and a bit of sunshine.

2005 - Foundation Ceremony

Isselburg

Jama'at Ahmadiyya, Germany

Photo / Data: Jama'at Ahmadiyya, Germany

Hadhrat Khalifatul Masih V[aba] lays the foundation stone for Nasir Mosque in Isselburg, Germany, on September 26, 2005.

German and Arabic welcome slogans greet visitors of the Isselburg foundation ceremony.

Jama'at Ahmadiyya, Germany

2007 - Inauguration Ceremony

A welcome arch in the colors of the German flag was erected in front of Nasir Mosque on the occasion of its opening on January 3, 2007.

Jama'at Ahmadiyya, Germany

Hundreds of attendees, some of which are shown in this photograph, gather inside Nasir Mosque on the occasion of its opening ceremony.

Berlin

Three artists' renditions of the Khadija Mosque, planned for construction in the city of Berlin.

Dr. Detief Dezernbirzk, MP of Germany, is addressing attendees of the foundation stone-laying ceremony of Khadija Mosque in Berlin on January 2, 2007.

Commenting on *Jama'at* Germany, German Member of Parliament, Dr. Detief Dezernbirzk, remarked:

"*Jama'at* Ahmadiyya is like an open book. Its operations are an example for others to follow. Its youth not only speak good German language but they are getting higher education and mix well with the German people. He further said that he knows *Jama'at* Ahmadiyya for a long time and when he heard on television that the people of Helnsdorf were opposing *Jama'at* Ahmadiyya he could not believe [it]."

Details Concerning the Early Planning for the Khadijah Mosque

In a Friday sermon dated December 29, 2006, *Hadhrat Khalifatul Masih V* [aba] related the historic beginning of this mosque by narrating a statement by *Hadhrat Khalifatul Masih II* [ra]:

On February 2, 1923, Hadhrat Khalifatul Masih II [ra] *remarked on the construction of the Ahmadiyya mosque in Berlin, Germany:*

'After much thought, I have decided that the Mosque that is being constructed in Germany be made entirely with the financial contributions of the women of our Jama'at[...]It is often the case that husbands exert control over the the income of their households, and they do not have much cash left after they take care of the financial responsibility of the family. But women always have something left over in the form of their jewelry. It is for this reason that husbands take help from their wives during dire circumstances. It is for this reason nobody should wonder where women will find money to sacrifice. Women can give their financial contribution by giving up their jewelry.'

After narrating this statement of *Hadhrat Khalifatul Masih II* [ra], *Hadhrat Khalifatul Masih V* [aba] continued his sermon:

During the time of the second Khalifa, the Lajna in Germany contributed some seventy thousand francs. This money allowed the Jama'at to purchase land for the Mosque. However, the value of the franc plummeted, and the money eventually could not be used to fund completely the construction of the Mosque. As a result, the project remained closed for decades. During the time of fourth Khalifa, the Lajna in Germany pledged to make a mosque of their own in following with the second Khalifa's directives. Hadhrat Khalifatul Masih IV [rh] *granted the Lajna in Germany permission and named the mosque "Khadijah Mosque."*

In 2005, a plot of land was purchased in the city of Helnsdorf. The permission to build the Mosque was granted by the local authorities – the "Bezirksamt" – but the residents turned against that idea and opposed the construction. This opposition continued for a long time until the Interior Minister of Berlin reassured the residents by commenting: 'We have done much investigation and found the Ahmadiyya Muslim community to be a very peaceful organization. We have not found a single incident of lawlessness by this Jama'at.' With permission finally granted, the Lajna in Germany began the construction of the Khadijah Mosque in earnest.

Over 80 years after the original appeal of the second *Khalifa, Hadhrat Khalifatul Masih V* [aba] laid the foundation stone for the Khadijah Mosque in East Berlin on January 2, 2007, and said:

My main objective, and desire, that has brought me here was to lay the foundation stone of the Mosque of Berlin. From the minarets of our mosques, the rays of spiritual light of the last and the perfect religion of Allah will spread in all directions. These mosques will become the symbols of peace in this country.

IRELAND
Jama'at established in 2001

A view of Ha'Penny Bridge, in Dublin, Ireland.

ABOUT IRELAND

Just west of Great Britain, the country of Ireland occupies five-sixths of the island of Ireland in the North Atlantic Ocean. Of the 4.1 Million residents of Ireland who subscribe to a religion, 88% are Roman Catholic, 3% are of the Church of Ireland, and 2% are other types of Christians. The GDP is 187 billion with a per capita GDP of $45,000.

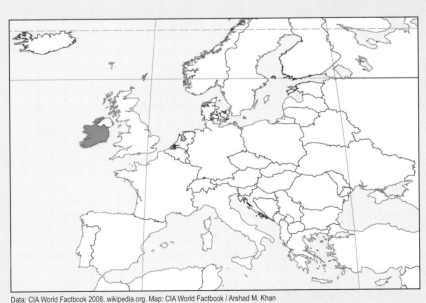

Donegal
Galway   Dublin
Limerick
Cork

Data: CIA World Factbook 2008, wikipedia.org. Map: CIA World Factbook / Arshad M. Khan

The Mission House of the Ahmadiyya Muslim Community of Ireland is located in the city of Galway.

Maulana Ibrahim Noonan, Ameer and Missionary-In-Charge Ireland, with members in front of the Mission House in Galway.

Dr. Aleemuddin Ahmad, National President, Jama'at Ireland.

On Tabligh Day at the Mission House in Galway, visitors read books of the Ahmadiyya Muslim Community.

Above: Hadhrat Khalifatul Masih IV [rh] converses with guests after his inaugural address at the Mission House in Galway. At left: Hadhrat Khalifatul Masih IV [rh] enjoys a walk with members of the Ireland Jama'at.

KOSOVO

Jama'at established in 1947
www.islam-ahmedia.org

A winter view of Kosovo's capital city, Pristina.

ABOUT KOSOVO

Kosovo, which declared its independence from Serbia on February 17, 2008, is the newest country in the world. This small southeast European nation is about 11,000 km² with a population of 2.1 million. 88% of the inhabitants are of Albanian ethnicity, and Albanian is the official language. The population includes Muslims, Serbian Orthodox, and Roman Catholics. The GDP of Kosovo is US $3.2 billion with a per capita income of US $1,800.

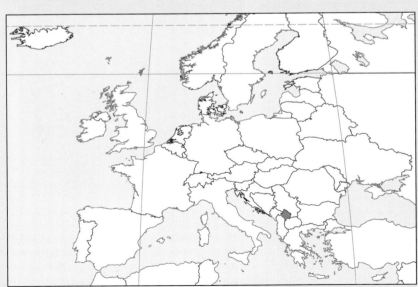

Data: CIA World Factbook 2008, wikipedia.org. Map: CIA World Factbook / Arshad M. Khan

Glimpses: Jalsa Salana, Kosovo

A group photo after Jalsa Salana Kosovo in 2007. Standing in the center (with green cap) is Amir Jama'at Germany. Standing to his right (with striped tie and black prayer cap) is Missionary Javaid Iqbal Nasir; and standing to the left of Amir Jama'at Germany is Mr. Musa Rustemi, the Amir of the Kosovo Jama'at.

Attendees of the Jalsa Salana, Kosovo in 2007.

Missionary Javaid Iqbal Nasir addresses the 2007 Jalsa gathering.

Another view of the 2007 Jalsa Salana in Kosovo.

Mr. Musa Rustemi, Amir Jama'at Kosovo, addressing attendees of the 2006 Jalsa.

Construction of the First Jama'at Center in Kosovo

All photos: Jama'at Ahmadiyya, Kosovo

In these photos, members of Majlis Khuddamul Ahmadiyya, Kosovo, are performing Waqare Amal duties to help prepare the concrete slab for the construction of the first Jama'at Center in Kosovo. Clockwise, from the top left: 1. A cement mixer arrives at the site; 2. A khadim takes a break from laying the re-bar skeleton for the slab by opening up a snack; 3. Khuddam distribute the cement evenly as it runs down the sluice from the cement mixer; 4. A khadim smooths out a portion of the slab.

"God desires to found a community of the faithful to manifest His Glory and Power.[...] He shall strengthen them with His own Spirit, and bless them, and purify them."

— Hadhrat Mirza Ghulam Ahmad[as], March 4, 1889.

THE NETHERLANDS
Jama'at established in 1947
www.ahmadiyya-islam.nl

The famous Peace Palace, the official home of the International Court of Justice, located at The Hague. The site of more international legal institutions than perhaps anywhere else in the world, The Hague is the city housing the official seat of government for The Netherlands, despite the fact that it is not the capital city.

ABOUT THE NETHERLANDS

Bordering the North Sea, the Netherlands is located between Belgium and Germany. It is almost twice the size of the state of New Jersey. The population is 61.6 million, and over 50% are Christian, 5% are Muslim, and 41% have no declared religion.

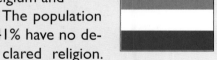

The GDP is $683.9 billion, and the per capita GDP is $38,600. The Netherlands is a founding member of NATO and the EEC. The Kingdom of the Netherlands was formed in 1815. In 1839, Belgium seceded and formed a separate kingdom.

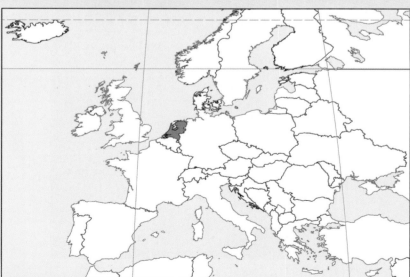

Data: CIA World Factbook 2008, wikipedia.org. Map: CIA World Factbook / Arshad M. Khan

Groningen
Amsterdam
The Hague
Utrecht
Middel-
Maastricht

The Mobarak Mosque in The Hague, Netherlands. This mosque was constructed in 1955 by funds donated by Ahmadi Muslim ladies of Lajna Imaillah, Pakistan. They collected Rs. 143,664. The initial scheme was made on May 12, 1950, the foundation was laid on May 20, 1953, and the inauguration was performed by Ch. Muhammad Zafrullah Khan^{ra} on December 9, 1955.

An Eid ul Adhea gathering at Mobarak Mosque, The Hague, Netherlands, circa 1965.

Ahmadi Muslims in Holland: Historic Highlights

(with contributions from Mr. Hamid Karim Mahmud, Missionary, Nunspeet, Holland)

1947 — *Jama'at* Ahmadiyya is registered in Holland.

1948 — *Hafiz* Qudratullah arrives from Pakistan as the first Missionary of *Jama'at* Ahmadiyya to Holland.

1953 — The first translation of the Holy Qur'an in the Dutch language is published. Chaudhry Muhammad Zafrullah Khan [ra] lays the foundation of Mobarak Mosque at The Hague.

1955 — *Hadhrat Khalifatul Masih II* [ra] arrives on June 18 and offers prayers for the completion of Mobarak Mosque at The Hague. On December 9, Chaudhry Muhammad Zafrullah Khan [ra] inaugurates the mosque, an event covered by the press. The funds for this mosque were donated by *Lajna Imaillah*, Pakistan.

1957 — Sir Abubakar Tafawa Balewa, a Minister in the Government of Nigeria, visits the Hague Mosque and discusses preaching activities in Holland with Sir Zafrullah Khan [ra].

1958 — Prince Fahd bin Faisal visits Mobarak Mosque to offer prayers.

1980 — *Hadhrat Khalifatul Masih III* [rh] arrives in Holland on August 4, and stays for three days. On August 5, he holds a press conference at the Dutch Parliament Press Room, where he is welcomed by officials of the Dutch Parliament. Over a dozen media representatives gather to ask *Huzoor* [rh] several questions.

1981 — *Hadhrat* Mirza Tahir Ahmad [rh], prior to his *Khilafat*, delivers a Friday Sermon at Mobarak Mosque.

1985 — On September 13, *Hadhrat Khalifatul Masih IV* [rh] inaugurates Baitun Noor Mosque in Nunspeet, Holland.

2008 — *Jama'at* Ahmadiyya Holland purchases a large center in Amsterdam. At present, two missionaries, Mr. Naeem Ahmed Warraich and Hamid Karim Mahmud, are serving the Holland *Jama'at*, and Mr. Hibatunnoor Verhagen is the current Amir *Jama'at* for Holland. The *Jama'at* Holland publishes a Dutch monthly magazine called *Al-Islaam*. *Jama'at* Holland is observing *Khilafat* Jubilee celebrations. For the sixteen *Jama'at* chapters in Holland, thirty-six *Khilafat Jalsas* are being organized in different cities.

Majlis Khuddamul Ahmadiyya, Karachi, Pakistan

The Missionary-In-Charge, Hafiz Qudratullah, Imam of the Hague Mosque, is seen in this circa 1962 photo delivering the Eidul Fitr sermon to the Ahmadi Muslim congregation.

Majlis Khuddamul Ahmadiyya, Karachi, Pakistan

Hafiz Qudratullah Sahib giving a gift to the Saudi prince in Holland.

Jama'at Ahmadiyya, The Netherlands

Hadhrat Mirza Tahir Ahmad [rh] *is seen here delivering a Friday sermon at Mobarak Mosque in 1981.*

Sir Chaudhry Muhammad Zafrullah Khan [ra] breaks ground for the construction of a new mosque in The Hague, Netherlands in 1953. The mosque, known as Mobarak Mosque, was constructed in 1955.

Sir Chaudhry Muhammad Zafrullah Khan [ra] greets the Honorable J. M. A. H. Luns, the Dutch Minister for Foreign Affairs, featured in the Dutch newspaper Het Vaderland on Feb 6, 1961.

Hadhrat Khalifatul Masih II [ra] Visits Holland

Hadhrat Khalifatul Masih II [ra] visits the famous Westbroekpark in The Hague on June 30, 1955. He is accompanied by his personal physician, Dr. Hashmatullah Khan and Jama'at Ahmadiyya missionaries.

This 1955 photograph shows Hadhrat Khalifatul Masih II [ra] leaving Mobarak Mosque at The Hague after offering prayers for the completion of its construction. On his left is Sahibzada Mirza Mubarak Ahmad, Secretary for Ahmadiyya Foreign Missions.

Hadhrat Khalifatul Masih III [rh] Visits Holland

Jama'at Ahmadiyya, The Netherlands

Hadhrat Khalifatul Masih III [rh] visits the Binnenhof in August, 1980. The Binnenhof is the site within The Hague where the Dutch Parliament has met since 1446. He is seen here conversing with Mr. de Beaufort, a member of the Dutch House of Commons.

Hadhrat Khalifatul Masih IV [rh] Visits Holland

Jama'at Ahmadiyya, The Netherlands

Hadhrat Khalifatul Masih IV [rh] with members of Jama'at Ahmadiyya, Holland, during his visit to the country in 1985.

Hadhrat Khalifatul Masih IV [rh] talks to attendees of a press conference held at the Hotel Veldzicht in Nunspeet, Holland in September 1985.

Hadhrat Khalifatul Masih V [aba] Visits Holland

Hadhrat Khalifatul Masih V [aba] presides over a session of the 26th Jalsa Salana Holland, held in 2006.

Checking his watch en route to the Jalsa site, Hadhrat Khalifatul Masih V [aba] illustrates his commitment to the cause of the Promised Messiah[as], who was told by divine revelation: "You are that Honorable Messiah whose time will not be wasted."

Hadhrat Khalifatul Masih V [aba] conducts a children's class on the occasion of his visit for Jalsa Salana, Holland in 2004.

The Visit of the Queen of the Netherlands at The Hague in 2006, on the Occasion of the 50th Anniversary of Mobarak Mosque

Preparations for Her Majesty's Arrival

Jama'at Ahmadiyya, The Netherlands

A view of Mobarek Mosque, as preparations are being made for Queen Beatrix's arrival.

Jama'at Ahmadiyya, The Netherlands

Under a sign that says, "Welcome, Your Majesty," children wave from inside the Mobarek mosque.

Jama'at Ahmadiyya, The Netherlands

The audio team makes preparations inside Mobarak Mosque.

Jama'at Ahmadiyya, The Netherlands

Preparations being made for the food reception just outside the mosque.

50th Anniversary Proceedings with Her Majesty

Three members of Nasiraat (young girls' group) make a presentation before Her Majesty.

The Amir of Jama'at Holland gives a welcome address.

Her Majesty is presented with a five volume Commentary of the Holy Qur'an.

Her Majesty enjoys a tour of the permanent photo exhibition inside Mobarak Mosque.

Members of Lajna Imaillah (Ahmadiyya ladies' organization) meet with Her Majesty.

Her Majesty departs from Mobarak Mosque.

Commemorative stamp issued by The Netherlands featuring Her Majesty Queen Beatrix.

NORWAY
Jama'at established in 1957

A panoramic view of Vestpollen, Lofoten Island, Norway. Despite being situated north of the Arctic Circle, Norway has mild temperatures and represents one of the world's most unusual climactic anomalies.

ABOUT NORWAY

From the 9th to the 11th centuries, Viking culture dominated the land now delineated as the Kingdom of Norway, and the Viking communities became united in the 10th century and embraced Christianity in 1030. After a period of expansion, Norway became unified at turns with Denmark, then Sweden, until Norway broke away in 1905. During World War I, the country remained neutral, but after Nazi occupation during World War II, the country embraced protection under NATO and was one of the founding members of the United Nations. Today, Norway's nearly 5 million inhabitants live in a democratic, constitutional republic that boasts vast oil and gas reserves and a national welfare system. The per capita GDP of the country is US $55,600, making it one of the wealthiest countries in the world.

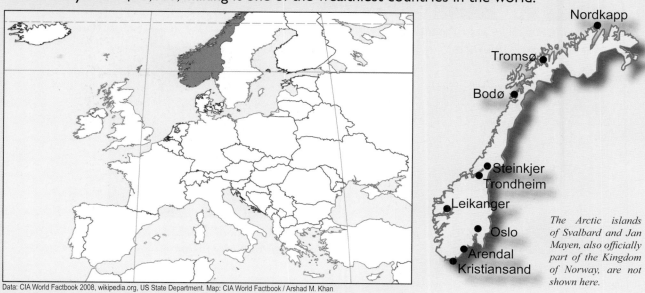

The Arctic islands of Svalbard and Jan Mayen, also officially part of the Kingdom of Norway, are not shown here.

Data: CIA World Factbook 2008, wikipedia.org, US State Department. Map: CIA World Factbook / Arshad M. Khan

A view of the Noor Mosque in Oslo, Norway.

Zartasht Munir, Ameer of the Ahmadiyya
Muslim Jama'at in Norway.

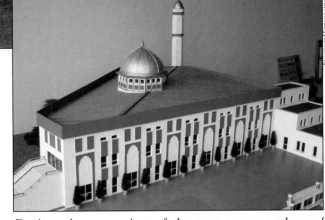

Designer's conception of the new mosque planned
for construction by Jama'at Ahmadiyya Norway.

Shahid Mahmood Kahloon,
Missionary-in-Charge for Norway.

Syed Kamal Yusuf served as the
first Ahmadi Muslim missionary to
Scandanivia.

Ahmadi Muslims in Norway: Historic Highlights

1932
Hadhrat Khalifatul Masih II [ra] sees in a vision that the residents of Norway, Finland, Sweden and Hungary are waiting to receive the message of Ahmadiyyat. This vision manifests itself as reality when a new convert from Sweden requests Huzoor [ra] to open a mission in the Scandanavian countries. Huzoor [ra] later would give permission of this activity during his July 22-25, 1955, tour in London.

1957
Noor Ahmad Truls Bolstad becomes the first Norwegian to become an Ahmadi Muslim.

1958
Syed Kamal Yusuf arrives in Norway on August 28 as a missionary serving all of Scandinavia. He establishes a headquarters in the capital city of Oslo.

1979
In December, a spacious building is purchased by the Ahmadiyya Muslim Community in Norway.

1980
Hadhrat Khalifatul Masih III [rh] inaugurates the this building as a mosque on August 1, during Friday prayers. On August 2, the citizens of Oslo congratulate Huzoor [rh] on the inauguration of this mosque.

Missionary Syed Kamal Yusuf leads Eid prayers in Oslo, Norway; circa 1962.

1982
Hadhrat Khalifatul Masih IV [rh] arrives in Norway on July 31. On August 5, he addresses members of the press and on August 6, he conducts the first *Majlis e Shura* (Executive Meeting of the Consultative Body) of Norway.

1986 to 1996
Hadhrat Khalifatul Masih IV [rh] visits Norway in 1986, 1987, 1991, 1993, and 1996. On June 24, 1993, he initiates a scheme to build a mosque at Nordkapp, stating in his sermon: "Today, we are making history. This history has no significance or value in the sight of worldly people. But today, I tell you that there are some histories which are preserved in the heavens rather than on earth… This small group which has come here today has no standing in the sight of the world, but calling Almighty God to witness, I say that a time will come when the history preserved in the heavens shall descend to the earth, and not only the people of Norway but the peoples of every other nation shall recall these days with pride and remember when a small group of humble ones came here, in fulfillment of the prophecy of the Holy Prophet Muhammad[sa] and proclaimed the name of the one God and offered Friday prayers here."

2005
Hadhrat Khalifatul Masih V [aba] arrives on September 19 in Oslo, and stays at the Ahmadiyya Muslim mission house. He addresses a reception held in his honor, which is attended by several government officials and dignitaries.

2006
The 24th Norway *Jalsa Salana* is held on September 16-17 at Marienlyst School in Oslo. Almost 800 people attend the auspicious event. Maulana Mubarak Ahmad Tanweer, from Germany, represents the *Markaz* (Ahmadiyya Muslim headquarters), and representatives of several of the major political parties in Norway also attend. During this event, the *Lajna Imaillah* (Ahmadiyya Muslim Ladies' Auxiliary) in Norway showcases a special exhibit on the meaning and significance of the word *jihad* in Islam, describing its use and misuse in popular culture.

2007
The 25th Norway *Jalsa Salana* is held on October 27-28 in Leto Hall, Ullensaker, located 45 km outside the capital city Oslo. Approximately 800 guests attend the *Jalsa* from different parts of Norway and other locations in Scandinavia. Mr. Naimatullah Basharat, the Ameer and Missionary of the Ahmadiyya Muslim Community in Denmark, represents *Markaz* (Ahmadiyya Muslim headquarters) at this occasion. Among the distinguished guests in attendance is the Mayor of the Ullensaker municipality, Mr. Harald Espelund. One government representative speaks on behalf of the Prime Minister of Norway, who sent his regards to *Jama'at* Ahmadiyya Norway. During this year's *Jalsa*, the *Lajna Imaillah* prepare a special exhibit on *Khilafat*, which is enjoyed by attendees.

Glimpses of the Visits of the *Khulufa* to Norway

Mr. Albert Nordengen, the Mayor of Oslo, Norway, meets with Hadhrat Khalifatul Masih III [rh] on August 2, 1980.

Circa 1986. Members of the Ahmadiyya Muslim Community in Norway pose for a group photo with Hadhrat Khalifatul Masih IV [rh].

A group photo of members of Jama'at Ahmadiyya, Norway, with Hadhrat Khalifatul Masih V [aba].

PORTUGAL

Jama'at established in 1957

A sunset view of Belém Tower. Located where the Tagus River, the longest river on the Iberian peninsula, empties into the Atlantic Ocean, the Belém Tower was constructed to defend the river entrance. Located in the Belém district of Portugal's capital city of Lisbon, the tower is a UNESCO World Heritage Site.

ABOUT PORTUGAL

Having been under Roman, Germanic or Arab/Berber rule for nearly twelve centuries, Portugal gained its national identity in 1140 under the monarchy of King Afonso I. In the 15th and 16th centuries, Portugal became an international colonial power. A "corporate" authoritarian government established in 1926 ended in 1974, after a bloodless coup by the military. A new constitution was ratified in 1976. Of Portugal's 11 million inhabitants, nearly 85% are Roman Catholic. A member of the European Union since 1986, Portugal's per capita GDP is about US $24,000.

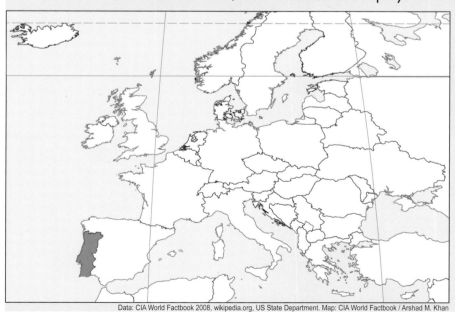

Data: CIA World Factbook 2008, wikipedia.org, US State Department. Map: CIA World Factbook / Arshad M. Khan

Jama'at Ahmadiyya, Portugal

Jorge Sampaio, the President of Portugal (1996-2006), meets with Hadhrat Khalifatul Masih IV[rh].

Jama'at Ahmadiyya, Portugal

A view of part of the library within the Ahmadiyya Mission House in Portugal.

Jama'at Ahmadiyya, Portugal

Members of the Majlis-e-Amila (Executive Body) for Jama'at Ahmadiyya, Portugal.

SPAIN
Jama'at established in 1946
www.alislam.org/spanish

A beautiful view at sunset of the Palace at Alhambra, with the Sierra Maestra Mountain range seen in the distance. Located in Granada, Spain, the Alhambra Palace has been listed as a UNESCO World Heritage Site.

ABOUT SPAIN

Spain remained neutral in World War I and II, but was caught in its own Civil War (1936-1939). Spain suffered from the the dictatorship of Francisco Franco until his death in 1975. The country gradually gained stability and has become a strong economic nation of Europe. Almost 40.5 million people live in Spain. The GDP of Spain is US $1.4 trillion, and the per capita GDP is $33,700. Most of its citizens adhere to Catholicisim (94%). After 744 years of Christian rule, Basharat Mosque was built in 1980.

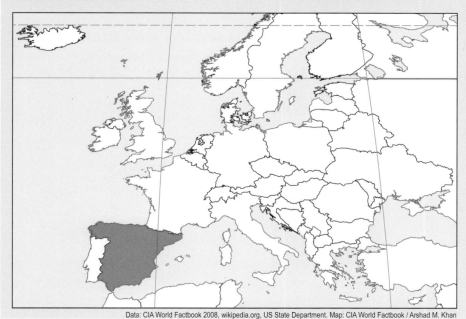

Data: CIA World Factbook 2008, wikipedia.org, US State Department. Map: CIA World Factbook / Arshad M. Khan

A view of Basharat Mosque, which is located in Pedro Abad, Spain.

*Mr. Mubarik Ahmad Khan,
Ameer Jama'at Spain*

*Mahboob ur Rahman Shafique Ahmad,
Missionary serving Madrid, Spain*

*Mr. Sayad Abdullah Nadeem Shah,
Missionary-in-Charge, Spain*

*Abdul Saboor Numan, Missionary
serving Valencia, Spain*

*Malik Tarik Mahmood, Missionary
serving Barcelona, Spain*

The Foundation Stone Ceremony for Basharat Mosque in Spain

Hadhrat Khalifatul Masih III [rh] visits the site assigned for the construction of Basharat Mosque, Spain.

Hadhrat Khalifatul Masih III [rh] lays the foundation stone for Basharat Mosque.

Hadhrat Khalifatul Masih III [rh] addresses the Jama'at during the foundation ceremony for Basharat Mosque. At Huzoor's immediate right stands Maulana Karam Ilahi Zafar, first Missionary to serve Spain. The late Maulana Sheikh Mubarak Ahmad is seen at far left in the photograph.

Hadhrat Khalifatul Masih III [rh] leads the Jama'at in congregational prayers during the foundation ceremony of Basharat Mosque.

Amor Para Todos, Odio Hacia Nadie

Members of the Jama'at pose for a group photograph with Hadhrat Khalifatul Masih III^{rh} on the occasion of the foundation ceremony for Basharat Mosque, Spain, in 1980.

The Inauguration Ceremony for Basharat Mosque in Spain

A historic photograph of Hadhrat Khalifatul Masih IV^{rh} on the occasion of the inauguration ceremony for Basharat Mosque, Spain, in 1982. Seated on Huzoor's right is Sir Muhammad Zafrullah Khan^{ra}, who served as President of the United Nations General Assembly (1962-1963) and also as the President of the International Court of Justice at the Hague (1970-1973). Seated to Huzoor's left is Dr. Abdus Salam, 1979 Nobel Laureate in Physics.

Ahmadi Muslims in Spain: Historic Highlights

711 General Musa sent Tariq bin Ziad with 7000 Berbers and 300 Arabs to retaliate against this tyranny. King Roderick prepared an army of 100,000 men to fight back. On July 19, 711, a fierce battle took place where Muslims troops, led by Tariq bin Ziad, succeeded in defeating the standing army of the King of Spain.

786 The mosque of Córdoba is erected.

1000 The population of Muslim inhabitants in Spain reaches its peak.

1492 Fall of Granada and the Arab/Berber Muslim rule in Spain

1835 Birth of the Promised Messiah [as]

1889 Birth of *Jama'at* Ahmadiyya

1908 *Hadhrat* Ahmad [as] passes away and *Khilafat e Ahmadiyya* begins.

1914 *Hadhrat Khalifatul Masih I* [ra] passes away and *Hadhrat* Mirza Bashiruddin Mahmud Ahmad [ra] takes this office.

1934 The *Tehrike Jadid* Scheme for the propagation of Islam is initiated.

1936 Malik Mohammad Sharif is sent as a missionary to Spain. However, since the country is confronted with civil war, he is directed to move to Italy instead.

1946 Two missionaries, Maulana Karam Ilahi Zafar and Mr. Mohammad Saqi, arrive in Spain. However, due to the civil unrest preceding the partition of India and Pakistan, it is decided to close down the mission in Spain. As a result, Mr. Saqi is sent to Trinidad. Mr. Zafar, however, requests *Hadhrat Khalifatul Masih II* [ra] to keep the mission open and volunteers to meet his expenses by working odd jobs. Permission is granted, and Mr. Zafar settles in Madrid and begins his missionary work by selling homemade perfume on a small cart in weekly open markets.

Majlis Khuddamul Ahmadiyya, Karachi, Pakistan

Missionary Karam Ilahi Zafar (at left), the Ahmadiyya Muslim Missionary in-Charge in Spain, is conversing with members of the Spanish military; circa 1962.

1970 *Hadhrat Khalifatul Masih III* [rh] arrives in Spain on May 25 and stays until June 1.

1975 After 31 years, the military dictatorship ends with the death of Francisco Franco, and a fresh round of democratic rule begins.

1980 The Government of Spain enacts a new ruling on July 5, in which religious freedom is granted to all adherents of various faiths. October 10 marks the happy occasion of establishing a mosque in Spain after 744 years, as the foundation stone of the Basharat Mosque is laid in Pedro Abad. The event marks the first such installation in Spain after the enactment of the new ruling. The Mayor of Pedro Abad attends the function and remarks that the event is of great significance for Pedro Abad's history, especially in light of the fact that the Ahmadiyya group was the first to benefit from the recent ruling granting religious freedom.

1982 *Hadhrat Khalifatul Masih IV* [rh] makes his very first trip (as Khalifa) to Spain and inaugurates the Basharat Mosque on Friday, September 10. At this occasion, there is a renewal of *Ba'ait* (Initiation) for the first time outside Pakistan. The First International *Shura* (consultative body session) is also held.

1985 Between October 11-15, *Hadhrat Khalifatul Masih IV*[rh] pays a second visit to Spain. In this trip, *Huzoor*[rh] addresses a press conference at Basharat Mosque, the Bulgarian Ambassador meets *Huzoor Aqdas*[rh] in Madrid and discusses the issues facing Bulgaria, and a large-scale seminar is organized at Hotel Alhambra Palace, where *Huzoor*[rh] addresses the intelligentsia of the country.

1990 During his third visit to Spain (March 9-15), *Hadhrat Khalifatul Masih IV*[th] addresses a group of city and other government officials at a dinner arranged by *Jama'at* Ahmadiyya Spain at the Gran Captain Hotel. The Civil Governor also visits Basharat Mosque for a personal *Mulaquat* with Huzoor Aqdas[rh]. On March 15, *Huzoor*[rh] delivers his famous lecture "An Elementary Study of Islam" at the University of Seville.

1992 During his fourth visit to Spain (May 18 - June 2), *Huzoor*[rh] attends the *Seville Expo'92*, the Universal Exposition organized on Cartuja Island in Seville. The Governor of Seville also dines with *Huzoor*[rh]. During this visit, BBC also records an interview with *Huzoor*[rh].

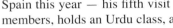

www.foundationexpo88.org, Creative Commons License.

1995 A Mission House in Algeciras is opened this year and, because of its location on the Gibraltar Pensinsula, this center becomes the source of the introduction of Ahmadiyyat in Morocco. During *Huzoor's*[rh] visit to Spain this year — his fifth visit to the country — he meets with *Jama'at* members, holds an Urdu class, and has some sightseeing tours.

Hadhrat Khalifatul Masih IV[rh] *attended Expo'92 in Seville, Spain.*

2003 Missions in Barcelona and Valencia are opened.

2004 *Jama'at* Ahmadiyya Spain welcomes *Hadhrat Khalifatul Masih V*[aba] during his first visit to Spain (Dec 31, 2004 - Jan 16, 2005). *Huzoor*[aba] traveled to Spain by road from France. He stayed at a hotel the first night and visits Pedro Abad on January 1. During his visit, Huzoor Aqdas[aba] addresses the 20th *Jalsa Salana* of *Jama'at* Ahmadiyya Spain. This *Jalsa Salana* was also especially noteworthy because a special message was sent for the occasion by the Prime Minister of Spain, José Luis Rodríguez Zapatero. This is the first time that the Head of the Spanish government sent a special message for such an occasion. This year marks the first time that any standing *Khalifatul Masih* attends the *Jalsa Salana* of Spain. This year also marks the first time that portions of *Jalsa Salana* Spain are televised worldwide via Muslim Television Ahmadiyya. Huzoor Aqdas[aba] launches an initiative to build an Ahmadiyya Muslim mosque in Valencia in the near future, and in all cities the *Jama'at* is currently engaged in with respect to *Tabligh* in the longer term. *Huzoor Aqdas*[aba] reiterates *Hadhrat Khalifatul Masih III*'s statement: "*The selection of this place to build the House of Allah is not made by me or by [Missionary] Karam Ilahi. Instead, the selection of this place has been done by Allah Himself, and this piece of land has been selected for the House of Allah. Insha'Allah, Allah's promise will be fulfilled, and the day will dawn when the sun of Islam and Ahmadiyyat will rise on this land.*" (*Al Fazl*, November 28, 2003).

2005 The Mission House at Valencia is purchased, and the plans for building a mosque begin. With this new purchase, *Jama'at* Ahmadiyya Spain has Mission Houses in Madrid, Barcelona, Pedro Abadand Valencia. Five Ahmadiyya Muslim Missionaries are working in the country.

The inauguration Ceremony of Basharat Mosque in Pedro Abad, Spain.

Maulana Karam Ilahi Zafar:
The Pioneering Ahmadi Muslim Missionary of Spain

Extract from the first Friday Sermon in Basharat Mosque by Hadhrat Khalifatul Masih IV [rh]

Jama'at Ahmadiyya, Spain

Hadhrat Khalifatul Masih IV [rh] delivers the Friday sermon at Basharat Mosque, Pedro Abad, Spain, on September 10, 1982.

"What I meant was the sacrifices given by Brother Karam Ilahi Sahib Zafar and his family. For a long time, this family made untiring efforts to serve Ahmadiyyat in times when the government was very strict, and it would not let even Christian missionaries preach. Under such circumstances, when there was no way for the *Jama'at* to help him, the financial situation was tight and the government had rigid rules and laws preventing the *Jama'at* from helping him in any way, he devoted himself with much zeal, and *Hadhrat Musleh Mauood* [ra] accepted his sacrifice. *Hadhrat Musleh Mauood* [ra] accepted it, and at the same time Allah's love accepted it also. It is the sweetness of the same fruit of sacrifice that we enjoy today.

I had an opportunity to visit Spain a long time ago, and I saw something that registered in my heart and memory for ever. It was a small mobile cart on which he [Missionary Karam Ilahi Zafar] would sell homemade perfume which he made himself. He would take care of *Jama'at* needs as well as his personal expenses from the little money he would make that way. It was in 1957 that I visited Spain along with Mir Mahmood *Sahib*. It was such a mobile cart that sometimes there was no space available for it to be parked. When the opposite parties found out about it, they would come and damage the cart. A few sympathetic shopkeepers would give him some space temporarily to park and sell. But after a little while, he had to leave and find another space.

His way of preaching was that he would sell his homemade perfume, would pay his personal expenses, and then whatever he could save, he would use it to order *Jama'at* literature on his own. There were times when his home was attacked by enemies. I saw myself the marking on the *Jama'at* sign board of stones that were pelted by people at it from time to time. The few new Ahmadies who accepted Islam used to meet in secret, like the people of "*Kahf*". People used to tell on them, and the enemies would come and attack them. They [newly convert Ahmadis] saved their lives and respect with much hardship.

Along with the homemade perfume, he [Missionary Karam Ihahi] also kept a small spray pump. When we got there he told us, "Look this is how I do my *Tabligh*." He would start spraying the perfume through the pump, and, out of curiosity, people would gather around him.

www.alislam.org/spanish

Maulana Karam Ilahi Zafar, shown here at the time of Hadhrat Khalifatul Masih II ra.

The Eastern fragrances he sold stirred much interest. He would tell people, "You see, this fragrance will not last on you for long. It might scent your clothes and garments for a few days, but then it would disappear after those garments are washed. It will go away in one, two or three or four days. But, I have another perfume whose fragrance is everlasting and never goes away. It will stay with you in this world, and it will stay with you in the world hereafter. If you want to find out more about this perfume of everlasting fragrance, then here is my business card. You can come over whenever you like and meet me. I will show what that fragrance is, and how you can get it." Some people would buy the perfume and go away, but others would take the card also. This is how some opportunities of preaching would come his way.

Jama'at Ahmadiyya, Spain

Hadhrat Khalifatul Masih IV rh holds his daughter steady for this photograph, which was taken at Pico de Mulhacén, continental Spain's highest mountain. Missionary Karam Ilahi Zafar is also pictured (center, wearing a turban).

Missionary Karam Ilahi Zafar, the Ahmadiyya Muslim Missionary-in-Charge in Spain, stands with delegates to the International Librarians' Congress, held in Madrid; circa 1960.

Hadhrat Khalifatul Masih V[aba] presides over the 20th Jalsa Salana of Spain

Jama'at Ahmadiyya, Spain

Hadhrat Khalifatul Masih V[aba] leads silent prayers during the 20th Annual Jalsa Salana of Spain.

Jama'at Ahmadiyya, Spain

The Ahmadiyya Missionaries who serve Spain meet with Hadhrat Khalifatul Masih V[aba].

Jama'at Ahmadiyya, Spain

Hadhrat Khalifatul Masih V[aba] making some notations during his visit to Alhambra Palace in Granada, Spain.

SWEDEN
Jama'at established in 1956
www.ahmadiyya.se

Photo: stock.xchng. User: mamil. Data: wikipedia.org.

A view of the "Ice Hotel" in the village of Jukkasjärvi, Sweden. Containing over eighty rooms, the Ice Hotel is sculpted entirely of ice blocks and is reconstructed from scratch every year. The popular tourist attraction is open only from December to April each year.

ABOUT SWEDEN

Sweden, which joined the European Union in 1995, has a long history of armed neutrality and economic success. The Scandinavian country is 450,000 km² with a population of 9 million. 87% of the inhabitants are Lutheran, and Swedish is the official language. The GDP of Sweden is US $432 billion with a per capita income of US $36,900.

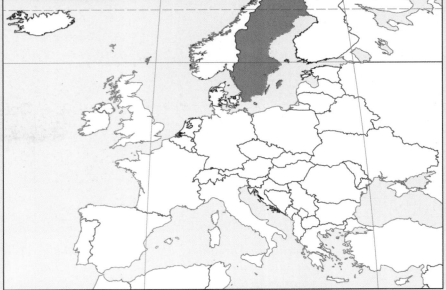

Data: CIA World Factbook 2008, wikipedia.org, US State Department. Map: CIA World Factbook / Arshad M. Khan

A view of Nasir Mosque, which is located in Göteborg, Sweden. It was built in 1975 and reconstructed in 1999.

A glimpse of the preparations being made to welcome Hadhrat Khalifatul Masih V [aba] at Nasir Mosque in Sweden in 2005.

Ahmadi Muslims in Sweden: Early Historic Highlights

1922 — *Hadhrat Khalifatul Masih II* [ra] sees a vision in which the people of Norway, Sweden, Denmark and Hungary are waiting for Ahmadiyyat. (*Al-Fazal*; July 3, 1956).

1955 — A Swedish man named Mr. Gunar Erickson meets *Hadhrat Khalifatul Masih II* [ra] and requests him to open an Ahmadiyya Mission in these countries. *Huzoor* [ra] accepts this request while at a conference in London, (July 22-24). (*Al-Fazal*; October 6, 1979)

1956 — On April 12, Syed Kamal Yousuf is sent to Sweden to open an Ahmadiyya Muslim Mission House. Accompanying him is Chaudhry Abdul Lateef. A place is rented, and the task of propagation begins. Syed Kamal Yousuf finds himself evicted from scores of rental properties, as he has a large host of people who visit him. The first Ahmadi in Sweden is Mr. Erickson, who becomes and joins the Ahmadiyya Muslim Community on August 7. He is a dedicated member and becomes an honorary Missionary of the *Jama'at*. He starts the first monthly magazine, *Active Islam*, which is published in three languages.

1969 — In April, Missionary Bashir Shams, who is temporarily staying in Denmark, receives a telephone call from a Yugoslavian man working in a small town near Denmark. Missionary Shams visits him upon his request, and when the two meet, the man relates: "I saw a dream that an angelic person with a thick white beard and wearing a turban came to me, and he had a paper in his hand known as *Ba'ait* paper. I have the feeling that this paper is the entry permit to Paradise." Mr. Shams showed him the picture of *Hadhrat Khalifatul Masih III* [rh]; he was overwhelmed and exclaims that this is the person who he saw in his vision. Missionary Shams explains to him the tenets of Islam and describes the *Ba'ait* Form. Without hesitation, he accepts and signs. *Hadhrat Khalifatul Masih III* [rh] advises the Missionary to stay in Sweden for another three months, during which time twenty-five more individuals more go on to accept Islam/Ahmadiyyat. (*Tehrik e Jadid*, July, 1969, page 21). The first meeting of European Missionaries is held in Sweden on Sept. 28 and is chaired by *Hadhrat Khalifatul Masih III* [rh].

1975 — *Hadhrat Khalifatul Masih III* [rh] lays the foundation for Nasir Mosque on September 27, 1975.

1976 — The inauguration of Nasir Mosque is held on August 20 by *Hadhrat Khalifatul Masih III* [rh]. Over forty Swedish newspapers cover the event.

1981 — On August 27, after a long struggle and persistent efforts, the Justice Department of Sweden gives written permission to the Ahmadiyya Muslim Missionary, to solemnize *Nikah* (marriage) ceremonies and naming rituals in the country.

1982 — On August 8, 1982, *Hadhrat Khalifatul Masih IV* [rh] arrives in Göteborg on his first visit to Sweden and stays for a few days. He addresses a press conference, meets with Ahmadi families, and responds to media questions.

On September 17, 2005, *Jama'at* Sweden arranged a reception dinner in honor of *Hadhrat Khalifatul Masih V* [aba]. Addressing the reception's attendees, he stated that Allah has mentioned in the Holy Qur'an that the foundation of a Mosque must be based on "*Taqwa*" (fear of God). The Holy Qur'an tells us to respect mosques as well as all places of worship regardless of religious affiliation. The mosque is dedicated to the worship of one God. It is intended to be a place of peace and love. This teaching of the Holy Qur'an embodies the goals of the Ahmadiyya *Jama'at* when it establishes mosques all over the world. [...]Our mosques are solely for the purpose of worshiping one God and for the establishment of peace. The purpose of our mosques is neither to provide beds for terrorism nor to generate hatred toward others. Our mosques are exclusively for the worship of our Creator and as such are open to all who seek to worship. *Huzoor* [aba] said that the reality of our *Jama'at* is that our hearts are full of love and acceptance for all of humankind, and we do not seek to express our ideology through words alone, but through actions. The Ahmadiyya *Jama'at* is taking active steps everyday in service of humanity. It is the belief of this *Jama'at* that if a person does not respect and fulfill the rights of humankind, then the rights of God never can be fulfilled. *Huzoor* [aba] said that it is the duty of all Ahmadis across the world to emulate this philosophy through their conduct. It is the duty of every Ahmadi to win the fellow hearts of humankind through peace and love. It is the duty of every Ahmadi to adopt *Taqwa* and to in turn love all of humanity. May Allah make this mosque a symbol of peace, a place of love and tranquility. (Extracted from *International Al-Fazal*, November 4, 2005).

© Bogdan Lozar | Dreamstime.com

SWITZERLAND

Jama'at established in 1946
www.ahmadiyya.ch

An early morning of Lake Thun, which is located in central Switzerland (see map, below right). The Swiss Alps are reflected in the tranquil lake waters, as does the famous Oberhofen Castle, which dates back to the Middle Ages.

ABOUT SWITZERLAND

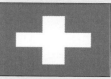

Switzerland started as a coalition of three local territories in Central Europe, beginning in 1291. In 1499, this confederation sought independence from the Roman Empire, and, in 1803, it emerged as a sovereign country. At the present time, it has 26 districts. As a neutral country, Switzerland did not participate in either of the World Wars. It joined the United Nations in 2002. The country's 7.55 million inhabitants contribute to creating a GDP of US $255.5 billion, with a per capita GDP of US $34,000.

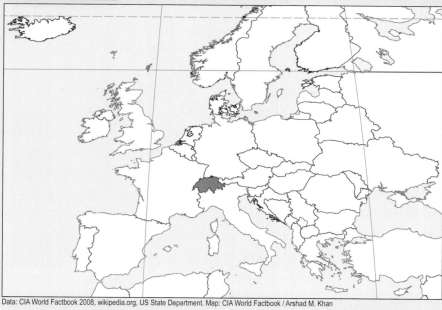

Data: CIA World Factbook 2008, wikipedia.org, US State Department. Map: CIA World Factbook / Arshad M. Khan

Ahmadiyya Mosques Around the World **245**

Mahmud Mosque, Zürich, Switzerland

Mr. Sadaquat Ahmad, the Imam of Mahmud Mosque.

Hadhrat Nawab Amtul Hafeez Begum Sahiba^{ra}, daughter of Hadhrat Mirza Ghulam Ahmad ^{as}, is laying the foundation stone of Mahmud Mosque in Zürich, Switzerland.

The Mayor of Zürich, Switzerland (standing at right) is seen here visiting Mahmud Mosque.

Majlis Khuddamul Ahmadiyya, Karachi, Pakistan

Hadhrat Khalifatul Masih II ^{ra} visited Switzerland during his second European tour and is seen here with a group of Ahmadi Muslims in Switzerland. Mr. Shaikh Nasir Ahmad, the Missionary for Switzerland, is standing at Huzoor's immediate left.

Jama'at Ahmadiyya, Switzerland.

Hadhrat Khalifatul Masih III ^{rh} is seen here with some Jama'at members in Switzerland.

Hadhrat Khalifatul Masih III ^{rh} addresses a press conference in Zürich.

Hadhrat Khalifatul Masih III ^{rh} is seen here in Switzerland conversing with Chaudhry Mushtaq Ahmad Bajwa, the Ahmadiyya Missionary serving Switzerland, and Sahibzada Mirza Mubarak Ahmad, Secretary of Ahmadiyya Muslim Foreign Missions.

Hadhrat Khalifatul Masih V ^{aba} (standing, center) in a 2004 group photo with members of the Majlis e Amila (Executive Body) of the Ahmadiyya Muslim Community of Switzerland.

Ahmadi Muslims in Switzerland: Historic Highlights

1946
The *Jama'at* sends three Ahmadi Muslim missionaries – Shaikh Nasir Ahmad, Chaudhry Abdul Latif and Ghulam Ahmad Bashir – to Germany. Due to visa difficulties, however, the missionaries arrive instead in Switzerland on October 13. Abdul Lateef and Ghulam Ahmad Bashir are sent to Holland, and Shaikh Nasir Ahmad remains in Switzerland.

1954
Shaikh Nasir Ahmad begins learning German and attains fluency to the extent that he translates the Holy Qur'an into German, complete with prefatory notes. A copy of this new translation is presented to the President of the Swiss Confederation, Rodolphe Rubattel in the Parliament House.

Majlis Khuddamul Ahmadiyya, Karachi, Pakistan

Members of the Ahmadiyya Community in Zurich, Switzerland, after offering Eid ul Fitr prayers, circa 1962. Standing in the center (with prayer cap) is Mr. Sheikh Nasir Ahmad, Missionary in-Charge in Switzerland.

1955
Hadhrat Khalifatul Masih II ra visits Switzerland twice this year. He lands in Geneva on May 8 and stays a month for medical consultation and treatment. On June 5, the *Jama'at* arranges a gathering in which *Huzoor* ra speaks briefly with members. On June 8, *Huzoor* ra gives an interview on Swiss television and departs for London on June 10. During his second visit on August 26, *Huzoor*ra comes to Zürich for medical treatment and stays at Bellvoir Park. On August 29, he addresses a press conference which was translated into English by *Hadhrat* Sir Muhammad Zafrullah Khan[ra] and into German by Shaikh Nasir Ahmad. On August 31, *Huzoor*ra gives a lecture at a local school introducing Islam and then leaves for Pakistan on September 2.

1962
The foundation of Mahmud Mosque is laid in Zürich.

1963
On June 22, *Hadhrat* Chaudhry Muhammad Zafrulla Khan[ra] inaugurates the Mosque.

1967 to 1980
Hadhrat Khalifatul Masih III rh visits Switzerland six times during his *Khilafat*: July 1967, April 1970, August 1973, September 1976, May 1978, and July 1980. In these visits, he addresses press conferences, meets with *Jama'at* members, and gives advice to individuals. Dr. Sigmund Widmer, then Mayor of Zürich, gives *Huzoor* rh a warm welcome at the Municipal Building in 1980.

1982 to 1992
Hadhrat Khalifatul Masih IV rh also visits Switzerland six times. The first visit was prior to his being *Khalifa*, and the other five visits were made between 1982-1992. In 1985, *Huzoor* rh holds a question and answer session at a reception that was arranged by the *Jama'at* at Nova Park Hotel. Guests from all walks of life participate and enjoy this session. In 1987, he gives his famous "Revelation, Knowledge and Truth" lecture at the prestigious University of Zürich. This lecture becomes the source of his later masterpiece book *Revelation, Rationality, Knowledge and Truth*. Shaikh Nasir Ahmad has the honor of translating the lecture simultaneously into German language. The auditorium is the same one in which Winston Churchill gave his famous "Let Europe Rise" lecture. In 1988, a 25-year "Silver Jubilee" celebration is held, and extensions are made for a women's area and office space on the mosque property. The last visit of *Huzoor*rh takes place in 1992, when he attends the first and the last day of *Ijtema* of *Majlis Ansarullah*, delivers the opening and closing addresses, and holds a question and answer session. During his 1992 tour, *Hadhrat Khalifatul Masih IV* rh advises the *Jama'at* to acquire another parcel of land, as the mosque had become insufficient for the needs of the *Jama'at*. Accordingly, the *Jama'at* successfully purchases a 6,727 m^2 plot of land about 54 km from Zürich in the municipality of Wigoltingen. This land already had a three-story structure with 15 rooms and two halls.

2004
Hadhrat Khalifatul Masih V aba visits Switzerland in September, where he addresses the *Jalsa Salana* of Switzerland. Over 1,050 members from ten different countries attend the Jalsa – the largest attendance for a *Jalsa* in Switzerland since 1983.

© Darren Baker | Dreamstime.com

The Big Ben clock tower and the Houses of Parliament in London, England, as viewed at night from Westminster Bridge.

ABOUT THE UNITED KINGDOM

Britain was one of the leading colonial powers until the mid-20th century; its domain stretched over one-fourth of the earth's surface. By the latter half of the twentieth century, most colonies had declared independence from British rule. Britain is one of the founding nations of NATO and a member of EU. 60.9 million strong, the U.K. has a GDP of 2.147 Trillion and enjoys a per capita of $ 35300. Over 71% people are Christian and 2.9%, Muslim.

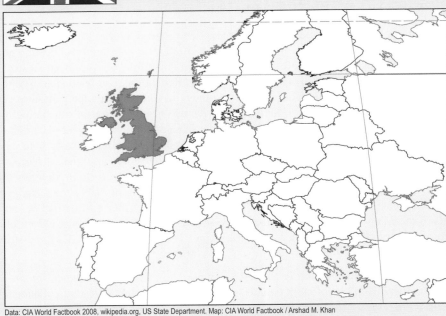

Data: CIA World Factbook 2008, wikipedia.org, US State Department. Map: CIA World Factbook / Arshad M. Khan

Britain's "Firsts"

*Ch. Fateh Muhammad Sial,
the First Missionary to U.K.*

*Mr. G. Sparrow, the First Ahmadi
resident of U.K. He joined in 1913.*

The U.K. Jama'at's Current Leadership

*Rafiq Ahmad Hayat,
Amir, Jama'at U.K.*

*Maulana Ataul Mujeeb Rashid,
Missionary-in-Charge, U.K.*

Britain's Recent Past

*Aftab Ahmad Khan,
Former Amir, Jama'at U.K.*

*Ch. Hidayatullah Bangvi,
Former Officer, Jalsa Salana U.K.*

Ahmadi Muslims in the United Kingdom: Historic Highlights

1912 The United Kingdom *Jama'at* is established this year. The first missionary sent to the country is Choudhry Fateh Mohammad Sial[ra].

1914 As per the instructions of *Hadhrat Musleh e Mauood*[ra], Choudhry Sial[ra] acquires a house on 63 Melrose Road, establishing the first Ahmadiyya Mission House in the U.K.

1916 Qazi Mohammad Abdullah[ra] is sent for two years to London to serve the community.

1918 Mufti Mohammad Sadiq[ra] arrives in the U.K. and stays until 1920. This year, through his efforts, Mr. Sparrow is the first British resident to become an Ahmadi Muslim.

1919 Choudhry Fateh Mohammad Sial[ra], the first Ahmadiyya missionary sent to the U.K. in 1912, returns to serve the UK this year, along with Abdul Raheem Nayyar[ra].

1920 Mubarak Ali arrives in the U.K. and remains in the country for three years. Choudhry Fateh Mohammad Sial[ra] works diligently to obtain land for a mosque and succeeds in buying a parcel of land with a built-in house for the price of £2,223.

1924 *Hadhrat Khalifatul Masih II*[ra] arrives in London in July to attend the Wembley Conference, and Chaudhry Muhammad Zafrullah Khan[ra] reads *Huzoor*'s essay entitled, "Ahmadiyyat the True Islam" to the conference attendees. On October 19, *Huzoor*[ra] lays the foundation stone of the Fazl Mosque in London and delivers his first address at the mosque on October 24. This year, *Huzoor*[ra] establishes England as the host country for the publication of *The Review of Religions* magazine.

1925 On May 11, Malik Ghulam Farid is appointed as *Imam* of the London Mosque and begins working with Abdul Rahim Nayyar[ra].

1926 On October 3, Shaikh Abdul Qadir, member of the Indian Delegation for the League of Nations, inaugurates the Fazl Mosque.

1933 Abdur Raheem Dard, at the instruction of *Hadhrat Khalifatul Masih II*[ra], persuades *Qaid e Azam*, Mohammad Ali Jinnah, to transfer his residence from England to India in order to help promote a separate state for the Muslims. At a reception held in England in his honor, *Qaid e Azam* remarks that at *Hadhrat Khalifatul Masih II*'s request, he felt compelled to return to India.

1940s *Maulana* Jalal ud Din Shams spearheads Tabligh efforts in London and peacefully holds many public debates. He also publishes his famous book entitled, *Where did Jesus die?*.

1961 *The Muslim Herald* starts its publication from the U.K.

1963 The first *Jalsa Salana* (Annual Gathering) of the U.K. Ahmadiyya Muslim Community is held.

1970 Mahmud Hall was built adjacent to the London Mosque to cater to the expanding needs of the *Jama'at*.

1978 *Hadhrat Khalifatul Masih III*[rh] makes a tour of the U.K., and announces the establishment of five new mission houses in England. He also participates in a conference on the crucifixion of Jesus[as].

1980 *Hadhrat Khalifatul Masih III*[rh] makes another tour of the U.K. this year and announces the establishment of Ahmadiyya Mission Houses in Bradford, Huddersfield, Manchester, Birmingham and Southall.

1984 *Hadhrat Khalifatul Masih IV*[rh] emigrates from Pakistan, marking a new era of *Jama'at* progress worldwide, and arrives in London to a warm welcome by the Ahmadiyya Muslim Community. The *Jalsa Salana* (Annual Gathering) of the U.K. *Jama'at* is transformed into an international *Jalsa Salana*, and a huge influx of people from all over the world participate in the auspicious gathering. *Huzoor*[rh] delivers the first Friday Sermon on May 4, after migration. On August 25th this year U.K. *Jalsa* was held with *Huzoor's* presence.

1985 — *Hadhrat* Chaudhry Zafrullah Khan[ra] passes away.

1986 — In March, *Huzoor*[rh] introduces *Syedna Bilal* Fund, and in October he draws attention to the plight of El Salvador. The response from the *Jama'at* to alleviate their suffering is overwhelming.

1987 — Among other tours, *Huzoor*[rh] travels to USA and addresses *Jalsa Salana* USA. In this trip he lays the foundation of Baitul Hameed Mosque in Los Angeles and inaugurates mosques in Tucson and Portland, Oregon.

1988 — Invitation to *Mubahila* and its main results: the miraculous reappearance of Aslam Qureshi and the end of Ziaul Haq's regime in Pakistan.

1989 — *Huzoor*[rh] travels to USA and Canada and addresses their respective *Jalsas Salana*.

1991 — *Huzoor*[rh] travels to Qadian. This is the first time any *Khalifa* goes to Qadian since the partition of Pakistan from India in 1947.

1992 — This year, Friday sermons and *Jalsa Salana* U.K. were broadcast via MTA (Muslim Television Ahmadiyya). *Huzoor*[rh] tours Canada and inaugurates Baitul Islam in Toronto, Canada. For the first time, *Huzoor*[rh] addresses Jalsa Qadian in December live from U.K. via MTA.

1993 — The first International *Ba'ait* is added to the *Jalsa* U.K. Program.

1994 — MTA daily broadcasting begins. *Huzoor*[rh] travels to the U.S. and inaugurates Baitur Rahman in Silver Spring, Maryland.

1995 — The humanitarian relief organization, Humanity First, is established.

1998 — *Huzoor*[rh] travels to the West Coast of United States and inaugurates Baitul Baseer Mosque in Silicon Valley, California. This was *Huzoor's*[rh] last visit to the United States.

1999 — *Huzoor*[rh] lays the foundation of Baitul Futooh Mosque on October 19.

2001 — *Huzoor*[rh] delivers news at the UK *Jalsa* that Ahmadiyyat has spread to each of the 54 countries on the African continent.

2003 — *Huzoor*[rh] introduces the Maryam *Shaadi* Fund for the financial support of economically-disadvantaged brides. On April 19, he passes away. The *Jama'at* elects *Hadhrat* Mirza Masroor Ahmad[aba] to be *Khalifatul Masih V*, who begins his office on April 23. The funeral prayers are arranged for our late *Huzoor*[rh], and the entire proceedings are shown live on MTA to a worldwide audience.

2005 to 2007 — Fifteen new mosques are established during this nineteen-year period in various parts of England, including Darul Barkat in Birmingham, Baitul Futuh in London (Europe's largest mosque), Baitul Mu'eed in Cambridge, Baitus Subhan in Croydon, Baitul Ahad in East London, Earlsfield Mosque in Earlsfield, Baitur Rahman in Glasgow, Baitun Noor in Hounslow, Baitus Salam in Islamabad, Bait ul Ikram in Leicester, Darul Aman in Manchester, Baitul Shukoor in Oxford, Baitul Islam in Scunthorpe, and the Ahmadiyya Center in Tooting.

Greater London

1 City of London
2 City of Westminster
3 Kensington & Chelsea
4 Hammersmith & Fulham
5 Wandsworth
6 Lambeth
7 Southwark
8 Tower Hamlets
9 Hackney
10 Islington
11 Camden
12 Brent
13 Ealing
14 Hounslow
15 Richmond upon Thames
16 Kingston upon Thames
17 Merton
18 Sutton
19 Croydon
20 Bromley
21 Lewisham
22 Greenwich
23 Bexley
24 Havering
25 Barking & Dagenham
26 Redbridge
27 Newham
28 Waltham Forest
29 Haringey
30 Enfield
31 Barnet
32 Harrow
33 Hillingdon

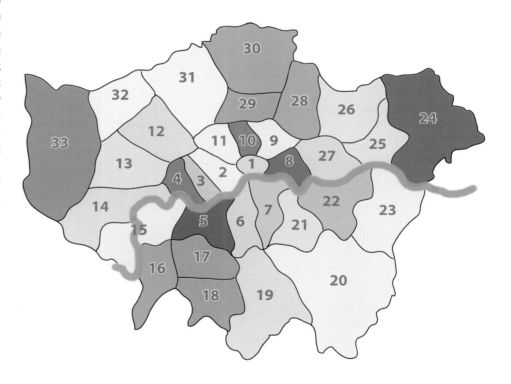

The City of London and its 32 Boroughs

Map of London drawing and art work by Arshad Khan, adapted from wikipedia.org. Data: wikipedia.org.

This stunning photograph of London, taken by Mr. David Iliff from the Golden Gallery in St. Paul's Cathedral, showcases the cityscape near the River Thames. For more of Mr. Iliff's amazing photos, please visit http://en.wikipedia.org/wiki/User: Diliff.

I saw in a vision that I was standing on a pulpit in the city of London and was setting forth in a well-reasoned address in the English language the truth of Islam. Thereafter, I caught several birds that were sitting upon small trees and were white in color, and their bodies resembled the bodies of partridges. I interpreted this vision as meaning that though I would not be able to travel to that country, my writings would be published there, and many righteous English people would accept the truth. (Izala Auham, pages 515-16)

Hadhrat Khalifatul Masih II[ra] during his trip to London in 1955.

This pair of photos courtesy of Jama'at Ahmadiyya, United Kingdom.

Greater London

The first mosque to be built in London (constructed in 1924), the Fazl Mosque is now an important city landmark.

A group of schoolchildren pay a visit to the London Mosque in 1987. Mr. Ataul Mujeeb Rashed, the Missionary in Charge of the U.K. Jama'at, is standing at the back left.

The Foundation Ceremony for the Fazl Mosque In London

Jama'at Ahmadiyya, United Kingdom

A glimpse of the historic foundation stone laying ceremony for the London Mosque. Hadhrat Khalifatul Masih II ra performed the ceremony on October 19, 1924.

Inscription on the London Mosque

IN THE NAME OF ALLAH THE MOST BENEFICENT AND THE MOST COMPASSIONATE. WE PRAISE AND INVOKE HIS BLESSINGS ON HIS PROPHET THE EXALTED ONE. WITH THE GRACE AND MERCY OF GOD; HE ALONE IS THE HELPER.

Verily, my prayer, my sacrifice, my life and my death are for Allah, the Lord of all the worlds.

I, Mirza Bashiruddin Mahmud Ahmad, Khalifatul Masih II, Head of the Ahmadiyya Community which has its headquarters at Qadian, Punjab, India, lay the foundation stone of this mosque today, the 20th of Rabiul Awwal, 1343 Hijra, to seek the pleasure of God so that His name be glorified in England and that the people of this country may also partake of the blessings which have been vouchsafed to us. I pray to God that He may accept this humble and sincere effort of all the members of the Ahmadiyya Community, both women and men, and that He may provide means for the growing prosperity of this mosque, and may He make it forever and ever a centre for promulgating the views of purity, piety, justice and love; and may this place prove a sun of spiritual light radiating forth in this country and in all the countries around the blessed beams of the Heavenly light of the Holy Prophet Muhammad, the Chosen One of God and Seal of the prophets, and of Ahmad, the Promised Messiah, the prophet of God, the Vicegerent and the reflection of Muhammad (may peace and the blessings of God be upon them both). Amen. 19.10.1924.

Greater London

The London Borough of Merton

Baitul Futuh Mosque

www.baitulfutuh.org

Jama'at Ahmadiyya, United Kingdom

Baitul Futuh Mosque is located in Morden, a town in the London borough of Merton.

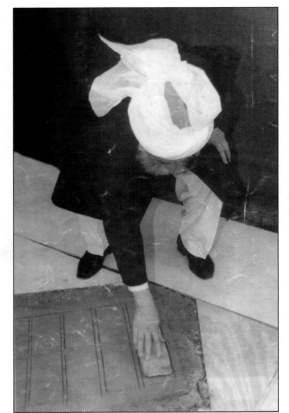

Left: Hadhrat Khalifatul Masih IV^{rh} is laying the foundation stone of Baitul Futuh Mosque on October 19, 1999. Above: The architect's sketch of Baitul Futuh Mosque.

Baitul Futuh Mosque has been named the 49th best building in the world, according to "The Independent" magazine, dated October 18-24, 2003. The periodical states: "Its 50-foot steel dome and 100-foot minaret are an exotic addition to this South London suburb."

Members of Parliament and other distinguished guests visit Baitul Futuh Mosque on April 19, 2007.

Speaking at a dinner held to celebrate the inauguration of Baitul Futuh Mosque in London, *Hadhrat Khalifatul Masih V*[aba] said: "Islam teaches us to always be mindful towards God Who is our Creator and to always keep His memory fresh in our hearts and to deal with His creation with love, affection, harmony and tolerance. This is the sum total of the teaching given to us by Muhammad, the Holy Prophet of Islam[sa]. So, if this is the teaching of this religion, how can slogans of hatred be shouted from the rooftops of its mosques that are supposed to be the places of worship of its followers?"

The Founder of Ahmadiyya Muslim community, *Hadhrat* Mirza Ghulam Ahmad[as], the Promised Messiah, states:

"A true Muslim, who is aware of the teachings of his faith, will always remain sincere and obedient to the government under whose benign shadow he lives his life in peace. Religious difference does not prevent him from true obedience and compliance." (*Tohfa Qaisariya*, p. 29). [...] As I said earlier, man has been created for only two purposes and they are that man should worship the One and only God and to interact kindly with God's creation. To achieve these objectives, mosques are built. In view of this objective, the Ahmadiyya Muslim community is pressed into the building of mosques in all corners of the world. Just as with those mosques, this mosque of the Ahmadiyya community is a symbol of peace. I urge you, that irrespective of your faith, creed, race or nationality, you should create in your own areas an atmosphere of peace, and help a suffering humanity."

Baitul Futuh Mosque

Hadhrat Khalifatul Masih V ^{aba} at the inauguration of Baitul Futuh mosque. Seated with him are the Amirs of Germany, USA, UK, and Ghana.

Hadhrat Khalifatul Masih V ^{aba} receives sweets from a young Tifl at the inauguration of Baitul Futuh Mosque.

Greater London

Baitul Ahad, East London

Baitus Salam, Southall

Baitun Noor, Hounslow

Baitus Subhan, Croydon

*Jamia Ahmadiyya, U.K.,
Colliers Wood*

Gillingham

Jama'at Ahmadiyya, United Kingdom

In September, 1982, Nasir Hall opened in Gillingham.

Oxford

Jama'at Ahmadiyya, United Kingdom

Baitul Shukoor, Oxford.

Jama'at Ahmadiyya, United Kingdom

Birmingham

Darul Barakaat opened in 2004 in Birmingham, U.K to widespread press coverage.

Hadhrat Khalifatul Masih V[aba] concluded his inaugural address with this beautiful prayer:

"O Allah we are one, we are one in the building of the mosque and in congregational prayers. And we are one even after we come out of the mosque because it is your commandment that Muslims are brothers to each other. We Ahmadis are fortunate that we have accepted the Imam of the Age to uphold your unity. And O God, you have strengthened us with *Khilafat* after the Messiah of the age. You have kept us as one and have given us solace and tranquility and strength. We pray by seeking your Grace and earnestly request that you keep this beauty with us. Give us the ability to be grateful to you and remain true worshippers. The house we have built to uphold your *Tauheed* (Unity) and worship, pray that we are able to frequently visit it and populate it." (Inauguration address of *Hadhrat Khalifatul Masih V*[aba], October 1, 2004. Reproduced in *Al-Fazl International*, September 30-October 7, 2004)

Jama'at Ahmadiyya, United Kingdom

Bradford

Baitul Hamd in Bradford, U.K.

Manchester

Darul Aman Mosque

Sheffield

Baitul Aafiat Mosque

Huddersfield

Baitus Samad Mosque

Hartlepool

Jama'at Ahmadiyya, United Kingdom

Nasir Mosque, in Hartlepool, U.K.

Hadhrat Khalifatul Masih V^{aba} performs the groundbreaking ceremony for Hartlepool Mosque.

Other Historical Pictures in the U.K.

Hadhrat Khalifatul Masih III[rh] is being interviewed by a reporter. Seated next to him is Chaudhry Muhammad Zafrulla Khan[ra].

Hadhrat Khalifatul Masih III[rh] with other elders of the Jama'at. Sahibzada Mirza Tahir Ahmad[rh] is seen standing in the back, Ch. Muhammad Zafrulla Khan[ra] is seated at Huzoor's[rh] left, and M.M. Ahmad Sahib at his right. Maulana Abdul Malik Khan is seated on the extreme right.

All photos this page: Jama'at Ahmadiyya, United Kingdom

Hadhrat Khalifatul Masih IV[rh] delivers an historic address on the occasion of the Jama'at Ahmadiyya Centennial celebration on March 23, 1989.

North America

Ahmadiyyat was introduced to the North American continent in 1921, with the pioneering efforts of *Hadhrat* Mufti Muhammad Sadiq [ra]. With its introduction into Canada by 1963, the *Jama'at* had grown into scores of individial chapters across the continent. The 100th anniversary of the founding of the *Jama'at* was marked by its introduction in the country of Guatemala in 1989.

Photos clockwise from upper left: Jama'at Ahmadiyya, USA; Jama'at Ahmadiyya, Canada, Jama'at Ahmadiyya, USA; Jama'at Ahmadiyya, Canada; Jama'at Ahmadiyya, USA; Jama'at Ahmadiyya, Guatemala.

CANADA

Jama'at established in 1963
www.ahmadiyya.ca

A painting of Baitul Islam Mosque by Martha Eleen, presented at the LOOP Gallery in Toronto in January, 2007

ABOUT CANADA

Canada, which became a self-governing nation in 1867, is the second largest country in the world (smaller only to Russia), comprising nearly 10 million km² of total area. Over 33 million people live in Canada, of which nearly 60% speak English and 23% speak French (both official languages). 43% of the population is Roman Catholic, followed by Protestants (23%), other Christian demoninations (4%) and Muslims (2%). The GDP of Canada is US $1.4 trillion, with a per capita income of US $38,200.

CIA World Factbook

Toronto, Ontario, Canada

Baitul Islam Mosque in Vaughan, near Toronto, Canada.

Scenes of Hadhrat Khalifatul Masih V^{aba} arriving at Baitul Islam Mosque in 2005.

Maulana Naseem Mahdi,
Missionary-in-Charge, Canada

Lal Khan Malik
Amir of Canada

baitul islam

We are extremely grateful to God Almighty that He enabled us to undertake this sacred project of building a House of God in this beautiful country. There is a special reason and it carries historic importance in construction of this mosque, of which the audience is unaware. People of this place are also unaware of why we have come here and what are our intentions in building this beautiful mosque. During these days, places of worship have become the hub of political activity and the center of subversive movements... I would like to make it abundantly clear that wherever we shall build mosques and places of worship, they will all be for the sacred cause explained by the Holy Qur'an. They will not be built to spread enmity, hatred or terrorism. They will strive with every nerve to establish love and peace in their surroundings. This is only due to the fact that we are a peace-loving community. (Excerpt of an address by *Hadhrat Khalifatul Masih IV*[rh] at the foundation laying ceremony of Baitul Islam Mosque, *Ahmadiyya Gazette Canada*, Nov-Dec 2003, page 49).

Peace Village, Ontario, Canada

Jama'at Ahmadiyya, Canada

Huzoor's [aba] tour of Peace Village in June, 2005.

Peace Village, adjacent to Baitul Islam Mosque

Jama'at Ahmadiyya, Canada

www.peacevillage.ca

Aerial view of Peace Village. The first phase of housing construction (comprising 260 homes on a 50-acre parcel of land) was complete in 2000. The village includes parks and playgrounds.

Ahmadiyyat in Canada: A Brief Timeline

1940 Shaikh Karam Deen settles in Nova Scotia and becomes the first Ahmadi in Canada.

1963 The seed of Ahmadiyyat is sown in Montreal, where the first *Jama'at* is established. Dr. Khalifa Abdul Momin becomes the President.

1966 A *Jama'at* is established in Toronto. Mian Ataullah is named the President. The Ahmadiyya Movement in Islam is officially registered with the government of Ontario.

1967 Syed Tahir Ahmad Bukhari becomes the first Amir of the Canadian *Jama'at*.

1974 Barrister Abdul Aziz Khalifa becomes National President of the Canadian *Jama'at*.

1976 *Hadhrat Khalifatul Masih III* [rh] makes his first visit to Canada (August 8-11, 1976). *Huzoor* [rh] holds a press conference and unveils plans for the establishment of a mission house in Canada. A conference with representatives of all *Jama'ats* is held in Toronto.

Jama'at Ahmadiyya, Canada

Hadhrat Khalifatul Masih III [rh] *at a press conference during his visit to Canada.*

1977 Syed Mansoor Ahmad Basheer arrives on March 22 and becomes the first Missionary to Canada. He establishes the first Canadian mission in Toronto.

The first *Jalsa Salana* Canada is held on December 25-26 in Toronto.

Syed Mansoor Ahmad Basheer starts a religious quarterly journal entitled *The Light*. This could not be continued after his departure in 1980.

1979 The first mission house in Calgary is purchased in January, and the first mission house in Saskatoon is purchased in June.

1980

Hadhrat Khalifatul Masih III[rh] makes his second visit to Canada (September 4-11) with trips to Calgary and Toronto (where he leads Friday prayers).

Hamidullah Shah (the President of the Calgary *Jama'at*) distributes the Holy Qur'an to communities in the Arctic Circle near the North Pole. *Huzoor*[rh] expresses his pleasure at this effort by presenting the gift of the *Commentary of Surah Al-Fatiha* (written by *Hadhrat Ahmad*[as]) to the Calgary *Jama'at*.

On September 8, 1980, *Huzoor*[rh] visits the Calgary mission house at 12th Avenue. He also participates in an educational dialogue with professors from the University of Calgary.

On November 12, 1980, Muniruddin Shams arrives in Canada as the second missionary.

1982

Buildings are purchased in Montreal (Al Nusrat Mosque) in January and Vancouver (Bait-u-Dua) in October. Saeed Ahmad Azhar is stationed in Calgary and Maulana Ali Haider Uppal is assigned to Vancouver, British Columbia.

1985

Naseem Mahdi arrives on May 5 as the third Missionary-in-Charge of Canada. A 25-acre parcel of land is acquired in December in Maple, Canada. The property features a three-story house with 22 rooms and 18 bathrooms with two halls and a double garage.

1986

On September 20, *Hadhrat Khalifatul Masih IV*[rh] lays the foundation stone of Baitul Islam Mosque in Toronto.

1992

On October 17, *Hadhrat Khalifatul Masih IV*[rh] inaugurates Baitul Islam Mosque.

Nine proclamations are issued by municipalities all across Canada, declaring October 17, 1992, as "Ahmadiyya Mosque Day" and October 16-23 as "Ahmadiyya Mosque Week."

Huzoor's[rh] Friday Sermon on October 16 from Baitul Islam Mosque becomes the first live worldwide telecast on MTA.

Jama'at Ahmadiyya, Canada

Hadhrat Khalifatul Masih IV[rh] *during a visit to Canada in June, 1989, for Ahmadiyya centennial celebrations.*

1992-2007

In these fifteen years, *Hadhrat Khalifatul Masih IV*[rh] visits Canada in 1994, 1996 and 1997. Peace Village is built in 1997, and a building is purchased in Hamilton (Masjid Al Noor). Jamia Ahmadiyya Canada is inaugurated in Mississauga in 2003. *Hadhrat Khalifatul Masih V*[aba] visits Canada for the first time, in 2004. He visits again in 2005 and lays the foundation of Baitur Rahman in Vancouver, Masjid Noor in Calgary, and a mosque in Bramptom. He also inaugurates Baitul Mahdi in Durham.

Jama'at Ahmadiyya, Canada

A view of of the tree-flanked entrance to Baitul Mahdi, located in Durham.

Jama'at Ahmadiyya, Canada

Huzoor ^{aba} with Naseem Mahdi, Amir and Missionary-in-Charge of Canada, during silent prayers on the occasion of the inauguration of Baitul Mahdi in Durham (June 29, 2005).

Brampton, Ontario, Canada

Jama'at Ahmadiyya, Canada

Future mosque in Brampton

Jama'at Ahmadiyya Canada

Jama'at Ahmadiyya, Canada

Huzoor ^{aba} laying the foundation stone of the new mosque in Brampton (above) and leading silent prayers during the foundation stone ceremony on July 2, 2005 (right).

Montreal, Quebec, Canada

Jama'at Ahmadiyya, Canada

Al-Nusrat Mosque in Montreal. The building was purchased by the Canadian Jama'at in 1982.

Hadhrat Khalifatul Masih III [rh] visited the Calgary Mission House on September 8, 1980.

Calgary, Alberta, Canada

Jama'at Ahmadiyya, Canada

Jama'at Ahmadiyya, Canada

An artist's rendition of the new mosque currently under construction in Calgary.

Jamia Ahmadiyya Canada

Jama'at Ahmadiyya, Canada

Jamia Ahmadiyya at Baitul Hamd in Mississauga, Ontario.

Huzoor[aba] with Mubarak A. Nazir, Principal, Jamia Ahmadiyya, Canada, on June 30, 2004.

Jama'at Ahmadiyya, Canada

Jama'at Ahmadiyya, Canada

Huzoor[aba] with Naseem Mahdi (Amir), Missionaries, staff, faculty and students at Jamia Ahmadiyya Canada on June 30, 2004.

Visit of Hadhrat Khalifatul Masih III [rh] to Canada, 1980

All photos on this page: Jama'at Ahmadiyya, Canada

Huzoor [rh] speaking with a reporter.

Huzoor [rh] addressing the Jama'at.

Visit of Hadhrat Khalifatul Masih IV [rh] to Canada, 1989

Huzoor [rh] during a Question/Answer session.

Huzoor [rh] with a press reporter.

Visit of Hadhrat Khalifatul Masih V [aba] to Canada, 2005

Huzoor [aba] with the Prime Minister of Canada on June 30, 2005

Lal Khan, Naib Amir of Canada, greets Huzoor [aba] as he arrives in Canada on June 4, 2005.

The Influence of Hadhrat Mirza Ghulam Ahmad [as]

The Honorable Paul Martin, Canadian Federal Minister of Finance, addresses the Annual Ahmadiyya Convention, Canada.

At the occasion of the 2000 *Jalsa Salana* in Canada, Mr. Paul Martin (the current Canadian Prime Minister and then Canadian Federal Minister of Finance) shared a few thoughts with the attendees of the *Jalsa*. He mentioned that he was to attend the G-7 Conference in Japan at the month's end and his department gave him some briefings and notes for this meeting. Simultaneously the *Jama'at* sent him an invitation to the Canadian *Jalsa* along with some literature. Included in this package was *Hadhrat* Ahmad's[as] last book entitled *Message of Peace*. He read through this book, and was so overwhelmed by its presentation that he discarded the notes his department gave him for the meeting and instead used *Huzoor*'s concept of a 'global village'. After reviewing the notes provided by his own department, Martin said:

"I had read the same thing expressed in a way that it is much more powerful, a vision of what the world was all about, what we had to do...it was articulated in a way that could never be expressed by any bureaucrat or any department of finance. It occurred to me that my notes for today should be the very notes written by a great man in 1889 in a small village in northern India. *Hadhrat* Ahmad [as] wrote: 'when distances had shrunk and when followers of all religions had drifted away from pure faith, that he had been sent to all mankind to re-establish a close relationship with the one true God, that this would be the only way for man to peace. All other ways and variance with this one would only lead to restlessness and disorder and the world would be assailed by all manners of calamity until man hearkens to this call.'

Understand, this was written in 1889, and if indeed the world had listened to these words, there would have been no World War I and there would have been no World War II. There would not have been war in Korea, there would not have been war in Vietnam, and there would not have been the financial calamities that occurred in the last 45 years. So let me tell you how powerful this message is and how it must be heard by everybody. When the finance ministers meet together in Japan at the end of this week and the beginning of the next, my message may be expressed in the dry and arid words of the department of finance, but at the same point in that meeting, I am going to tell my colleagues there of this meeting and how the world must listen to this message."

The Ahmadiyya Gazette, Canada, Nov. 2000, page 83.

Jama'at Ahmadiyya, Canada

Huzoor [aba] with Imam Naseem Mahdi and other Missionaries of Canada.

Guatemala
Jama'at established in 1989

A pyramid temple in the ancient Mayan ruins of Tikal in Guatemala, which date back to the 4th century B.C.

Raymond Ostertag

ABOUT GUATEMALA

Guatemala attained independence from Spain in 1821. Located in Central America south of Mexico, Guatemala is approximately 109,000 km^2 with a population of 13 million; most of the inhabitants speak Spanish or various Native American dialects (The Mayans flourished in this region in the first century A.D.) Roman Catholicism is the primary faith. The GDP of Guatemala is US $31 Billion, with a per capita income of $5,400.

CENTRAL
AMERICA

Guatemala

Jama'at Ahmadiyya, Guatemala

Hadhrat Khalifatul Masih IV^{rh} with the President of Guatemala, Mr. Jorge Serrano Elias, in 1991.

Jama'at Ahmadiyya, Guatemala

Baitul Awwal Mosque in Guatemala, inaugurated by Hadhrat Khalifatul Masih IV^{rh} on July 3, 1989.

THE UNITED STATES OF AMERICA
Jama'at established in 1920
www.ahmadiyya.us

Sundown at Joshua Tree National Park in California, USA. The Joshua tree is unique to the deserts of the southwestern United States.

ABOUT THE UNITED STATES of AMERICA

The United States of America became a sovereign nation after gaining its independence from England in 1776. The fifty states of the USA comprise over 9.8 million km^2 of total area with a population of 304 million, of which 75% are Protestant or Roman Catholic and less than 1% Muslim. The GDP of the United States is nearly $14 trillion with a per capita income of $ 46,000.

CIA World Factbook

Jama'at Ahmadiyya, USA

Hadhrat Mirza Masroor Ahmad[aba], before his Khilafat (center), with Sahibzada M.M. Ahmad (left) and Maulana Shaikh Mubarak Ahmad in 1997

Ahmadiyyat in America: Spiritual Colonization

"The pioneers in the colonization of American land are always looked back upon with great honor and respect. Their work was temporal, but now, my dear brothers and sisters, Allah the Almighty has made you the pioneers in the spiritual colonization of the Western world. If you will work with the same love, zeal, sincerity and loyalty as they did, your honor and respect and name will be still greater than theirs, as you will have moreover the reward of the Last Day and Allah's pleasure, the grandeur and beauty of which no one can estimate here in this world."

Hadhrat Mirza Bashiruddin Mahmood Ahmad [ra]
The Muslim Sunrise (inaugural issue), July, 1921.

The First Ahmadi Muslim Missionaries to the United States

Hadhrat Mufti Muhammad Sadiq [ra]
1920-23

Hadhrat Maulvi Muhammad Din [ra]
1923-26

Sufi Mutiur Rahman Khan Bengalee
1928-48

"My dear friends and children! No country and no people are absolutely without seekers for truth. The voice which was taken as the babble of a madman by many, began to attract some of those who were destined to be the pioneers and torch-bearers of truth in the United States of America. Maybe some of them have left this world, their spirits might be hovering over your heads just now seeing you in the seed which is being sown by God in the wilderness, as well in some well-prepared soil, to grow in time and become heavy crop to give a new life to millions and millions of people of your country."

Hadhrat Mirza Bashiruddin Mahmud Ahmad [ra]
(On the occasion of the 2nd Annual Convention of the Ahmadiyya Community, USA in 1949)

Ahmadiyyat in America: Visits of Khulafa

Hadhrat Khalifatul Masih III^{rh} with members of the American delegate to Rabwah in 1973.

Hadhrat Khalifatul Masih III^{rh} greeted by Rehmat Jamal, President L.A. Jama'at, in San Francisco, 1980.

Hadhrat Khalifatul Masih III^{rh} and Dr. Muhammad Sadiq in the U.S.

Hadhrat Khalifatul Masih III^{rh} in the US (1980).

Hadhrat Khalifatul Masih IV^{rh} during the inauguration of the Yousuf Mosque in Tucson.

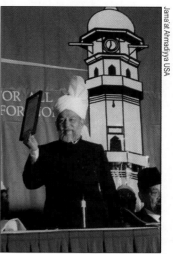

Hadhrat Khalifatul Masih IV^{rh} conducting an Ameen Ceremony (recognizing the completion of the first reading of the Holy Qur'an) with children at Baitur Rahman Mosque in 1998.

Huzoor^{rh} receiving a token of appreciation at the U.S. Jalsa Salana in 1994.

Hadhrat Khalifatul Masih IV^{rh} with M.M. Ahmad, Amir USA, at a reception at Capitol Hill, Washington DC.

Hadhrat Khalifatul Masih IV^{rh} greeted by Dr. Ahsanullah Zafar, then Naib Amir USA.

Hadhrat Khalifatul Masih V^{aba} addresses the U.S. Jalsa Salana live from London via 2-way satellite transmission, 2006. Left: The U.S. Jalsa audience watches Huzoor^{aba} on a large screen. Simultaneously (right), a monitor at the Jalsa shows Huzoor^{aba} addressing the U.K. audience at Fazl Mosque, London.

Ahmadiyyat in America: Leadership

Dr. Ahsanullah Zafar (Amir USA, 2003-Present)

Dr. Ahsanullah Zafar is the present Amir of the U.S. *Jama'at*. He was born in Sargodha, Pakistan in 1943 and attended Talimul Islam (TI) High School in Rabwah. He would go on to medical school in Lahore and complete a residency in radiology in New Jersey in 1974. He was appointed Amir after the passing of M.M. Ahmad in 2003. As a dedicated leader, Dr. Ahsanullah Zafar has been instrumental in the growth and success of the U.S. *Jama'at* over the last several years.

Sahibzada M.M. Ahmad (Amir USA, 1989-2002)

Born in Qadian, India in 1913, Sahibzada Mirza Muzaffar Ahmad was the grandson of *Hadhrat* Ahmad [as]. He became Amir of the U.S. *Jama'at* in 1989 after retiring from an illustrious career in public service, which included assignments as Deputy Chairman of of the Planning Commission for Pakistan and Executive Director of the World Bank. As Amir for thirteen years, the U.S. *Jama'at* made unprecedented achievements in financial sacrifice and the number of Ahmadiyya chapters grew rapidly. M.M. Ahmad Sahib passed away in 2002.

Imam Shaikh Mubarak Ahmad (Amir USA, 1983-1989)

Maulana Shaikh Mubarak Ahmad was born in District Multan, Pakistan in 1910. After several years working as a missionary in Africa, he was appointed Amir and Missionary-in-Charge of the U.S. *Jama'at* in 1983 and immediately undertook the task of establishing five mosques in the United States under *Hadhrat Khalifatul Masih IV*'s [rh] scheme. He retired in 1990 but still actively served Jama'at in various capacities until his demise in 2001. He was well-versed in several languages and authored over 20 works. He defended Islam against the attacks of Reverend Dr. Graham in the 1960s.

Imam Ataullah Kaleem (Amir USA, 1977-1983)

Maulana Ataullah Kaleem was born in Amritsar in 1922. He spent 19 years as a missionary in Ghana and 6 years in Rabwah before becoming Amir and Missionary-in-Charge of the U.S. *Jama'at* in 1977. Several missions were established in the United States during his six-year tenure. Maulana Kaleem authored 18 books including *The Synopsis of Religious Preaching (Parts 1,2 and 3)* and started the Urdu journal, *Al-Noor,* and the *Ahmadiyya Gazette* while in America. He later served as Missionary-in-Charge of Germany. He passed way in 2001 after a long life dedicated to Islam.

Ahmadiyyat in America: Current Missionaries

Imam Inamul Haq Kauser

Imam Daud Hanif
Missionary-in-Charge, USA

Imam Shamshad Nasir

Imam Mubashar Ahmad

Imam Azhar Haneef

Imam Irshad Malhi

Imam Chaudhry Munir Ahmad

Imam Zafar A. Sarwar

Imam Mirza Yahya Luqman

Imam M. Zafrullah Hanjra

Imam Ziaul Haq Zaki

Ahmadiyyat in America: Amir, Naib Amirs and Auxiliaries

Imam Daud Hanif

Dr. Ahsanullah Zafar
Amir, USA Jama'at

Munir Hamid

Dr. Nasim Rehmatullah

Dr. Zaheer A. Bajwa

Zinda M. Bajwa

Dr. Hamid ur Rahman

Wasim Malik

Dr. Shahnaz Butt, Sadr;
Lajna Imaillah, USA

Munum Naeem

Dr. Faheem Younus,
Sadr; Majlis
Khuddamul Ah-
madiyya, USA

Dr. Wajeeh Bajwah,
Sadr; Majlis
Ansarullah, USA

Silver Spring, Maryland

Headquarters for the Ahmadiyya Muslim Community, USA

A view of Baitur Rahman Mosque, located in Silver Spring, Maryland.

The original 8.75 acre parcel of land on which Baitur Rahman Mosque would later be built was obtained in the mid-1980s. *Hadhrat Khalifatul Masih IV*[rh] laid the foundation on October 9, 1987. Following years of fund-raising (half the donations were contributed by the Association of Ahmadi Doctors), the mosque broke ground in 1993 in a ceremony presided by the late Sahibzada Mirza Muzaffar Ahmad, Amir of the US *Jama'at*. Baitur Rahman Mosque was formally inaugurated by *Huzoor*[rh] during the U.S. Jalsa Salana in 1994. With separate floors for the men's and ladies' prayer halls, the mosque has a capacity for a combined 1300 worshippers. National Headquarter offices are situated in the basement level.

Left: Hadhrat Khalifatul Masih IV[rh] *with M.M. Ahmad, Amir of USA, during the 1994 Jalsa Salana in Silver Spring, Maryland. Right: The late M.M. Ahmad laying the foundation of Baitur Rahman Mosque in 1993.*

Baitur Rahman

by Sayyarah Hikmat

A citadel of peace, solace and calm.
A vibrant place of magical wonder and charm.

Gone are all my fear of cares as I enter
The beautiful mansion, majestic, grand!

It is an abode of God whose blessings are showered on us day by day.
The call for prayer awakens your soul from sloth and slumber.
It stirs the embers of your soul into a Divine fire!

There is no more talk of material profit and loss in these turbulents times of chaos.
From this mosque is raised the voice of harmony, love and peace!

The Friday sermon is an invitation to the doors of Islam.
In immaculate English, it sounds like the pattering rain!

The Advocates of the Messiah[as] (I meet in the mosque), my brothers and sisters
Whose faces are radiant with Divine light, whose souls are enveloped with angelic spirit!

In the Holy Month of *Ramadhan*, the atmosphere is permeated with God's glory!
You experience a sense of fulfillment where ego gets crushed

And you transcend into a spiritual universe with angels, Divinity and the Word of God!
This world and its museum show seems empty, futile and hollow!

Willingboro, New Jersey

Jama'at Ahmadiyya USA

Baitul Nasr in Willingboro, New Jersey

In 1984, members of the New Jersey *Jama'at* acquired a 2.5 acre plot of land where the mission house was situated. In 2007, Baitul Nasr was completed on the same site through the contributions of the Willingboro *Jama'at* members.

Hamid Khan for *The Ahmadiyya Gazette, USA*: Jan 2007

Hamid Khan for *The Ahmadiyya Gazette, USA*: Jan 2007

Colorfully carpeted rows with individually demarcated spaces greet worshippers entering the prayer area of Baitul Nasr.

Dr. Ahsanullah Zafar, Amir Jama'at USA, addresses a gathering at Baitul Nasr.

Chicago, Illinois

Baet ul Jaamay located in Glen Ellyn, Illinois, about 20 miles east of Chicago.

Masjid Baet ul Jaamay

Falahud Din Shams

All praise belongs to Allah who gave us the opportunity to build a beautiful mosque in the metropolitan Chicago area. It is only through His mercy and grace that this kind of accomplishment takes place.

It was *Hadhrat Khalifatul Masih IV* [th] who personally took an interest in the mosque to be constructed at this location. In 1997, while he was visiting Chicago for the foundation laying ceremony, he met with the architect over his renderings and gave his comments and approved to proceed with the project.

It is also with great gratitude that I must mention the enthusiasm and vigorous work that our late Amir of USA, Sahibzada M.M. Ahmad did in reference to this mosque. His guidance and keen interest was a major factor in accomplishing the completion of this huge project. After he became ill, it was our current Amir, Dr. Ahsanullah Zafar, who continued to support this project with the same vigor.

We witnessed many signs throughout this project. It was a miracle how the zoning process went smoothly. There was opposition but nothing compared to what other organizations faced in the area. The highlight was when the pastor of a local church across the street stood up in front of the zoning board, without our prior knowledge, in favor of the project.

Construction on the mosque began in 2001, at which time *Hadhrat Khalifatul Masih IV*[th] gave the name, Al Masjid Baet ul Jaamay. It was complete three years later, and in April of 2004 the formal inauguration took place.

Baet ul Jaamay has 21,000 square feet of space on two floors for men and women. Half the space on each floor is divided into a prayer area and meeting area. The mosque has two full-sized kitchens, several offices, a childcare room and a library.

The House of Gathering

by Qasim Rashid

In a time come and gone, on a warm summer day
I watched as the groundwork for His house was laid.

To gather mankind, it was titled Jaamey
So aptly invoked by our blessed Raabay [rh].

And throughout our struggles, and throughout our plights
It remains as a beacon of hope in the night.

A beacon of honor, of God, of His proof
To answer those seeking Islam in its truth.

For if you watch close, you might see it, that glimmer
That vision forseen by Khilafat, that shimmer.

Of the moment that comes in the future one day
When all mankind gathers, at Baet ul Jaamay.

Below: the original Sadiq Mosque. Right: The new Sadiq mosque adjacent to the original property

The Sadiq Mosque, on 4448 Wabash Street in Chicago's southside neighborhood, was the first Ahmadiyya mission house established in the United States (1920) by the first USA missionary Hadhrat Mufti Sadiq Ahmad [ra]. This location served as *Jama'at* headquarters until 1948. In 1994, the house adjacent to the original property was purchased. The new Sadiq Mosque was inaugurated by *Hadhrat Khalifatul Masih IV*[th] on October 23, 1994.

Texas

Houston

The Ahmadiyya Gazette, USA: May-June 2004

Baitus Samee Mosque in Houston, Texas

Baitul Samee sits on a 5-acre mosque property which was purchased and donated by Mohammad Younus Chaudhary in 1996. The foundation was laid by *Hadhrat Khalifatul Masih IV*[th] in 1998 and construction completed in 2 phases by 2003. The total facility, which includes a community center with halls and offices, can accomodate over 800 people.

"Allah be praised who enabled the Houston *Jama'at* to put up a beautiful mosque. May Allah bless this mosque and all those who have contributed towards its completion... I pray that may He extend all the blessings associated with the mosque to the region and the city and to each and every member of the Ahmadiyyat *Jama'at*... your work has just begun. The completion of the mosque has signaled that all of you should embark upon the job of winning sincere worshippers with view to populating the mosque."

- A message by *Hadhrat* Mirza Masroor Ahmad, *Khalifatul Masih V*[aba] on the occasion of the inauguration of Baitus Samee Mosque in Houston, Texas

Our Lady Texas, Listen Closely
Dedicated to Baitus Samee Mosque

by Bilal Rana

Stirring beneath her soil
Permeates a hidden gold
Laden, a spirit centuries old
Waiting to be found
Eager to erupt
Like the rich sands of desert Arabia.

She too
Has her First House
Where all unite to pray
Jews and Christians too
Believer and sinner alike
Light, Endless Light.

How strange! How ecstatic!
That here, I express
But in fact I am being told
That God listens, wordlessly
But in truth is shouting!
And it is I who am listening.

Hadhrat Khalifatul Masih IV[rh] lays the foundation for Baitus Samee Mosque on June 30, 1998

Hadhrat Khalifatul Masih IV[rh] with Munum Naeem, President Houston Jama'at and Muhammad Younus Chaudhary during the foundation of Baitus Samee

Dallas

Baitul Ikram, Dallas, Texas

In 1996, the Dallas *Jama'at* acquired five acres of land in Allen, Texas located 10 miles north of Dallas. *Hadhrat Khalifatul Masih IV*[th] gave the name Baitul Ikram. The foundation was laid in 2002 with a brick received from *Huzoor*[rh]. Within five months, the first phase was complete and inaugurated by Dr. Ahsanullah Zafar, Amir, USA. Baitul Ikram, with 4900 square feet of space, consists of two large prayer halls, a library, two offices, a kitchen and a childcare room. Two additional phases are planned.

Ohio

Columbus

Masjid Bait-ul-Nasir

Baitul Nasir near Columbus, Ohio was constructed in 2007. This was the last American mosque constructed during the first century of Khilafat.

Jama'at Ahmadiyya USA

The original mission house in Columbus, Ohio was acquired in 2001.

Baitul Nasir in Columbus, Ohio was built in 2007. It was the last U.S. mosque constructed during the first century of Khilafat. Local members of the Columbus Jama'at contributed entirely to the construction of Baitul Nasir. It has a capacity for 500 worshippers.

Dayton

The original site for the Fazal Mosque in Dayton, Ohio was acquired in 1952, and the Fazal Mosque was constructed in 1972 (the first mosque built in the U.S.). Sufi Mutiur Rahman Bengali, the 3rd missionary sent to the U.S., worked from this historic mosque.

Jama'at Ahmadiyya USA

The Fazal Mosque in Dayton, Ohio

The Cleveland chapter began in the late 1930s. Mr. Sayed Abdul Rahman and his family were the first local Ahmadis to actively serve the *Jama'at* in the area. As the chapter grew, twelve families contributed to the purchase of a church in Bedford, Ohio, which was renovated and converted to Baitul Ahad Mosque in 1986. The present structure is a 5000 square foot, 2 story building with a basement. It consists of meeting rooms, a large prayer room, a stage, a closed circuit TV and sound system, as well as a satellite system for national and international communication. There is also an apartment for visiting missionaries. One of the most prominent features of the building is the large golden dome on top that was custom built in the Islamic tradition. The Cleveland *Jama'at* was blessed with the visits of *Hadhrat Khalifatul Masih IV*[th] who also visited the mosque.

Cleveland

Baitul Ahad near Cleveland, Ohio

The late Dr. Muzaffar Ahmad Zafr, former Amir and Naib Amir USA, was a tireless worker, a dedicated leader and a devoted servant of *Khilafat-e-Ahmadiyya*. His eloquent speeches on propagation were inspiring to audiences of all ages. He would take charge of security arrangements whenever the *Khalifa* would visit the United States. *Hadhrat Khalifatul Masih IV*[th] once said, "He was so active that whenever I visited the U.S. he was always in charge of my security, as far as human efforts were concerned. It appeared he never slept in those days. Whenever I came out he was always there." Dr. Zafr served the Ahmadiyya Community as Naib Amir for many years. He lead the American delegation to Rabwah and Qadian frequently and represented North America at the International *Ba'ait*. He passed away on Friday, November 15, 1996 in his hometown of Dayton, Ohio.

Detroit, Michigan

The new Detroit mosque

Hadhrat Khalifatul Masih IVth laying the foundation for the Detroit Mosque in 1987

The original Detroit mission house

Al-Muzaffar

by Omar F. Ahmad

No towering domes or sleek minarets--
Al-Muzaffar is plain, but such is its charm.

No arches spanning o'er marble steps--
Victorious it stands; God kept us from harm.

No flowers blooming in lofty gardens--
Remember the day when the arsonists failed ?

No water splashing from pristine fountains--
They suffered their fate in a fiery jail.

No grand mehrab facing hallowed halls--
The Messiah's opponents thought they'd won.

No silk tapestries adorning the walls--
But they'd forgotten his servants acted as one.

No couches, cushions, or carpets spread out--
We did not respond with a list of demands.

No treasures of man, no shame or doubt--
God helped us rebuild it--with our own hands.

The First Ahmadi Martyr in the U.S.

Four days prior to the 35th to be held at Oakland University in Michigan, on August 8, a devoted worker of the Ahmadiyya community, Dr. Muzaffar Ahmad, was shot and martyred at his home in Canton, Michigan. The following morning, the Detroit Mission House was set on fire. Oakland University refused to host the Jalsa out of fear. *Hadhrat Khalifatul Masih IVth* instructed the US Jama'at not to cancel the Jalsa. It was held in Belleville, Michigan on August 12-13 and attended by1000 Ahmadies.

"Muzaffar is alive even today ! Nay, he got a life far greater than that he had ! O Muzaffar ! Peace be on to you ! At your back are millions of Muzaffars ready and anxious to move forward and take your place. O you who quenched the flame of Muzaffar's life, you have given him a cup of everlasting life to drink. To him life is granted, and to you nothing but death."

Hadhrat Khalifatul Masih IVth,
August 12, 1983

Dr. Muzaffar Ahmad

California — Silicon Valley

Baitul Baseer in Milpitas, California (Silicon Valley)

Sajid Maqsood

Hadhrat Mirza Tahir Ahmad, *Khalifatul-Masih IV*[rh], visited the Silicon Valley (located in northern Callifornia) and inaugurated the Baitul Baseer Mosque in Milpitas, California, on Friday, July 1, 1998.

On July 3, 1998, *Hadhrat Khalifatul-Masih IV*[rh] addressed a gathering of more than 1,000 people including more than 100 guests. The mayors of Milpitas and Fremont, the chief of staff of the Santa Clara Board of Supervisors, and many other local leaders were present. In his address, *Hadhrat Khalifatul Masih IV*[rh] said that Islam was not a territorial religion but it ruled over the hearts and minds of the faithful. He observed that in the context of the present world situation Islam is misunderstood to be a territorial religion and the responsibility for this misconception "lies squarely on the shoulders of Muslim scholars, who live in the modern times but actually belong to medieval ages". He said that the mission of the Ahmadiyya Muslim Community is "to rehabilitate the original values of Islam". He noted that "the key that opens up all hearts is the key of the love of God; it is the key to the submission to God." *Hadhrat Khalifatul-Masih IV*[rh] declared that the doors of Baitul Baseer Mosque, like the doors of every other Ahmadi mosque, remain open to anyone who wishes to worship and pay homage to the unity of God. This short but thought-provoking address was listened to with rapt attention. The event was covered by local television and newspapers.

Wasim Malik

Huzoor [rh] *escorted by Wasim Malik President, San Jose Jama'at during a visit in 1998.*

Wasim Malik

Hadhrat Khalifatul Masih IV [rh] *delivering the inauguration speech for Baitul Baseer with the Mayor of Milpitas, California on the stage in 1998.*

Los Angeles

Baitul Hameed Mosque in Chino, California, 30 miles east of Los Angeles.

Baitul Hameed Mosque: Groundbreaking Ceremony - 1987

The original mission house in Chino, California was purchased in the mid 1980s. *Hadhrat Khalifatul Masih IV*[rh] laid the foundation for the mosque in 1987, and later inaugurated Baitul Hameed Mosque in 1989. On April 19, 2003, members of the *Jama'at* gathered to mourn the passing of *Hadhrat Khalifatul Masih IV*[rh]. During the prayer service lead by Imam Inamul Haq Kauser, Missionary of Los Angeles, a structure fire broke out rendering it inoperable. The mosque is currently undergoing a massive reconstruction and renovation, to be completed in late 2008, *Insha'Allah.*

Local members of the Ahmadiyya community in Los Angeles collectively pray at the groundbreaking ceremony of Baitul Hameed Mosque in 1987.

Seated first row from left to right: Dr. Hamidur Rahman (seated behind him is Dr. Muzzafar Ahmad Zafr), Chaudhry Munir Ahmad, Sahibzada M.M. Ahmad, Hadhrat Khalifatul Masih IV[rh], *Rehmat Jamal, Sheikh Mubarak Ahmad, and Anwer M. Khan. From center left to right: Ashraf Rajput, Dr. Gulzar Ahmad, Inayatullah Khan and Amir ud Din.*

Dr. Hamid ur Rahman

Hadhrat Khalifatul Masih IV^{rh} at Yosemite Falls. From left to right: Karl Reichhold (a new convert), Dr. Hamid ur Rahman (President, L.A. Jama'at), Huzoor^{rh}, Faiz Rahman and Chaudhry Munir Ahmad, Missionary serving Los Angeles.

"The best way to express thanks to Allah is to increase our level of prayer at every occasion when a mosque is built. There is no meaningful or better expression of thanks than this."

Excerpt from the Friday sermon of *Hadhrat Khalifatul Masih IV^{rh}* on October 30, 1987.

Baitul Hameed Mosque: Foundation Ceremony - 1987

Dr. Hamidur Rahman

Dr. Hamidur Rahman

Far left: Hadhrat Khalifatul Masih IV^{rh} lays the foundation of Baitul Hameed Mosque. Immediate left: Huzoor^{rh} leads silent prayers during the ceremony.

THE ORANGE COUNTY Register

SATURDAY   **OCTOBER 24, 1987**   **25 CENTS**

Saturday, October 24, 1987   The Orange County Register   **B7**

Muslim sect lays foundation of mosque in Chino

Spiritual leader visits from Pakistan to lead ceremony

By Scott Fagerstrom
The Register

CHINO — They believe in one God — Allah — and in his prophet Mohammed.

They pray five times a day, bowing in the direction of Mecca.

They observe the holidays and dietary laws of the Koran, which they consider God's word.

They consider themselves Muslims, although their doctrine differs from more traditional Muslim teachings.

About 10 million people — including about 100 Orange County families — are members of the Ahmadiyya Movement, a rapidly-growing sect whose members consider themselves faithful followers of Mohammed.

Local members of the movement are planning to build California's first Ahmadi mosque in Chino, dramatically raising the profile of what has been an obscure sect.

Construction of the mosque, expected to take six to eight months, officially began at 4 p.m. Friday, when Hazrat Mirza Tahir Ahmad, spiritual leader of the movement and the founder's grandson, laid the foundation stone at the site of the mosque, 11941 Ramona Ave.

The group's unique teachings about Christ (they believe he survived the Crucifixion and lived to old age in what is now India) and a 19th century teacher named Hazrat Mirza Ghulam Ahmad (they consider him a prophet) are rejected by most Muslims.

Anwer Khan, general secretary of the Los Angeles area chapter, said Ahmad's visit from Pakistan is as significant to area Ahmadis as the pope's visit was to Catholics.

The 11,000-square-foot mosque, with traditional dome and minarets, will provide space for youth and adult Koran studies, as well as Islamic observances, he said.

"We are very excited," said Khan. Until now, members of the 15-year-old Los Angeles chapter have had to worship in parks or public auditoriums, he added.

The Ahmadiyya Movement was born in India in 1889, when the group's founder prophesied that his teachings would lead mankind into a golden age.

Muslims traditionally have believed that Christ was taken up to heaven after the Crucifixion, and also that Mohammed was the final prophet. Ahmadis say the traditional Islamic doctrine about Jesus' death and about the meaning of Mohammed's status are misinterpretations of the Koran.

Such points of contention might seem minor to non-Muslims, but in some parts of the Muslim world, Ahmadis are persecuted for their doctrines, Khan said. In Pakistan, for instance, the government punishes Ahmadis for identifying their faith as an Islamic movement, he added.

Khan, 42, a marketing manager for Beckman Instruments, said he left Pakistan in 1971 to escape such persecution. He now lives in Brea.

Ahmad is staying in Orange County this weekend, but for security reasons the Ahmadis will not reveal his exact location.

Hazrat Mirza Tahir Ahmad
Grandson of sect's founder

News of the foundation ceremony of Baitul Hameed Mosque appeared prominently in the local press.

Ahmadiyya Mosques Around the World   **299**

Baitul Hameed Mosque - 20 Years

Ahsan M. Khan

In a small California town, circa 1987 --
A spectacular blessing arrived from the heavens.

Five new mosques in America was the Khalifa's [rh] scheme
And in a matter of years, it was no longer but a dream.

After months of withstanding dissension from neighbors,
The Jama'at of Los Angeles tasted the fruits of its labor

The first shovel was struck, the first brick was laid --
Ahmadies rejoiced—A House of God would be made.

Huzoor blessed us with a visit, and planted the seed.
With Divine inspiration, he named it Baitul Hameed.

Two years later, in triumphant jubilation,
Hundreds gathered for the momentous inauguration.

A field once covered with insects and hay
Now filled with men, women and children eager to pray.

A Chino sky once silent at dawn,
Now rang with the call of Adhan.

Churches were visited, invitations were extended --
In a matter of months, the citizens were befriended.

The mosque was where the message was told.
Truthseekers from everywhere now entered the fold.

Not just a building, but a symbol of unity.
A beacon of peace in a righteous community.

Alas, we will never forget that April morning in 2003
As we mourned the loss of Hadhrat Khalifatul Masih [rh].

Our cries of sadness turned to screams of confusion.
Was our home burning down, or was this an illusion?

The ashes and flames may have stripped the brilliance,
But they could do nothing to destroy our resilience.

We prayed to Allah, and He heard our supplications,
And alas today, we witness the restoration.

As humble servants of Ahmad [as], truly are we blessed.
Indeed, *the sun of Truth will rise from the West.*

Baitul Hameed Mosque: Renovation Efforts - 2008

Mosque prepares to emerge from ashes

By Melodie Henderson

After spending nearly 20 years in a community that once opposed its presence and five years to recover from a fire that caused close to a million dollars in damage, Chino's Baitul Hameed Mosque strives to be a beacon of peace in the community.

Imam Shamshad Ahmad Nasir is featured in a news item about the renovation of Baitul Hameed Mosque in the local newspaper, The Chino Champion *(Sat., May 24, 2008 issue).*

Chino Champion clipping shown here under Fair Use policy.

Baitul Hameed Mosque is being newly renovated after being partially destroyed by a fire which occurred by accident in 2003. This is how it appears now as this book goes to press.

Ahmadiyyat in America: A Brief Timeline

1920 *Hadhrat* Mufti Muhammad Sadiq[ra], a devoted companion of the Promised Messiah[as], arrives in Philadelphia, becoming the first missionary to the U.S.

1922 The first Ahmadiyya Muslim Mission is established in Chicago, Illinois. *The Muslim Sunrise*, a quarterly magazine, is started.

1923-1926 *Hadhrat* Maulvi Muhammad Din[ra] becomes the 2nd missionary to arrive in the U.S.

1928-1948 *Hadhrat* Sufi Mutiur Rahman Khan Bengalee serves for 20 years as a U.S. missionary during which the *Jama'at* sees great progress in America.

1933 *Hadhrat* Chaudhry Muhammad Zafrullah Khan[ra] visits the U.S. and speaks at the World Faiths Conference in Chicago.

1948 The first *Jalsa Salana* (annual convention) is held in Dayton, Ohio.

1950 2141 Leroy Place in Washington DC is purchased and renamed American Fazl Mosque; it serves as U.S. *Jama'at* headquarters for 44 years. A mission house is acquired in Pittsburgh, Pennsylvania.

1952 A site is acquired in Dayton, Ohio, where later (in 1972) the first constructed Ahmadiyya mosque, the Fazal Mosque, is built.

1965 *Ayesha Magazine* is started by *Lajna Imaillah*, USA.

1972 The first *Majlise Shura* (consultative body) of the U.S. *Jama'at* meets at the *Jalsa Salana* in Lake Forest, Illinois. A mission house is acquired in St. Louis, Missouri.

Hadhrat Mufti Muhammad Sadiq[ra]

The cover of the inaugural issue of The Muslim Sunrise.

The American Fazl Mosque in Washington DC

The Fazal Mosque in Dayton, Ohio

Ahmadiyyat in America: A Brief Timeline

1975 A mission house is acquired in Baltimore, Maryland.

1976 *Hadhrat Khalifatul Masih III*[rh] makes his first visit to the United States and attends the Jalsa Salana at Drew University in Madison, New Jersey.

1980 *Hadhrat Khalifatul Masih III*[rh] makes his second trip to the United States.

Rashid Ahmad represents USA during an international Ahmadiyya conference. Rashid Sahib, from Milwaukee, Wisconsin is former President of Jama'at Ahmadiyya USA.

1982 The National Mosque Fund is initiated by *Hadhrat Khalifatul Masih IV*[rh], calling for the construction of 5 mosques in the US: Washington D.C., New York, Detroit, Chicago and Los Angeles, with an initial target of $2.5 million.

Mission House near Boston, Massachusetts

1983 *Hadhrat Khalifatul Masih IV*[rh] launches a divinely inspired scheme to invite people towards Islam, or *Da'wat Ilallah*.

1984 Mission houses are purchased in New York (Baitul Zafar), Zion and Boston.

1985 The Yousuf Mosque is built in Tucson, Arizona. A mission house is acquired in New Orleans, Louisiana.

The Zion Mission House

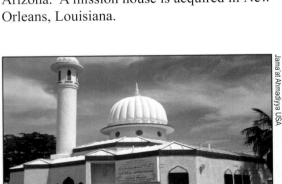

Yousuf Mosque, Tucson, Arizona

Baitul Zafar in Queens, New York

1987

Hadhrat Khalifatul Masih IV[rh] visits the U.S. and lays the foundation for future mosques in Washington D.C., Detroit and Los Angeles.

A mission house (Baitul Ahad) is established in Cleveland, Ohio.

1989

Baitul Rizwan is constructed in Portland, Oregon and inaugurated by *Hadhrat Khalifatul Masih IV*[rh] in 1989. Baitul Hameed Mosque near Los Angeles, California is also inaugurated by *Huzoor*[rh]. A mission house is aquired in Rochester, New York.

Baitul Rizwan, Portland, Oregon

1990

A building is purchased in Houston, Texas to be used as a mosque and mssion house.

1992

Mission house properties are purchased in St. Louis, Missouri, Charlotte, North Carolina and Milwaukee, Wisconsin.

1993

Bashir Afzal, president of the Ahmadiyya Community in New York, passes away.

Bashir Afzal, a former Baptist minister, studied Islam and Ahmadiyyat intensely. He eventually visited Rabwah and Qadian in the 1950s, at which time he devoted his life in the serve of Ahmadiyyat. He served as President of the New York Ahmadiyya community for 30 years and dedicated a lot of effort towards the spiritual training of new converts. He passed away on July 18, 1993 at the age of 90.

1994

Baitur Rahman Mosque in Silver Spring, Maryland is completed and inaugurated by *Hadhrat Khalifatul Masih IV*[rh]. Ahmadiyya headquarters are officially relocated. MTA North America is officially launched as Earth Station, broadcasting programs to Canada and the U.S. In 1995, www.alislam.org is started.

Huzoor[rh] inaugurates the newly renovated Sadiq Mosque in Chicago. The Van Buren Center is purchased near downtown Chicago.

1996

Properties are purchased in Bay Point, California; Milpitas, California near San Jose; and Hawthorne, California near Los Angeles.

Baitus Salam in Los Angeles

Mian Mohammad Hussain, born on March 2, 1905, is the oldest living Ahmadi in the United States. He was a former instructor at Taleemul Islam School in Qadian and a private instructor for Hadhrat Khalifatul Masih IV[rh]. *This 103 year old Moosi currently resides in Riverside, California.*

Ahmadiyyat in America: A Brief Timeline

1996 — Muhammad Sadiq, an early American Ahmadi convert, passes away.

1997 — A church building is acquired and converted to a mosque in Old Bridge, New Jersey (Baitul Hadi) and land for a future mosque is acquired in Dallas, Texas. In Albany, New York, a local Ahmadi family donates a school building to be used as a mosque.

1997 — Public meetings commemorating the centenary publication of *The Philosophy of the Teachings of Islam*, a divinely inspired writing of the Promised Messiah[as] are held throughout the US.

1998 — *Hadhrat Khalifatul Masih IV*[rh] attends the 50th US *Jalsa Salana* and inaugurates mosques in New Jersey and San Jose, and lays the foundation for the mosque in Houston, Texas. He delivers his final Friday sermon on U.S. soil on July 3, at the inauguration of Baitul Baseer near San Jose.

2000 — The 'Messiah 2000 Conference' is held in Zion, Illinois to celebrate the fulfillment of the prophecy pertaining to Dr. John Alexander Dowie. The function, presided by M.M. Ahmad, Amir USA, is attended by 1,500. Five grandsons of *Hadhrat* Ahmad[as] are also in attendance.

2003 — Humanity First, USA is established.

2003 — A mission house (Baitul Huda) is acquired in Long Island, New York. Another mission house is purchased in Brooklyn, New York.

2005 — Properties for mission houses are acquired in Syracuse, New York; Bronx, New York; Research Triangle, North Carolina; Seattle, Washington and Phoenix, Arizona.

2006 — Properties for mission houses are acquired in Orlando, Florida and Harrisburg, Pennsylvania *Hadhrat Khalifatul Masih V*[aba], in a live two-way MTA satellite transmission from London, addresses the U.S. *Jama'at* during the final session of the *Jalsa Salana*.

2007 — Church buildings are purchased for future mission houses in Austin, Texas and Hartford, Connecticut.

2008 — *Khilafat* Centenary celebrations take place all across the United States. The 60th U.S. *Jalsa Salana* takes place in Harrisburg, Pennsylvania.

Brother Muhammad Sadiq was born in Newark in 1912. He accepted Ahmadiyyat after reading books written by Missionary Sufi Mutiur Rahman Bengali. He was a dedicated and humble servant of Islam. Brother Sadiq was well-versed in the Holy Qur'an and had a profound love for *Khilafat-e-Ahmadiyya*. He passed away in New Jersey in 1996.

Baitul Huda, Long Island, New York

Imam Inamul Haq Kauser accompanies Hadhrat Khalifatul Masih IV[rh], *as he is greeted by Naib Amir, Muzaffar Ahmad Zafar during Huzoor's*[rh] *tour of the U.S. in 1996.*

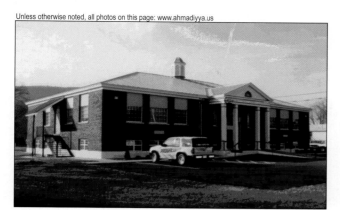

Mosque in Albany, New York

Phoenix Mosque

Baitul Aman, Connecticut

Baitul Naseer, Miami, Florida

New mosque under construction in St. Louis, Missouri.

Baitul Muqeet, Austin, Texas

Baitul Tahir in Brooklyn, New York

Baitul Hadi, Old Bridge, New Jersey

Ahmadiyya Mosques Around the World **305**

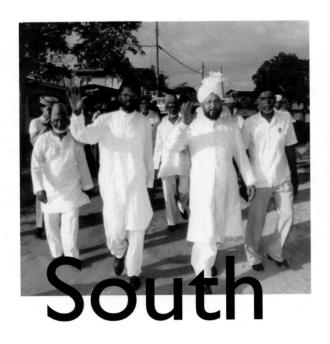

Photos clockwise from upper left: Jama'at Ahmadiyya, Trinidad & Tobago; Jama'at Ahmadiyya, Suriname; vivirlatino.com; Jama'at Ahmadiyya, Brazil.

South

The 1950's saw the message of Ahmadiyyat spread to the South American continent, beginning with its presence on the island nation of Trinidad & Tobago in 1952. Since then, the Jama'at has gradually expanded and is now active in several other countries, including, most recently, the French Antilles in 2002.

America

AHMADIYYA MUSLIM MOSQUES

BRAZIL
Jama'at Established in 1986

The blue morpho butterfly is indigenous to the Amazon rainforest in Brazil

www.chenowish.k12.or.us

Brazil

SOUTH
AMERICA

ABOUT BRAZIL

Brazil became an independent nation in 1822 after three centuries of Portuguese rule. In 1985, the military finally ceded and handed over the governance to civilian rulers. Brazil comprises a total area of 8,511,965 km². Portuguese is the official language, and the predominant religion (75%) is Roman Catholicism. The GDP of Brazil is US $1.3 trillion, with a per capita income of US $9,700.

CIA World Factbook

Jama'at Ahmadiyya, Brazil

The Petropolis Mission (about 60 km from Rio de Janeiro), purchased in 1989.

Ahmadiyyat in Brazil: A Brief Timeline

1986

Ahmadiyyat is established. Syed Mahmood Ahmad becomes the first President and Iqbal Ahmad Anjum, the first missionary, followed by Yousuf Yawson of Ghana.

1989

A mission house is purchased in Petropolis. *Hadhrat Khalifatul Masih IV*[rh] recognizes the Brazilian *Jama'at*'s achievement in a Friday Sermon.

Mrs. Aamina becomes the first Brazilian to accept Islam. She translates the Holy Qur'an into Portuguese, and *Hadhrat Khalifatul Masih IV*[r rh] graciously gives her the title 'First Female Ahmadi Missionary' *(Mujallah Lajna Imaillah Markaziyya, 1989)*.

1993

Waseem A. Zafar becomes Missionary-in-Charge of Brazil, a position he holds currently.

1994

The first *Jalsa Salana* in Brazil takes place and is held annually to present time.

2005

Khuddam and *Lajna* auxiliaries are established (Nadeem Tahir, *Sadr Khuddam*, and Anila Zafar, *Sadr Lajna*).

Syed Mahmood Ahmad, first president of the Brazilian Jama'at, addressing the Jama'at.

Waseem A. Zafar, Missionary-in-Charge, Brazil

Yousuf Yawson, an early missionary in Brazil

Abdul Rasheed, Vice President, Brazil Jama'at

Iqbal A. Najam, First Missionary to Brazil

Nadeem A. Tahir, Sadr, Khuddamul Ahmadiyya Brazil

Boys (Atfal) and girls (Nasirat) of the Ahmadiyya community in Brazil.

Guests and Jama'at members during the Jalsa Salana (annual convention) in Brazil, 2007.

French Antilles

Jama'at established in 2002

At the 2003 U.K. annual convention, *Hadhrat* Mirza Masroor Ahmad, *Khalifatul Masih V* [aba] shared the news that Ahmadiyyat has now spread to the French island of Martinique. A six-member delegation, which included Ashfaq Rabbani, the *Amir* of France, paid a visit to the island nation in 2002. During their stay, 10,000 pamphlets were distributed in ten cities and eleven propagation meetings were held. A live radio program lasting over one hour also was conducted, resulting in two *ba'aits* (conversions to Ahmadiyyat). A similar delegation lead by Rabbani established a mission house in Guadeloupe.

"This world is an island and a new island is being carved within it. The name of this island is Ahmadiyyat, the true Islam."

Hadhrat Mirza Tahir Ahmad [rh]

Ahmadi delegate to Guadeloupe in 2007

ABOUT MARTINIQUE and GUADELOUPE

Martinique and Guadeloupe are French islands located in the eastern Caribbean (commonly known as the French Antilles). Martinique is 1100 km² with a population of 426,000, and Guadeloupe (actually comprised of 5 islands) is 1600 km² with a population of 450,000. The predominant religion is Roman Catholicism. The official currency is the Euro. The French colonized both islands in 1635.

The Guadeloupe mission house

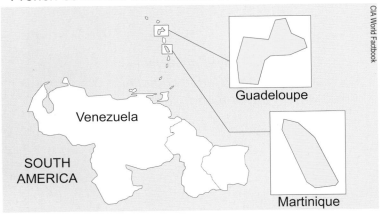

Guyana
Jama'at Established in 1956

Wikipedia

Kaieteur, located in central Guyana, is one of the tallest single-drop waterfalls in the world (251 meters). It is five times taller than Niagara Falls (USA) and twice as tall as Victoria Falls (Zambia).

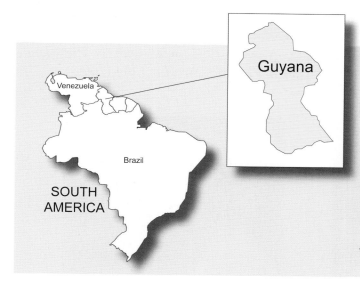

Venezuela

Guyana

Brazil

SOUTH AMERICA

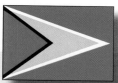

ABOUT GUYANA

Originally a Dutch colony, Guyana achieved independence from the United Kingdom in 1966. The country is 214,970 km² with a population of 769,000. English, Creole, Urdu, and Hindu dialects largely are spoken. 50% of the population is Christian, 35% Hindu and 10% Muslim. The GDP is US $ 897 million, with a per capita income of $ 5,300.

CIA World Factbook

Jama'at Ahmadiya Guyana

Baitul Noor in Guyana

Hadhrat Khalifatul Masih IV^{rh}, during his historic visit to Guyana in 1991, meets with the President of Guyana, Mr. Desmond Hoyt (left) and the Prime Minister of Guyana, Mr. Hamilton Green

Huzoor^{rh}, at a radio broadcasting station in Guyana, being interviewed by Maulana Abdur Rahman Khan, Missionary-in-Charge, Guyana, in 1991.

Maulana Abdur Rahman Khan, Missionary-in-Charge, Guyana in 1991.

Ahmadiyyat in Guyana: A Brief Timeline

1956

Mohammad Sharif Baksh, in his mid-teens, visited a bookstall in Guyana. A book about Ahmadiyyat intrigued him and subsequently led him to write a letter to *Hadhrat Khalifulatul Masih II*[ra]. He faced opposition when he shared what he had discovered and, based on the teachings of the Promised Messiah[as], he prayed for 40 days seeking guidance from Allah. One evening, while reflecting on Chapter 2, Verse 23 of the Holy Qur'an at a mosque in Sisters Village, Berbice, he experienced a true conviction in Ahmadiyyat. Baksh immediately wrote a letter of initiation to *Hadhrat Khalifatul Masih*[ra], and in so doing, he accepted Ahmadiyyat. A renowned businessman in Guyana, Baksh immediately began preaching Ahmadiyyat and a small *Jama'at* was established.

1959

Maulvi Bashir Ahmad Orchard became the first missionary to Guyana and actively propagated Islam. The local Imam of the Mosque in Sisters Village accepted Ahmadiyyat, followed by all the adherents of the mosque. Orchard Sahib would later establish a secondary school and start a tradition of *Jalsa Salana* (annual gathering) in Guyana.

Several missionaries were stationed in Guyana following Bashir Orchard's departure, including Ghulam Ahmad Nasim, Fazal Ilahi Basheer, Mohammad Siddique Nangli, Mohammad Aslam Qureshi (Shaheed), Hanif Yaqoob, Abdul Rahman Khan, Abdul Rasheed, Al-Hasan Bashir, and Ihsanullah Mangat (present),

Ihsanullah Mangat, Missionary-in-Charge, Guyana.

1991

The Ahmadiyya Muslim Community in Guyana is blessed with a historic visit by *Hadhrat Khalifatul Masih IV*[rh]. During his visit, Huzoor[rh] meets with the President of Guyana, Mr. Desmond Hoyte, and the Prime Minister, Mr. Hamilton Green.

Huzoor[rh] with Maulana Abdur Rahman Khan, Missionary-in-Charge Guyana, on arrival at Timehri Airport, 1991.

Suriname
Jama'at established in 1956

Jama'at Ahmadiyya, Suriname

Nasir Mosque in Suriname, established in 1971.

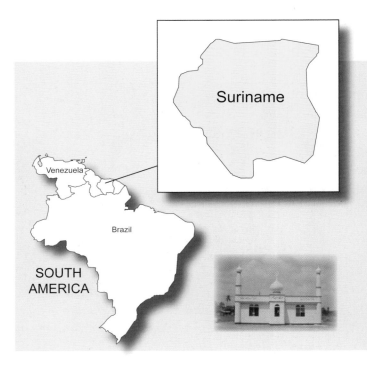

Suriname

Venezuela

Brazil

SOUTH AMERICA

ABOUT SURINAME

Suriname became a Dutch colony in 1667 and attained independence from the Netherlands in 1975. The country is 163,270 km^2 with a population of 470,000. Dutch is the official language, and English is spoken widely. Approximately 27% of the population is Hindu, 25% Protestant and 20% Muslim. The economy is dominated by the mining industry. The GDP of Suriname is US $3 billion, with a per capita income of $ 7,100.

CIA World Factbook

THE SPIRITUAL EXCAVATION OF SURINAME

Today, through God's help, for the first time in the history of Suriname, a successor of one sent by God, the Exalted, is speaking directly to you through this Friday Sermon. This historic event was to happen only once, and it has now happened, never to re-occur. If Allah so wills, Imams shall be sent by God, and they shall address the people of Suriname. They shall also deliver sermons, but the first time remains the first time. So you are fortunate in having become the witnesses to this historic occasion. It is essential that thanks be rendered for this. Thus, like Prophet Solomon[as], pray to God and render your thanks to Him by making sure your children also listen to this sermon in these very words. Do not be content by letting them hear summaries. By exposing them to this sermon, you shall be counted among those who took steps to protect

"I came here and saw that this Jama'at is made of great and sincere material. Indeed, this Jama'at is a mine of sincerity. But if mines are not excavated and valuable gems are not obtained therefrom, then of what benefit are they?"

their faith, who saved them from attacks of others, and who protected their moral values.

I came here and saw that this Jama'at is made of great and sincere material. Indeed, this Jama'at is a mine of sincerity. But if mines are not excavated and valuable gems are not obtained therefrom, then of what benefit are they? These gems remain mixed up in clay. There is in your midst such sincere material that if your missionaries and office holders take benefit from it and bring out their hidden treasures, then the whole area could benefit from your blessings and be filled with the light of Ahmadiyyat, by the Grace of Allah. May Allah Almighty grant you the capacity to do this. Ameen.

Excerpt from the Friday Sermon delivered by *Hadhrat Khalifatul Masih IV*[th] on May 31, 1991, at Baitul Nasir Mosque in Suriname. (*Al-Fazl*, September 23, 1991)

Hadhrat Khalifatul Masih IVth *and members of Jama'at Suriname with the President of Suriname during his historic 1991 visit.*

The President of Suriname meets with Hadhrat Khalifatul Masih IVth.

Ahmadiyyat in Suriname: A Brief Timeline

1956 The first mission house in Suriname is established on November 8.

1958 The first Ahmadi in Suriname, Abdul Aziz Jumman Baksh, accepts Ahmadiyyat on January 25, 1955. He would go on to study at Jamia Ahmadiyya in Rabwah and return as a missionary.

1971 The first mosque in Suriname, Baitul Nasir, is established and inaugurated by Maulana Fazal Ilahi Bashir. The land for the mosque was donated by Husaini Badola, the first president of the community.

1984 Masjid Nasar is established and inaugurated by Maulana Mohammad Siddique Nangli on February 19.

1991 *Hadhrat* Khalifatul Masih IV[RH] visits Suriname for a one-week tour.

1997 Maulana Hamid Ahmad Zafar oversees the construction of a mission house next to Nasar Mosque.

2002 On January 12, Maulana Hamid Ahmad Zafar initiates a weekly television program introducing Ahmadiyyat. The program has had a strong impact on the community and continues to this day.

2003 The Ahmadiyya Community in Suriname initiates a series of interfaith symposia on world peace and universal brotherhood, which continue to this day.

2006 In November, the 50th anniversary of Ahmadiyyat in Suriname is commemorated. Extensive programs are conducted, including the publication of a souvenir and translation of *Jama'at* literature and books into Dutch.

Jama'at at Ahmadiyya, Suriname

50 jaar
SURINAAMSE AHMADIYYA GEMEENSCHAP
1956-2006

Jama'at printed logo commemorating the 50th anniversary of Ahmadiyyat in Suriname (printed in Dutch)

Nasar Mosque in Suriname, established in 1984.

Mr. Samseer Sheikh Alibaksh, President, Suriname Ahmadiyya Community.

Laeeq Ahmad Mushtaq, Missionary-In-Charge, Suriname.

Members of the Ahmadiyya Community in Suriname on the occasion of the inauguration of Baitul Nasir by Maulana Fazal Ilahi Bashir and Husaini Badola, the first president of the community.

Trinidad & Tobago
Jama'at established 1952

© Derek Ramsey

The scarlet ibis is the national bird of Trinidad & Tobago and is featured on the Trinidad coat of arms. A newborn ibis is white in color. Its beautiful plumage takes on a scarlet color due to lifelong ingestion of crabs.

About Trinidad & Tobago

Trinidad & Tobago attained independence from the British Empire in 1962. The two islands comprise a total area of 5,128 km^2. English is the official language. The population is over 1 million; most of the inhabitants speak English, Hindi and French. Approximately 26% of the population is Roman Catholic, 23% Hindu and 6% Muslim. Due to its production of petroleum and natural gas, Trinidad is among the most prosperous in the Caribbean. The GDP of Trinidad & Tobago is US $ 23 billion, with a per capita income of $ 21,700.

CIA World Factbook

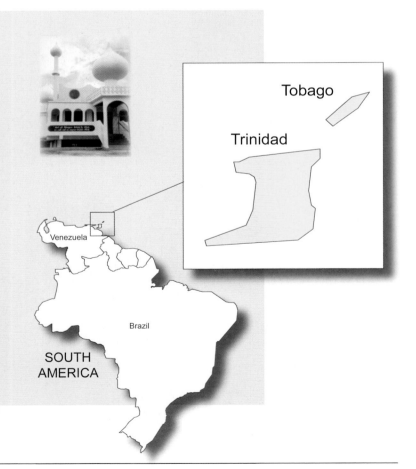

Venezuela

Brazil

SOUTH AMERICA

Tobago

Trinidad

All photos on this page: Jama'at Ahmadiyya Trinidad

Baitul A'ala, located in Caratal, Trinidad, was inaugurated on June 8, 1991, by Hadhrat Khalifatul Masih IVth during his historic visit.

Masjid Rahim in McBean was the first mosque established in Trinidad (1959).

Baitul Aziz in the northern region of Valencia was inaugurated in 1995.

Ahmadiyyat in Trinidad: A Brief Timeline

1952 The first seed of Ahmadiyyat in Trinidad is sown by the late Missionary Muhammad Ishaque Saqui.

1959 The first Ahmadi mosque in Trinidad, *Masjid* Rahim, is established in McBean.

1962 *Masjid* Nasir is established in Freeport.

1985 Mohammed Aslam Qureshi, a missionary in Trinidad, is martyred. The same year, *Masjid* Shahada in Siparia is established.

1991 *Maulana* Muhammad Saqui passes away. *Maulana* Hanif Yaqub assumes responsibilities as a missionary in Trinidad.

Hadhrat Khalifatul Masih IV[rh] makes his first visit to Trinidad. During his auspicious visit, Baitul A'ala Mosque in Caratal is inaugurated.

Huzoor[rh] appoints *Maulana* Ibrahim bin Yaqub as *Amir* and Missionary-in-Charge of Trinidad.

1995 *Masjid* Baitul Aziz is established in Valencia.

2003 *Masjid* Baitul Hamd is established in Icacos.

2007 Centenary Memorial Mosque is established.

Jama'at Ahmadiyya, Trinidad

The first missionary sent to Trinidad & Tobago, the late Maulana Muhammad Ishaque Saqui (right), is greeted by Maulana Ibrahim bin Yaqub at the Jalsa Salana (annual gathering) in 1990.

Jama'at Ahmadiyya Trinidad

Hadhrat Mirza Tahir Ahmad[rh], *on his way to inaugurate Baitul A'ala in 1991. On his right is Maulana Ibrahim bin Yaqub, Amir and Missionary-in-Charge of Trinidad & Tobago.*

AHMADIYYA MUSLIM MOSQUES

Oceania

Beginning in the 1920s, when Ahmadiyyat was introduced to the nation of Australia, *Jama'at* Ahmadiyya has greatly expanded its efforts in the continent of Oceania. Now, Ahmadiyya Muslim mosques and mission are in several island nations as well, including Tuvalu, the Solomon Islands, Tonga, Vanuatu, New Zealand and the Fiji Islands.

Photos counterclockwise from upper right: Jama'at Ahmadiyya, Fiji Islands; Jama'at Ahmadiyya, Australia, Makhzan-e-Tasaweer; Jama'at Ahmadiyya, Australia; Jama'at Ahmadiyya, Tuvalu.

AUSTRALIA

Jama'at established circa 1920's

The Aurora Australis ('Southern Lights'), here seen from Kangaroo Island in South Australia, occur as a result of geomagnetic storms.

ABOUT AUSTRALIA

In 1770, Captain James Cook claimed Australia in the name of Great Britain. Six colonies, formed in the 18th and 19th centuries, were federated in 1901 as the Commonwealth of Australia. Located between the Indian and South Pacific Oceans, Australia has an area of 7.68 million km² (slightly smaller than the United States), a population of 20.5 million, and a diverse representation of religious traditions: Christians: 68%, Buddhists: 2%, Muslims: 1.5%, Other: 28.5%. The GDP of Australia is U.S. $ 674.6 billion and the per capita income is $ 33,300

Sydney

Baitul Huda Mosque in Sydney, Australia, was inaugurated on July 14, 1989, by Hadhrat Khalifatul Masih IV^{rh}.

Hadhrat Khalifatul Masih V^{aba} visits with Jama'at staff members of the Hassan Moosa Khan library, located in Baitul Huda Mosque, Sydney, Australia.

The picturesque minaret and dome of Baitul Huda Mosque.

Mr.Mahmood Ahmad, Amir, Jama'at Australia.

Mr. Khalid Safiullah, Naib Amir, Jama'at Australia.

Mr. Nasir M. Kahlon, Naib Amir, Jama'at Australia.

Mr. Masood Ahmad Shahid, Missionary Sydney, Australia.

Sydney

Khilafat Centennial Hall: Foundation Ceremony

Dignitaries and guests gather with Hadhrat Khalifatul Masih V [aba] on the occasion of the foundation ceremony for the Khilafat Centennial Hall, located adjacent to Baitul Huda Mosque in Sydney.

Hadhrat Khalifatul Masih V [aba] and Respected Begum Sahiba lay the foundation stone for the Khilafat Centennial Hall in Sydney, Australia.

Brisbane

Hadhrat Khalifatul Masih V [aba] unveils a plaque commemorating the establishment of Baitul Masroor.

A view of one of the Mission House buildings constructed recently in Brisbane, Queensland, Australia, at the site of Bait ul Masroor.

Melbourne

The recently acquired building which serves as a new Ahmadiyya Center in Melbourne, Australia.

Adelaide

Hadhrat Khalifatul Masih V[aba] standing among members of Jama'at Ahmadiyya, Australia, on newly acquired land in Adelaide, Australia.

Hadhrat Khalifatul Masih V[aba] plants a Mulberry tree in Adelaide, Australia.

Hadhrat Khalifatul Masih V [aba] *stands with his entourage and members of Jama'at Australia in front of the famous, Sydney Opera House and adjacent picturesque downtown Sydney skyline.*

Hadhrat Ahmad's [as] advice to Sufi Hasan Moosa Khan [ra] of Australia, as related by Hadhrat Khalifatul Masih V [aba]

"**The foremost matter** mentioned in the letter was that following the pledge of *Bai'at*, consideration must be given to 'adorn' one's *Salat*....**The second counsel** in the letter to *Hadhrat* Sufi *Sahib* was to recite *Istaghfar* (seek forgiveness from Allah) in abundance while reflecting on one's sins and being mindful of the future...*Huzoor* [aba] reminded members that in December, 2005, the institution of *Wasiyyat* completed its one hundred years and...*Hadhrat* Sufi *Sahib* was the first ever *Moosi* (subscriber to the institution of *Wasiyyat*) outside of the Indian subcontinent. With his subscription of March, 1906, a centenary of the fruit of *Wasiyyat* in Australia has been reached. *Huzoor* [aba] said it was not just a coincidence that he should be visiting Australia at the time of the completion of exactly one hundred years of the first *Moosi* of Australia....*Huzoor* [aba] urged the earning Ahmadis of Australia to try and subscribe to the institution, firstly all the office holders, whether on a national or a local level, should reflect over this and the *Ameer Sahib* should look into this. *Huzoor* [aba] said that reading *Hadhrat* Sufi *Sahib's* account inspired him that each Ahmadi of Australia may become a *Moosi*. *Huzoor* [aba] said **the letter to Hadhrat Sufi Sahib also drew attention** to taking the message of Ahmadiyyat to others; certainly the current world situation demands that people are shown the way; we need to benefit others from the water of spirituality that has been granted to us."

From the Friday Sermon delivered by Hadhrat Khalifatul Masih V [aba]*, on 14 April, 2006, in Sydney, Australia (Source: www.alislam.org).*

Prelude to the 2006 Jalsa Salana, Australia

◄ *Traditional marquee tents are put up in preparation for Jalsa Salana Australia in front of Baitul Huda Mosque.*

A colorfully dressed Nasirat ul Ahmadiyya (Young Girls' group) stand eagerly waiting to welcome Hadhrat Khalifatul Masih V[aba] to Baitul Huda Mosque on the occasion of the 2006 Jalsa Salana, Australia.

Huzoor[aba] inspects the Langar Khana Masihe Mauood, Australia.

Huzoor[aba] in discussion with MTA officers.

Jalsa Highlights

Hadhrat Khalifatul Masih V [aba] leads the silent prayers following the flag hoisting ceremony marking the occasion of the 2006 Jalsa Salana, Australia.

A glimpse of the proceedings of the 2006 Jalsa Salana, Australia, which was opened with Juma (Friday) prayers led by Huzoor [aba].

Huzoor [aba] addresses guests and dignitaries attending a special banquet during the 2006 Jalsa Salana, Australia.

The Honorable Philip Ruddock, who was serving as Attorney General of Australia when this photo was taken (and who is now a Member of Parliament) greets Hadhrat Khalifatul Masih V [aba], during the special banquet held for dignitaries on the occasion of the 2006 Jalsa Salana, Australia.

The First Visit of Khalifatul Masih to Australia

Hadhrat Khalifatul Masih IV [rh] in discussion at the University of Canberra in 1983, where he delivered his famous lecture: 'Some Distinctive Features of Islam'.

The Spiritual Discovery of Australia

"Today, when we are laying the foundation stone of our first mosque and mission house, it is the greatest day in the history of Australia. The splendor of this day shall increase with the passage of time, and the day when Captain Cook stepped for the first time on the soil of this continent shall diminish and fade away before the glaring brilliance of this day. The time is not far away when the inhabitants of Australia will come in multitudes to pay homage to this mosque and, worshipping in this House of God, they shall remember the great day when a very humble servant of Islam laid the foundation stone of a very small mosque with earnest supplication. In this mosque's courtyard, they will pray, with tears in their eyes, for all those inner souls who offered wealth and life to construct this house of God, and wish they were present at that time and were among the pioneers who initiated the dominance of Islam in Australia."

— *Excerpt from the address of Hadhrat Khalifatul Masih IV [rh], delivered at the foundation stone ceremony of Baitul Huda Mosque in Sydney, Australia in 1983.*

Hadhrat Khalifatul Masih IV [rh] holds up a book about Australia's Aboriginal community, presented to him as a gift by the author, Burnum Burnam (standing next to Huzoor [rh]).

Local Aboriginal community members meet with Hadhrat Khalifatul Masih IV [rh].

Ahmadi Muslims in Australia: Historic Highlights

Mr. Sufi Hassan Moosa Khan^{ra}, the first Ahmadi Muslim in Australia.

1903 Mr. *Sufi* Hassan Moosa Khan becomes an Ahmadi Muslim when *Hadhrat* Ahmad^{as} accepts his *Bai'at* by written correspondence.

1921 Mr. Moosa Khan initiates a magazine entitled *The Muslim Sunshine. He* would receive extracts from Mufti Muhammad Sadiq^{ra}, the editor of *The Muslim Sunrise* (*The Muslim Sunrise*, Vol. 2, 1921).

1928 The first *Jalsa Salana* of Australia is held on December 28. Many non-Ahmadi guests participate in this *Jalsa*, in which Hassan Moosa Khan introduces the claims of *Hadhrat* Ahmad^{as} and narrates the history of Ahmadiyyat.

1979 Dr. Eijazul Haq requests permission from *Hadhrat Khalifatul Masih III^{rh}* to organize a *Jama'at* in Australia. Mirza Tahir Ahmad^{rh}, then serving as *Wakilut Tabshir*, suggests that names of individuals be proposed who could serve in various *Jama'at* capacities in Australia. Dr. Haq sends a few names and permission is granted from *Hadhrat Khalifatul Masih III^{rh}* to organize the *Jama'at*.

1983 Upon the instructions of *Hadhrat* Khalifatul Masih IV^{rh}, the Australian *Jama'at* acquires a 27 acre parcel of land in Sydney, Australia, and at this location *Huzoor^{rh}* lays the foundation stone of Bait ul Huda Mosque on September 30 (*The Weekly International Al-Fazal*, 12 May 06 issue, p. 1)

1984 Eighty individuals attend *Jalsa Salana* in Australia.

1985 On July 5, Shakil Ahmad Munir arrives in Australia to serve as the Ameer & Missionary-in-Charge. This year, a monthly magazine, called *Al-Huda*, begins circulation.

1986 A graveyard is acquired for the Ahmadiyya Muslim Community in Australia, and the first burial is for Shams ud Din.

1987 The Ahmadiyya Muslim *Jama'at* in Australia is formally registered on September 7.

Shakeel Ahmad Munir, the former Amir of Australia (left), standing with Mr. Maulana Mahmood Ahmad, the current Amir Jama'at Australia (right).

1989 On July 14, *Hadhrat* Khalifatul Masih IV^{rh} inaugurates Bait ul Huda Mosque in Sydney, Australia. (*The Weekly International Al-Fazal*, 12 May 06 issue, p. 1)

1991 Mahmood Ahmad arrives in Australia to serve as Amir and Missionary-in-Charge.

1996 Masood Ahmad Shahid arrives in Australia to serve as an Ahmadiyya Muslim Missionary, and has been serving the local Brisbane, Queensland *Jama'at* since 1997. Qamar Dawood Khokar also arrives in August, having been appointed to serve as an Ahmadiyya Muslim Missionary in Melbourne.

2006 *Hadhrat Khalifatul Masih V* ^{aba} inaugurates Baitul Masroor, which is located on a ten acre parcel of land in Brisbane. A guest house, mosque and mission house are located in Baitul Masroor. A 20-acre parcel of land is also acquired in Adelaide, which already has a five bedroom house on the premises.

FIJI ISLANDS

Jama'at established in 1960

Beauitful soft coral gardens on Taveuni, one island within the Fiji Islands group.

ABOUT FIJI

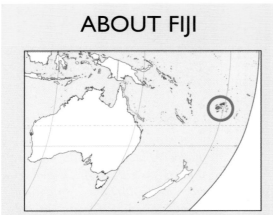

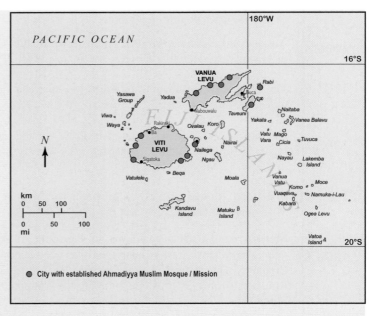

City with established Ahmadiyya Muslim Mosque / Mission

The Fiji Islands gained their independance from the British in 1970. The Islands are located in the South Pacific between Hawaii and New Zealand, and comprise an total area of 18,272 km². The population of the islands is about 1 million; most inhabitants speak English, Fijian or Hindi. Approximately 53% of the population are Christian, 34% Hindu, 7% Muslim and 6% of other faiths. The GDP of the Fiji Islands is US $3.4 Billion, with a per capita income of US $4,100.

Artwork: Arshad M. Khan, University of Texas Libraries / Data: Jama'at Ahmadiyya Fiji Islands.

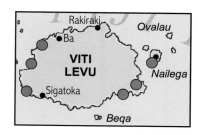

Viti Levu

On September 25, 1983, *Hadhrat* Khalifatul Masih IV [rh] laid the foundation stone for Rizwan Mosque in Sugar City, Latouka. The Mosque is located on highly elevated school grounds. It was built by two brothers, the late *Al-Haj* Mohammad Hanif and *Al-Haj* Shah Mohammad. The construction began in 1983 and was completed in 1984.

Hadhrat Khalifatul Masih IV [rh] places wet cement into the foundation site for Rizwan Mosque in Lautouka, Viti Levu, Fiji Islands.

The Aqsa Mosque was completed in 1972 and inaugurated by Missionary Incharge Mohammad Siddique Amritsari. *Al-Haj* Mohammad Ramzan Jhan donated funds to build the main floor of the mosque. The construction was done through *Waqar e Amal*. It has offices and missionary quarters on the ground floor.

Aqsa Mosque, Nadi, Viti Levu, Fiji Islands

Chaudhry Muhammad Zafrullah Khan [ra] laid the foundation stone of Mahmud Mosque in 1965. The Mosque officially opened in 1972. The late Mr. Mohammad Ayub Khan, who was serving then as President of the *Jama'at*, assisted with the Mosque's construction.

Mahmud Mosque, Maro, Viti Levu, Fiji Islands

Vanua Levu

Aiwane Mustafa Lajna Hall, Samabula, Vanua Levu

LAJNA CONTRIBUTIONS

The late Mrs. Maryam Bi donated a parcel of land in 1966 with the hope of building a mosque. On it, her children constructed Bilal Mosque, which is located in Nasarwaqa, Vanua Levu.

The Fiji Islands *Lajna Imaillah* (Ladies' Auxiliary) also worked together to construct the Aiwane Mustafa Lajna Hall, shown at the left.

CONSTRUCTING FAZL-E-UMAR

Maulana Ghulam Ahmad Farrukh laid the foundation stone for Fazl-e-Umar Mosque in 1974. It is one of the largest complexes in the entire country, housing a prayer hall, library, missionary quarters and guest house, printing press, and a half-dozen shops on the ground floor.

The original estimate for the mosque was $250,000, but with additional amenities, the facility amounted to $800,000. Fazl-e-Umar Mosque was inaugurated on September 18, 1983, by *Hadhrat* Khaliftaul Masih IV [rh].

Fazl-e-Umar Mosque in Samabula, Vanua Levu

"This is a great favor and blessing of Allah that today I am addressing this Friday Sermon from that area and country of the world which is considered the last corner of the world. From this perspective, we are experiencing the fulfillment of the promises made to the Promised Messiah [as] manifested in another way, first *Hadhrat* Ahmad's message reached the corner of the world through MTA [Muslim Television Ahmadiyya] and now it is being spread from the corners to the world over...on the occasion of *Jalsa Salana* Qadian, the Eid sermon and other addresses were transmitted from Qadian, and today, Allah has provided us the means to transmit from the corner of the world the message of *Hadhrat* Promised Messiah to the rest of the world. This is Allah's grace that we are able to see this bounty of Allah." -- *Hadhrat Khalifatul Masih V* [aba], April 25, 2006

GLIMPSES OF HUZOOR'S VISIT TO FIJI

Huzoor[aba] and his entourage meet the Honorable Ratu Joni Madraiwiwi, Vice-President of Fiji Islands, at the state office.

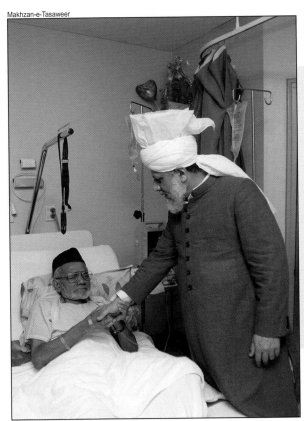

Master Mohammad Hussein, who translated the Holy Qur'an into the Fiji language, served as the country's missionary from 1978 to 1988. In 2006, while briefly hospitalized, he was visited by *Hadhrat Khalifatul Masih V*[aba].

HADHRAT KHALIFATUL MASIH IV[ra] ON THE DEVOTION OF FIJI AHMADIES

(Khutubat e Tahir, Vol II, pages 539-541)

"They have such a deep love for *Hadhrat* Promised Messiah[as], the like of which can only be seen for one's most beloved person. As I have mentioned before, when we met them face to face and talked about their spiritual reformation, we felt as if, in just a few days, a new nation had come into existence.

Thus, when the news of the Okara (Pakistan) reached them -- I cannot explain mentioned it in his speech It seemed they wanted to effect that it had left on they also mentioned at so have remained in a state seek Allah's forgiveness may He forgive all their the new beginning, which Allah help them make more

martyr of Nasir Ahmed of them -- the way it affected in words. Their Amir when he gave us a farewell. express the tremendous them. Other than that, many occasions that they of darkness, for which they and request for prayers that shortcomings. The new life, they have found now, may and more progress.

They told me that they cannot they are in now. They said they and now they know what Ahmadiyyat explain in words the condition have found a new identity in them is. Having experienced this, all of their members, including women, children, and the elderly, were ready to give their lives for the sake of Ahmadiyyat. They said that they were not exaggerating this fact, and even if they were to be slaughtered like goats, they would still be ready. They said that their wealth and social respect were all at my disposal and when I went back, I should go back with the assurance that by the Grace of Allah, whatever way I will call on them to serve the Jama'at, I will find them ready." — Friday Sermon, 21 October 1983.

Ahmadi Muslims in the Fiji Islands: Historic Highlights

1960 The Fiji Islands *Jama'at* is established in October, with Sheikh Abdul Wahid serving as the first Ahmadiyya Muslim Missionary to this region.

1962 A parcel of land, complete with a timber and iron building is purchased in Suva for the *Jama'at* and approved by the Center. A new *Jama'at* in Labasa is established.

1965 Maulana Rahim Buksh donates land to construct Mubarak Mosque, which is inaugurated by Sheikh Abdul Wahid on December 17. Sir Muhammad Zafrulla Khan [ra] visits the Fiji Islands, delivers a public lecture arranged by the Chief Minister, Ratu Sir Kamisese Mara, and lays the foundation of Mahmud Mosque at Maro. In April, a kindergarten program is formed in Lautoka.

1969 The first Ahmadiyya Muslim Primary School is established at Drasa Vitogo, Lautoka. Mohammed Hussain serves as its first schoolmaster.

1970 Maulana Ghulam Ahmad Farrukh inaugurates Nasir Mosque in Labasa.

1972 Maulvi Muhammad Siddique Amritsari inaugurates Mahmud Mosque, which is later completed under the leadership of Muhammad Ayyub Khan and his family.

1974 Maulana Ghulam Ahmad Farrukh lays the foundation of Fazle Umar Mosque in Samabula.

1977 Hamid Hussein donates a parcel of land to construct the Bilal Mosque, completed in 1978.

1983 *Hadhrat Khalifatul Masih IV* [rh], in his first tour of Southeast Asia, visits Fiji Islands during September 16-25. *Huzoor* [rh] inaugurates the largest mosque in the South Pacific, the Fazle Umar Mosque, on September 18, 1983. On September 25th, *Huzoor* [rh] visits the Ahmadiyya Primary School in Lautoka, and lays the foundation stone for the Rizwan Mosque on the school grounds. The mosque is later built by two brothers, *Al-Haj* Shah Mohammad and *Al-Haj* Mohammad Hanif, and their families. Mosque construction begins in 1983 and is completed in 1984.

1984 The Fiji Islands *Jama'at* establishes another primary school in a Housing Authority Area in Narere, Nasinu, 8 miles away from Suva City. Mr. Sadiq Hussain

1989 A new *Jama'at* on the remote island of Nailega is formed. A parcel of land with a house is bought and becomes the Mission House of Taveuni. *Hadhrat Khalifatul Masih IV* [rh] visits the Fiji Islands for the centenary celebrations and meets with new *Jama'at* members in Suva.

1993 On July 3, the Ahmadiyya Muslim College is founded by then Permanent Secretary of Education, Mr. Amraiya Naidu.

2002 Baitul Jaamey Mosque is built in Taveuni, the home of the International Date Line. Maulana Naeem Ahmad Cheema lays its foundation stone, and Nawab Mansoor Khan, Wakilut Tabshir Rabwah, inaugurates it in April. The *Jama'at* buys a 30 acre freehold land at Voloca, Labasa from Mr. Munif Buksh, son of the late Rahim Buksh.

Hadhrat Khalifatul Masih V [aba] *visits Baitul Jaamey in 2006.*

2003 An Ahmadiyya Muslim Secondary School is established, with voluntary overseeing done by Master Sadiq Hussain. The *Amir* and Missionary-in-Charge, Maulana Naeem Ahmed Cheema had laid the foundation stone. The school is now a full fledged secondary school.

2004 A new mosque is built on Rabi Island, which is populated mostly by Banabans who are of Kiribati origin. The Ameer and Missionary-in-Charge, Maulana Naeem Ahmad Cheema, lays the foundation of this mosque and also inaugurates this as Bait ul Mahdi Mosque. Master Sadiq Hussain provides voluntary service in building the mosque.

2006 *Hadhrat Khalifatul Masih V* [aba] arrives in the Fiji Islands on April 25. He addresses the *Jalsa Salana*, leads Friday prayers, visits many *Jama'ats*, holds meetings with the President of the country, attends receptions arranged by different organizations, and also has personal Mulaquats (meetings) with all *Jama'at* members. He also visits the Ahmadiyya Muslim Secondary School and inaugurates the Home Economics Block at the school. This year also marks the first live televised Friday Sermon to come from this corner of the world. Eleven satellites are used to transmit *Huzoor's* [aba] message globally.

Hadhrat Khalifatul Masih V [aba] *visits the official site of the International Date Line, at the 180° meridian.*

New Ahmadi Muslims in Neighboring Island Nations (Tonga, Vanuatu)

Tongan representatives meet with Hadhrat Khalifatul Masih V [aba] *on April 30, 2006.*

The first Ahmadi Muslim in Vanuatu.

NEW ZEALAND

Jama'at established circa 1912-1915

A view of Franz Josef Glacier in New Zealand. The glacier, some twelve kilometers in length, is part of the Southern Alps mountain range which runs along the western side of the country's South Island. A popular tourist attraction, the Franz Josef is a UNESCO World Heritage Site.

ABOUT NEW ZEALAND

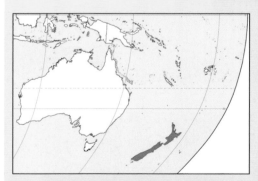

The Polynesian Maori reached New chieftains entered into a pact with Britain, they ceded sovereignty to Queen In that same year, the British The British colony of New 1907. New Zealand is 4.1 million over 50% of $112.6 billion and its per

Zealand in about 800 A.D. In 1840, their called the Treaty of Waitangi, in which Victoria while retaining territorial rights. began the first organized colonial settlement. Zealand became an independent dominion in located south east of Australia. The population is whom follow Christianity. The country's GDP is US capita income is US $27, 300.

Baitul Muqueet, Auckland, New Zealand

Hadhrat Khalifatul Masih V [aba] speaking with the representative of the Prime Minister of New Zealand, the Honorable Dr. Ashraf Chaudry (Member of Parliament).

Huzoor [aba] enjoying a lighthearted moment with his private secretary and Dr. Sorab, President of New Zealand Jama'at.

THE FIRST AHMADI MUSLIM IN NEW ZEALAND

Dr. Clement Wragge, the first Ahmadi Muslim in New Zealand

Professor Clement Wragge, an astronomer living in New Zealand, visited Lahore to give a lecture in 1908. Mr. Mufti Mohammad Sadiq [ra] also attended that lecture. Upon Mr. Sadiq's urging, Dr. Wragge met with *Hadhrat* Ahmad[as] on May 12, 1908, and found that all of the questions he asked him were met with answers that brought deep satisfaction. He met *Huzoor*[as] one more time, on May 18, 1908, about a week before *Hadhrat* Ahmad's sad demise. He later accepted Ahmadiyyat and thus bears the distinction of being the first Ahmadi Muslim living in New Zealand. (*Badar*, May 24, 1908, p 4; as chronicled in the Urdu text of *Tahrik-e-Ahmadiyyat*, Volume 2, p 543).

A FAMILY REUNION

Hadhrat Khalifatul Masih V[aba], during his Asian tour, visited New Zealand and expressed his desire to meet the children or grandchildren of Dr. Wragge. The New Zealand *Jama'at* was able to trace the whereabouts of his grandchildren, to whom they extended an invitation to meet with *Huzoor* Aqdas[aba]. Here, we show a few photographs of this special occasion.

Dr. Sohrab, President of Jama'at New Zealand, explains to Huzoor how he found Dr. Wragge's grave.

Dr. Clement Wragge's grandchildren met with Huzoor at the 17th Jalsa Salana New Zealand.

GLIMPSES FROM 17th JALSA SALANA

Hadhrat Khalifatul Masih V ^{aba} is greeted by Nasiraat (Young Ladies' Organization) as he enters the Jalsa Gah.

Huzoor ^{aba} delivering the final address.

Huzoor ^{aba} performs a "Hongi", a rubbing of the noses and sharing the breath of life, while presenting a gift to the Co-Leader of the Maori Party, Dr. Pita Sharples.

Huzoor ^{aba} distributes chocolates to eager Kiwi Atfal.

Huzoor ^{aba} hoisting the Jama'at flag alongside the New Zealand flag during the opening ceremony.

TUVALU

Jama'at established in 1987

A beach at Funafuti atoll, Tuvalu. This small island is the official capital of the island nation of Tuvalu.

ABOUT TUVALU

Tuvalu is one of the smallest countries of the world, with a total area of just 26 km² distributed among nine islands. Most of her 11,992 inhibitants are Protestant (97%); an adiditonal 1.7% are Seventh-Day Adventists; another 1% are Bah'ai.

The first Ahmadiyya Muslim Mosque in Tuvalu.

A Tuvaluan representative meets Hadhrat Khalifatul Masih V^{aba} on April 30, 2006.

Ahmadi Muslims in Tuvalu

Dr. Iftikhar Ayaz introduced Ahmadiyyat to Tuvalu; the first *Ba'ait* was in June, 1985. The first mosque and mission houses were constructed in 1992. In his first visit to the region, *Hadhrat Khalifatul Masih IVth* expressed a desire to spread Ahmadiyyat across the South Pacific Islands. Through Dr. Ayaz's efforts, the *Jama'at* was registered in 1987. *Hafiz* Jibraeel was sent from the Fiji Islands to Tuvalu for two years to train and teach new Ahmadis. Missionary Abdul Ghaffar, then stationed in Ghana, was subsequently posted to Tuvalu until 1998, helping the Ahmadi congregation grow to over 400. The translation of the Holy Qur'an and *Jama'at* literature was comprehensively undertaken in the Tuvaluan language.

Excerpts from Khaliftul Masih IV's (ra) address on the creation of the Tuvalu Jama'at

In Tuvalu, as soon as the *Jama'at* was registered, a big uproar took place. Many Christian opposition leaders raised serious objections against the registration in the National Assembly of Tuvalu. They criticized the government for allowing a new religion to hold its footing on the Island. This will create unrest and disorder in peaceful Tuvalu. Their opposition against the registration of *Jama'at* Ahmadiyya was very stiff. When this issue was raised in their Parliament, the Prime Minister of Tuvalu did not give any weight to their criticism and, in sharp contrast, fully supported *Jama'at* Ahmadiyya's right to get itself registered in Tuvalu. He said that the way we let Christians follow their religion, we as the Government of Tuvalu will follow the law of the land. We will not let Christians interfere in our law. *Jama'at* Ahmadiyya is legally registered here and the registration will stand as it is. On hearing such a bold statement, the Governor General of Tuvalu called the Prime Minister Sir Tamasi Poa Poa on the phone and congratulated him. He said that he was worried that the Prime Minister may take a milder position on the issue. But he did the right thing and made a right decision. Thus by the Grace of Allah, when Allah blesses us with successes, He also gives courage to hearts, through his angels, to make the right decision with justice. This is, however, so unfortunate and sad that some of our own Muslim countries do not practice the true and just teachings of Islam, while those who have no connection with Islam practice the principles of justice that in fact are Islamic principles. All the new Ahmadi initiations that have

> "The Prime Minister of Tuvalu fully supported Jama'at Ahmadiyya's right to get itself registered."

Hadhrat Khalifatul Masih IV rh with the Prime Minister of Tuvalu in London.

taken place in Tuvalu, by the Grace of Allah, are those of highly educated people. Among the locals who accepted Islam and Ahmadiyyat are also the President of the Public Service Commission and the police officer who was on security duty for the Governor General of Tuvalu. Both of these dear ones are present here in this *Jalsa Salana* [*Jalsa Salana* UK 1987] as the representative of Tuvalu. (At that point, *Huzoor*aba requested the two gentlemen to rise, so that the *Jama'at* may recognize them). *Huzoor*aba said that since the time they have accepted Islam, they have totally dedicated themselves to the service of Islam and Ahmadiyyat. They have good command of English, as well as of local languages. They have been engaged in the translation of Ahmadiyya literature in the local language. They also had an opportunity to translate many verses of Holy Qur'an in the local language. The police officer giving security duty for the Governor General, wrote me a letter just a few days before my arrival. He wrote that since the time he has joined the *Jama'at*, his interest in the police service has sharply declined. He was contemplating an early retirement. He requested me to allow him to take early retirement and then totally dedicate himself for the *Jama'at*. These are such amazing currents of blessings of Allah that are blowing in all directions. A plan for the construction of the mosque and the mission house in Tuvalu is in the final stages and the money needed for the project has already been sent. The work on the project will *Insha'Allah*, start soon.

— *Huzoor*'s (rh) address at *Jalsa Salana* U.K. on August 1, 1987.

Holding Fast by the Rope of Allah
The International Ba'ait and the Unity of Nations
by Imam Ataul Mujeeb Rashid, London, United Kingdom

"And hold fast, all together, by the rope of Allah and be not divided; and remember the favor of Allah which He bestowed upon you when you were enemies and He united your hearts in love, so that by His grace you became as brothers; and your were on the brink of a pit of fire and he saved you from it. Thus does Allah explain to you His commandments that you may be guided." (3:104)

As the above verse from the Holy Qur'an illustrates, Islam aims to unify humanity by eliminating mutual differences and discrimination. Islam is the flag bearer in carrying this message of unity to all nations of the world. This is not merely a claim; the true teachings of Islam provide a living proof in the person of the Prophet of Islam, Muhammad [sa]. Allah, in fact, instructs Muhammad[sa] in the Holy Qur'an to introduce himself as a messenger for all of humanity: *"Say, 'Oh mankind! Truly I am a Messenger to you all from Allah."* (*Al Araf*, verse 159). The extraordinary message that was given to him for the peace, security and international unity was for all nations and for all time.

Muhammad [sa] showed the entire world through his own practices, which are documented in the *Ahadith*, how to treat all nations of the world with grace and how to turn them into one nation through the peaceful teachings of Islam. He described such unity in familial terms, saying that "All humans created by God are brothers to one another" (*Masnad Ahmad*, v. 4, p. 369). All those people who came under the secure and peaceful shadow of Islam turned into brothers for each other.

This unity of humankind, which is the guarantee of salvation and success of mankind, is not a matter of ancient history. In the modern era,

Allah resurrected the spiritual means to unify humankind through the founder of the Ahmadiyya Muslim Community, *Hadhrat Mirza Ghulam Ahmad*[as] of Qadian, India — the Promised Messiah[as]. Under Divine direction, the Promised Messiah[as] laid the foundation of the *Jama'at* Ahmadiyya for the rejuvenation and establishment of Islam:

Maulana Ataul Mujeeb Rashid, Imam, Masjid London

"Allah, the most high and the lord of Majesty, has very much liked the system in which a large group of truthful people, after having beaded into one cord, appears as one nation among the creations of Allah" (*Majmoah Ishtiharat*, Vol. 1, p. 194).

In these latter days, which in fact are the continuation of the blessed time of the Prophet of Islam[sa], Allah has shown the destined unity of the nations of the world in a grand way through the establishment of *Jama'at* Ahmadiyya and the formal announcement of joining that *Jama'at*: the *Ba'ait*.

By the Grace of Allah, according to the teachings of Holy Qur'an and the practices of Prophet of Islam[sa], the system of *Ba'ait* has continued in *Jama'at* Ahmadiyya from the very beginning. The Promised Messiah[as] has invited all of humanity to spend some time with him to experience a pure and spiritual way of life:

"I have been told by Allah that those people who

are the seekers of truth and want to find the path of true faith, true spiritual purity, and love of Allah, and those who want to get rid of the impure, rebellious and ignorant life style, they should do Ba'ait at my hand" (Advertisement, December 1, 1888, *Majmoa Ishtiharat*, Vol. 1, p. 188).

The first *Ba'ait* was taken by the Promised Messiah[as], after receiving permission from Allah, on March 23, 1889, in the city of Ludhiana, India. This day is remembered as the date when the foundation of *Jama'at* Ahmadiyya was laid. The Promised Messiah[as] was sitting on a *"Darri"* (cotton spread) on the floor, in the corner of the room. Among the men, the first person to perform *Ba'ait* was *Hadhrat Hakeem Maulvi* Nooruddin[ra]. On that day, forty fortunate individuals received the honor to perform *Ba'ait* at the hands of the Promised Messiah[as]. Those who performed *Ba'ait* stated that they went through a unique spiritual experience at that time. A new and pure change was taking place in them from within. This small group of forty people, in fact, constituted the initial wave of the millions of people who were to join the Ahmadiyya *Jama'at* in later years.

The system of *Ba'ait* has since continued to operate throughout the world. After the establishment of the system of *khilafat*, the tradition continued in Pakistan. Soon, the honor of performing *Ba'ait* at the hands of the *khalifa* continued in other countries around the world. On December 28, 1992, at the occasion of *Jalsa Salana* Qadian, *Hadhrat Khalifatul Masih IV*[rh], addressed the gathering via Muslim Television Ahmadiyya (MTA) directly from London. After this session, eight new prospects, who were present in London, performed *Ba'ait* at his hands. This was the first time in the history of Ahmadiyyat that the *Ba'ait* ceremony was simultaneously transmitted via MTA. Ahmadi members of the *Jama'at* watched that ceremony all over the world. And while they were thousands of miles away from the *khalifa*, they were able to reaffirm their own *Ba'aits* simultaneously. This "International *Ba'ait*" was organized at the request of a newly converted Englishman in London. Describing this event,

Hadhrat Khalifatul Masih IV[rh] stated:

"Of all the interesting things I remember, the one thing that specially caught my attention, and I was told that members of the *Jama'at* also feel the same way, is the International *Ba'ait*. This is first time ever in history that a *Ba'ait* was being done at one place and at the same time all over the world tongues were busy in repeating those words, hearts were pounding and with one sound a pledge of faithfulness was done. This created a unique effect on the souls and hearts of those taking part in the *Ba'ait*. I think this was a way destined by Allah to show his expression. This did not happen accidentally. Our last year was decorated by Allah with that *Ba'ait*. The crown of International *Ba'ait* decorated it. It has been told that *Jama'ats* all over the world also reaffirmed their *Ba'aits* simultaneously and entered into a new age of faithfulness, dedication and service to mankind. This is the fulfillment of that *Ba'ait*. I can see that in future, *Insha'Allah*, *Ba'aits* will take place in the same way. When the *Ba'ait* will be taken in one *Jalsa*, then millions of *Ba'aits* will be reaffirmed at other places. The idea of millions of *Ba'aits* that I presented once is not a matter too far in the future, or just a dream or speculations. I feel that its time is very near."

(Daily *Al Fazl*, January 1, 1993).

A similar incident occurred on May 30, 1993, on the occasion of the Annual *Ijtema* (Gathering) of Khuddamul Ahmadiyya (Ahmadiyya Muslim Youth Association) in Germany. Seventy-one individuals of thirteen different countries took *Ba'ait* at the hands of *Hadhrat Khalifatul Masih IV*[rh]. This ceremony also was televised on MTA. In this way, an opportunity was made available to Ahmadis all over the world to re-affirm their *Ba'ait* also.

After those two initial opportunities, the historical debut of the International *Ba'ait* took place in 1993, during the *Jalsa Salana* in the United Kingdom. This was the first regular ceremony of International *Ba'ait*, in which more than two hundred thousand individuals were blessed with the opportunity to take part in the *Ba'ait* ceremony through MTA. All Ahmadi men, women and children around the world also were able to re-affirm their *Ba'aits*. Since this was the occasion of International *Ba'ait*, and without any doubt it was a unique incidence in the history of Islam, *Hadhrat Khalifatul Masih IV*[rh], delivered a heartwarming and faith-rejuvenating address before the International *Ba'ait*:

"Since the time the earth and the Heavens have been created, no eye has ever seen such a scene where people of many countries and nations, took bait at the hand of one man simultaneously. This is the first incidence in the history of Islam. And if Allah willed, this system will always continue in future. The target for the Ba'ait for the next year will be twice the number of Ba'aits this year. Every year this target will be increased double fold.

The idea of an International Ba'ait came to my mind when in the beginning of the year I was informed that ten thousands Ba'aits may take place this year. There was only little time left until the inauguration of Jalsa Salana. I thought that by the end of last year a target of one hundred thousand Ba'aits was given to the Jama'ats. Now very little time is left. How will the target be achieved? Then I prayed to Allah and a thought was put in my heart and I understood the road map to the International Ba'ait. I was told by Allah to prepare Jama'at, so they may take part in the International Ba'ait. All Jama'ats were then given new targets of Ba'aits.

There is no element of boasting or arrogance in my heart at this historical event. I feel the greatest humbleness in my heart. I am a humble person. May Allah cover my weaknesses, forgive me and change my weaknesses into good deeds."

(Daily *Al Fazl*, August 15, 1993, p. 1).

After the address, *Huzoor*[rh] went to the place of the *Ba'ait* ceremony. He sat on the floor and joined five individuals who represented the five continents of the world. Before commencing this new tradition of the *Jama'at*, he remarked:

"The long coat that I am wearing today is the blessed coat of The Promised Messiah[as]*. It is green in color, although due to the passage of such a long time, it has faded a little. I will take Ba'ait from you in the capacity of an insignificant servant of the founder of Ahmadiyya movement."* (Daily *Al Fazl*, August 15, 1993, p. 2).

In this way, under the shade of the blessings of Allah, the first historic International *Ba'ait* took place. It has become a milestone in the journey of progress and victory of Islam and Ahmadiyyat, and history will always remember it. On that particular day, a golden chapter was written in the history of Islam. It was a chapter of victory that still continues today and will continue forward. *Insha'Allah.*

First International Ba'ait ceremony held in 1993 at U.K. Jalsa Salana when 204,308 individuals entered the fold of Islam/Ahmadiyyat from 84 countries representing 115 nationalities of the world.

Glossary
Foreign words and phrases used in transliteration in this book

Ahmadiyya. Of or pertaining to Ahmadiyyat (an *Ahmadi* = follower of Ahmadiyyat)

Amir. President (*Naib Amir* = Vice-President)

Ansarullah. An Ahmadiyya auxiliary of men over forty years of age.

Begum Sahiba. 'The respected lady'

Ba'ait. A formal rite of initiation and allegiance into the fold of Ahmadiyyat.

Da'ee. Preacher; *Daee Ilallah* program = an initiative to engage in preaching.

Hadhrat/Huzoor. 'your honor' or 'the honored one'

Hafiz. One who commits Quranic text to memory. (plural = *huffaz*)

Holy Qur'an. The most authoritative and sacred text of Muslims.

Ijtema. A gathering.

Jalsa Salana. Annual gathering

Jama'at. An Ahmadiyya organization.

Ka'aba. The site located at the Sacred Mosque in Makkah (the first house of worship)

Khalifa. A successor of the prophet of God. (plural = *khulafa*).

Khalifatul Masih. Khalifa of the Messiah; for our context, the successor of the Promised Messiah[as]

Khilafat. The institution of successorship in Islam.

Khuddam. An Ahmadiyya auxiliary organization of men between 15-40 years of age.

Lajna Imaillah. An Ahmadiyya auxiliary of women over 16 years of age.

Majlis. A 'body of people' or a 'group'

Majlis e Irfan. A question/answer session with *Khalifatul Masih*.

Masih e Mauood. 'The Promised Messiah'

Masjid. Mosque (*Masjid e Nabawi*. Prophet's Mosque).

MTA. Muslim Television Ahmadiyya, the 24 hour live international satellite channel of the Ahmadiyya Muslim Community.

Musleh e Mauood. 'The Promised Reformer'. A name given to Khalifatul Masih II[ra].

Promised Messiah. *Hadhrat* Mirza Ghulam Ahmad[as] of Qadian (b.1835, d.1908) whose advent was foretold by the Prophet Muhammad[sa].

Qibla. Direction towards which a Muslim faces during *Salat*.

Sahibzada. 'respected son'

Salat. The ritualistic form of worship in Islam

Tafseer e Kabeer. A large commentary of the Holy Qur'an by *Hadhrat Khalifatul Masih II* [ra] (*Tafseer e Sagheer* is a shorter commentary written separately).

Guide to Abbreviations for Arabic Salutations

aba	*'ayyada hullah ta'ala binasrihil aziz'*: 'may Allah strengthen him with His mighty help'
as	*'alaihis salaam'*: 'peace be upon him'
ra	*'radhi allahu 'anhu'* (or *'anha'*): 'may Allah be pleased with him (or her)'
rh	*'rahimullahu ta'ala'*: 'may Allah shower His Mercy on him/her'
sa	*'salla'illahu alaihi wa sallam'*: 'may the peace and blessings of Allah be upon him'

Annotated Bibliography
Further information about the references used for this pictorial

Collections

- *Malfoozat* [Sayings].

  A collection of the writings of the Promised Messiah[as].

- *Tarikh e Ahmadiyyat* [History of Ahmadiyyat] (Rabwah: Idaratul Musanifeen/Nizarat Isha'at, 1957-2005).

  A multi-volume Urdu language history of Ahmadiyyat as chronicled by *Maulana* Dost Muhammad Shahid, official historian of the Ahmadiyya Muslim Community. Volumes run from 1889-1957.

- *Khutbat e Mahmood, Khutbat e Nasir, Khutbat e Tahir* and *Khutbat e Masroor*.

  Various collections of Friday sermons of the *khulufa*.

Periodicals

- Daily *Al-Fazal* (Rabwah)

  Official Urdu language daily newspaper of the Ahmadiyya Muslim Community. Publication began in 1913.

- *Al Fazal International* Weekly (London)

  Official Urdu language weekly newspaper of the Ahmadiyya Muslim Community, United Kingdom.

- Weekly *Badar* (Qadian)

  Official weekly Urdu language newspaper of the Ahmadiyya Muslim Community, Qadian.

- *Ahmadiyya Gazette, USA*

  Official monthly English language magazine of the Ahmadiyya Muslim Community, USA.

- *Ahmadiyya Gazette, Canada*

  Official monthly English language magazine of the Ahmadiyya Muslim Community, Canada.

Books

- *Daura-e-Maghrib* [Western Tours], Rabwah: Ziaul Islam Press, 1980.

  An Urdu language narrative of *Hadhrat Khalifatul Masih II*'s [ra] historic tour of eleven countries in Western Europe, the United States and Canada.

- *Africa Speaks* (Karachi: 1980).

  An extensive account of *Hadhrat Khalifatul Masih III*'s [rh] tour of African countries.

- *Musleh Maud ka Safr e Europe*

  An Urdu language pictorial published in Pakistan in 1955.

- *Tehrik-e-Jadid: Jama'at Ahmadiyya Tarraqui ki Shahrah pur* [Jama'at Ahmadiyya's Journey to Progress]

  An annual assessment of the Jama'at's progress around the world. Volumes run from 1994 until 1999.

- *Hayat e Nasir Volume I (Life of the third Khalifa)*
- *Sawaneh Fazle Omar Volumes 1-5* *Life of the Second Khalifa*

Pictorials

- *"Mosques Around the World: A Pictorial Presentation"*

  A U.S.A. Souvenir published at the inauguration of Baitur Rahman Mosque in 1994.

- *Souvenirs of Jama'at Karachi*

  An annual showcase of Jama'at progress. Volumes run from 1954 to 1988.

- *Mujallah Of Lajna Markaziyya* A reservoir of information about *Jama'at* progress.

Acknowledgments

The Holy Founder of Islam [sa] has taught us the philosophy of gratitude by saying: 'One who is not thankful to people cannot be thankful to God'. In the light of this wisdom, we sincerely offer our appreciation to all the individuals who have extended a helping hand for the preparation of this pictorial.

The first and foremost, of course, is Allah who provided us with this great and historic opportunity and enabled us to meet the challenges of this task. Next, we thank our beloved *Imam, Hadhrat Mirza Masroor Ahmad*[aba], who guided us from the very beginning and advised us with regards to the content, arrangement and the layout in general. We are especially thankful for his prayers and his invaluable message which he provided for this pictorial.

We are very thankful to respected Chaudhry Hamidullah, *Wakil e A'ala*, for his great suggestions and critical improvements in the contents. We thank respected Mr. Rafiq Mir for his continued support in pursuit of the correct data. We cannot forget Mirza Khursheed Ahmad, *Nazir e A'ala*, Rabwah, for invaluable support and and advice.

We owe our gratitude to respected Abdul Majid Tahir, Additional *Wakilut Tabshir*, London, for the time he spent with us to execute *Huzoor's* [aba] instructions at every step of this book's preparation. His staff, including Mr. Akhlaq Anjum and Mr. Mirza Nasir Ahmad, were eager to assist us with critical telephone communications and other administrative help.

Sahibzada Mirza Fazal Ahmad deserves our special thanks for his excellent advice, support, encouragement and valuable contributions. In order to be able to present the *Jama'at* record faithfully, Khilafat Library, Rabwah, is an indispensable treasure. The use of its facilities during non-working hours, with full support, was extended by Chaudhry Sadiq and his staff, for which we are extremely grateful.

The instructions, suggestions and advice of our respected Amir, Dr. Ahsanullah Zafar, were great sources of motivation for this task. Respected Dr. Zaheer Bajwa was instrumental in getting this entire project presented for review and approval. *Imam* Daud Hanif assisted us in contacting a few countries in Africa, allowing us to collect material from their *Jama'at* chapters expeditiously; he also provided his valuable comments on the contents of this pictorial. Imam Khalid Tahir of Russia provided us the translation from the Russian letter of Leo Tolstoy after retrieving the letter from Russian libraries. We would also like to thank our contributors, listed below, for their valuable time and for their excellent articles. We also present a list of individuals from around the world who have helped us in various aspects of this pictorial presentation. May Allah shower His mercy upon all of them and forgive us for any omissions.

Contributors/Authors

Maulana Dost Muhammad Shahid
Imam Ataul Mujeeb Rashid
Imam Daud Hanif
Imam Shamshad Ahmad Nasir
Dr. Shanaz Butt *Sahiba*
Falahuddin Shams
Wasim Malik
Mir Daud Ahmad
Dr. Naseem Rahmatullah

Poetry

Saayrah Hikmat
Qasim Rashid
Bilal Rana
Omar Ahmad
Ahsan Khan

Jama'at Contacts

Albania: Shahid Ahmad Butt
Australia: Mahmood Ahmad
Austria: Mohammad Wahab
Bangladesh: Abdul Awwal
Belgium: Farid Yousuf
Bénin: Chaudhry Asghar Ali
Bosnia and Herzegovina: F. Sultan
Brazil: Waseem Zafar
Bulgaria: M. Ashraf Zia
Burkina Faso: N. Mahmood
Cambodia: Uung Kurnia, Dr. Surraya
Canada: Malik Lal Khan, Aslam Dawood
Côte d'Ivoire: A. Quyyum Pasha
Denmark: N. Basharat
Fiji Islands: N. A. Cheema
France: Ishtiaq Hadi
French Antilles: Ishtiaq Hadi, Shuaib Ahmad
The Gambia: Yankuba Sinayoko
Germany: Zubair Khalil, Shahid Abbasi,
        Haider Ali Zafar, Mobashira Ilyas
Ghana: Abdul Wahab and Amtul Shakoor Adam
Guyana: Abdul Rahman
India: Mubarak A. Dar,
Indonesia: Abdul Mukhlis
Ireland: Dr. Aleemuddin Ahmad
Israel: Maymood Odeh
Japan: Anees Ahmad
Kazakhstan:Amir *Jama'at* Kazakhstan
Kenya: Daniel Owino
Kosovo: Javed Nasir
Lesotho: Zaheer Ahmad
Liberia: Ahsan Mahmood
Madagascar: Iqbal Nasir
Malaysia: A. Basit
Mauritius: Basharat Naveed
Myanmar: Muhammad Sadiq
The Netherlands: Ahsan Mahmood
New Zealand: S. Raheem Kichilan
Niger: Amir *Jama'at*, Niger
Nigeria: Amir *Jama'at*, Nigeria
Norway: Shahid Dar, Zartasht Munir
Pakistan (Rabwah): Syed Khalil, Amtul Hai
Philippines: Sibt e Hasan
Portugal: Sohail Ahmad
Russia: Khalid Tahir

Sierra Leone: Usman Hashmi
Singapore: Hasan Basri
South Africa: Zaheer Ahmad
Spain: Sayed Shah
Sri Lanka: Abdul Aziz
Suriname: Laeeq Ahmad Mushtaq
Sweden: Yahya Khan
Swaziland: Iqbal Ahmad
Switzerland: Sadaquat Ahmad
Tanzania: Ch.Tahir Mahmood
Thailand: Imran Ahmad
Trinidad: Ibrahim Bin Yaqub
Tonga/Tuvalu: NA Cheema
Uganda: Usman Hashmi, Abdul Hamid
The United Kingdom: Rafiq Hayat, Omair
        Aleem, Naseer Ahmad Qamar and
        Dabeer Ahmad
The United States of America: Col. Fazal Ahmad
        Dr. Naseer Ahmad, Imran Jattala, Hanif
        Koya, Dr. Atif Malik, Monas Chaudhry
        and Amir Rehman

The Last Ahmadiyya Muslim Mosque
Built in the First Century of Khilafat-e-Ahmadiyya

Masjid Mubarak, in Abuja, Nigeria is the last Ahmadiyya Muslim Mosque to be constructed within the First Century of Khilafat for Jama'at Ahmadiyya. Hadhrat Khalifatul Masih V [aba] inaugurated this mosque in April, 2008.